Beyond

the

Sky

and

the

Earth

DOUBLEDAY CANADA LIMITED

Beyond the Sky and the Earth

A Journey Into Bhutan

Jamie Zeppa

Book design by Carla Bolte

Canadian Cataloguing in Publication Data

Zeppa, Jamie.
    Beyond the sky and the earth : a journey into Bhutan

ISBN 0-385-25693-0

1. Zeppa, Jamie. 2. Bhutan — Description and travel. I. Title.
DS491.5.Z46 1999   954.98   C99-930610-3

Published in Canada by
Doubleday Canada Limited
105 Bond Street
Toronto, Ontario
M5B 1Y3

Printed and bound in Canada

FRI   10 9 8 7 6 5 4 3 2 1

for my grandfather

Patrick Raymond Zeppa

and my grandmother

Florence Alice Zeppa

Acknowledgments

M any people have helped me write this book. I would like to thank Nancy Strickland, who gave me a room of my own as well as her generous and unfailing friendship; and my other WUSC–Bhutan friends, Mark LaPrairie, Grant and Dorothy Bruce, Anne Currie, Barb Rutten, Cam Kilgour, and Catherine McAdam, for their friendship in Bhutan and beyond. Many thanks to my agent, Anne McDermid, for her tireless commitment to this project over many months and many miles. I am very grateful to my excellent editors for all their work in shaping this book: Julie Grau at Riverhead in New York, Mari Evans at Macmillan U.K., and especially, Jill Lambert, who was there from the beginning. I am also indebted to the many others who read various drafts, made invaluable suggestions and kept me writing, especially Tshewang, Sheree Fitch, Karma S., Shirley-Dale Easley, Ruth Liddington, and Lesley Grant of Doubleday Canada. My writing companions in Thimphu, the women of WAGS, were a great source of strength, as was my mother, Judy Luzzi. Thanks also to my father, Jim Zeppa, and Minor Miracles, for providing space and time to work during the revision process. I would like to thank Sonam Wangmo for her story of the oracle in her father's temple at Sakteng; Jigme Drukpa, who provided the information on Bhutanese music and musical instruments throughout the book; and Chris Butters, for insights into Bhutanese architecture. Thank you to Susan Terrill, my dearest friend, who submitted the essay that won the award that started the process that became this book. I am also grateful to the Canada Council for the Arts for its generous financial assistance. Finally, I thank all my former students from Bhutan, wherever you are now, for being my very best teachers. Tashi Delek.

You must leave your home and go forth from your country
The children of Buddha all practice this way.

—*The Thirty-Seven Bodhisattva Practices*

Arrival

Teachers will find
themselves in
isolated settlements
in an isolated
country. Living
conditions may vary
from basic
to spartan.
The demands on
their personal
resources and
professional abilities
will be high.

—WUSC Briefing Kit
for Bhutan

A Remote Posting

*T*he doors of the Paro airport are thrown open to the winds. The little building and its single stripe of tarmac are set in the middle of dun-colored fields dotted with mounds of manure. The fields are carved into undulating terraces edged with sun-bleached grass; intricate footpaths lead to large houses, white with dark wooden trim. A young girl in an ankle-length orange-and-yellow dress, two horses, three cows, a crow in a leafless willow tree. An ice-blue river splashing over smooth white stones. A wooden cantilever bridge. Above the bridge, on a promontory, a massive fortress, its thick white walls tapering toward the top, a golden spire flashing on the dark red roof.

All around, the mountains rise and rise, pale gold and brown in the February light. At one end of the valley, beyond a wall of black, broken peaks, one white summit shimmers; at the other end, the mountains grow tamer, softly rounded and turning smoky blue in the distance. On the slopes I can see clusters of prayer flags, long narrow strips of white cloth raised on towering poles, floating in the wind.

This is what I flew into, leaving behind the cities of India sprawling over hazy plains. At first, the mountains were far below, plunging into narrow valleys thick with forest, dense, impenetrable. "Ladies and gentlemen," the pilot said, "we have now begun our descent into Paro," and the little plane dropped suddenly, leaving me gasping as we skimmed over ridges and dropped again, into one of the few valleys in Bhutan wide and flat enough to land a plane in.

The sun slips into the crevasse between two hills and the afternoon is over. The line at the visa counter moves slowly. I am the last one at the desk. The visa officer carefully inspects and then stamps my passport. My *bags are lying alone on the tarmac outside, beneath furiously snapping flags. I haul them in. I have arrived.*

On the shelf above the desk in my one-room apartment overlooking a strip mall in the northern suburbs of Toronto, there were two blue plastic trays, one filled with graduate-school application forms, and the other marked simply "other." In the "other" pile was an article entitled "Working Your Way Around Europe," a yellowing passport application form, and a newspaper ad: TEACHERS WANTED FOR OVERSEAS POSTS. It was 1988, I was twenty-three. Outside my one window, winter was melting into sludge. The ad announced positions in southern Africa and central America, but the one that caught my attention was for an English lecturer at a college in the Himalayan kingdom of Bhutan. Two years of teaching and overseas experience were required for the position. I had neither, but I showed the ad to my boyfriend, Robert, who had once been to South America on an international development seminar. "Don't you think it would be a great experience?" I asked.

"It does look good on a résumé," he said. But I hadn't meant that kind of experience. I wanted something outside of professional considerations and career connections, something that wouldn't fit on a CV. Robert and I had decided to get married but that would be several years in the future, when we were both finished with our studies. I was supposed to be starting a Ph.D. in English. But I kept wondering if I should do something else altogether. "I want to do something in the real world," I kept saying to Robert—to which I would invariably add, "whatever that means." It wasn't that my life felt unreal to me, it just seemed very . . . *small.* I was tired of reading theory and writing essays, and, except for a week on a beach in Cuba, I had never been anywhere.

A few days later in the library, I remembered the ad and looked up Bhutan. There were four or five books, thick-paged volumes with washed-out black-and-white photos, all published in the 1960s and early '70s. I took notes in the back of my journal: *Bhutan, small Tantric Buddhist Kingdom in the Eastern Himalayas. Bordered by Tibet in the north, India in the south and east, Sikkim to the west. Entirely*

4

mountainous (altitudes ranging from 150 to 7,000 meters above sea level). Capital: Thimphu. Language: Dzongkha, related to classical Tibetan, plus various other dialects. People: in north and west, of Tibetan origin; in the east, Indo-Mongolian; in the south, Nepali. National sport: archery. Government: hereditary monarchy, established 1907, replacing dual system of government with religious and secular heads. Closed to outside world for centuries. Never colonized.

Modern economic development had begun in Bhutan in the 1960s with the construction of a road linking Thimphu to the Indian border. Until then, the economy had been based on barter; money was virtually nonexistent, and taxes had been paid in kind. Thirty years later, the feudal nature of rural Bhutanese society seemed largely unchanged. Virtually everyone owned land, but, except for the lowlands along the southern border, the terrain was too difficult to permit much more than subsistence farming. Buddhism permeated daily life, and many families still sent one son into the monastery. Relatively few foreigners visited the country; foreign aid was limited, and tourism discouraged.

I skimmed snippets of a British emissary's journey through Bhutan in 1774, and then studied pictures taken in the 1970s. Two hundred years had not made much apparent difference. The photographs showed mostly mountains, darkly forested, a few stone and wood houses planted along the edges of cultivated fields. It was like the Brothers Grimm. Bramble fences, stone walls, a woodcutter, a haystack. Fortresses on hillsides, overlooking narrow river valleys. An old man in a dark knee-length robe standing in a flagstone courtyard. A woman leading a small, stout horse, two young children following, bent under backloads of sticks. A boy waving a switch at a herd of cows. A barefoot, bareheaded king.

The deadlines for various graduate schools got closer, and the jumble of applications grew larger. I kept thinking of those pictures that were like certain poems that leave a little hole somewhere inside you. I called the World University Service of Canada, the agency which had placed the ad, and asked for an application form for the posting in Bhutan.

"Where the hell is that?" my grandfather asked when I told him on my next visit to Sault Ste. Marie, the northern Ontario steel town where I had grown up. My parents had split up when I was two, and in the ensuing turbulence, my father's parents had ended up with custody of my brother and me. They had been caring guardians but overly protective, especially my grandfather. My grandmother had died of cancer the year before, and my grandfather, feeling his seventy-two years, was anxious to see my brother and me settled in our lives.

"What do you want to go Over There for?" he said.

The rest of the world was all one place to him. If you weren't here, you were Over There.

"It's the same Over There as it is here," he said, and then promptly contradicted himself by asking what was I, crazy, did I want to get myself killed or something?

I told him that I would be going Over There with a legitimate, government-funded agency that had a long history of placing volunteers around the world, so there was no need to worry.

He named several causes for worry. What if I got sick? What if I had a terrible accident? What if there was an earthquake, a flood, an epidemic, a war? What if, what if. He came up with a hundred stories of people who went off and never came back, dead of unnamed diseases, lost in jungles, swept away by rivers, fallen off mountains, fallen in love, never heard from again. I should have known; I had been raised on tales of worry and what if. "Don't take chances. Life is too short to live by your own experiences," my grandfather had told us countless times. "Learn from other people's mistakes."

"What about school?" he said. "What about your Ph.D.?" The Depression had cut short his own education before he reached high school, and the value of education was one of his favorite subjects — "education" meaning knowledge that could be practically applied to save you from a lifetime in the coke ovens. I could see what he foresaw for me — the future opening up, the path leading over a low rise just ahead into an assured future, a secure career, a good marriage. He wouldn't understand if I told him that my future seemed to be closing in, getting smaller and narrower and more rigidly fixed with each essay I completed.

He had spent his whole life making his world safer, smaller, more secure. The basement pantry was lined with tins of food we would never eat, he saved bottles, nails, envelopes, old wrapping paper, broken toasters, bits of wire, cloth and carpet. "You never know when you'll need it," he said. Caution was his religion: you never know, you can't be too careful, better safe than sorry. In his experience, change meant loss. His own parents had immigrated from Poland, making the dark, cold journey across the Atlantic, moving up through New York, Pennsylvania and Michigan, into Ontario. They settled in Sault Ste. Marie, in the shadow of Algoma Steel, but even after the Depression, when things got better, they were not at home in this harsh new unfinished world, this Canada, and talked longingly of Poland, in Polish, until they died. This is what happened when you uprooted yourself, my grandfather believed: you could not go back and yet you did not belong. He believed in staying put.

I sat in my old bedroom, looking out the small window at the steel plant, with its wire fences, enormous grids and towers, smoke stacks staining the sky all year round. We had grown up chanting the names of the mysterious places inside—coke ovens, coal docks, blast furnace, slag dump. We knew you could grow up and get a job there, make good money working three-to-eleven, eleven-to-seven. "Your father could have been making good money there now," my grandfather said, shaking his head. "Would have made something of himself by now." When my father went to Toronto after the divorce, we were in awe. If you grew up in Sault Ste. Marie, Toronto was the ultimate destiny. If you got all the way to Toronto, you did not have to come back. My mother was proof of this; after the divorce she had only gone to Europe, and then she had come back. We did not consider that she wanted to be close to her children, we thought she had just not gone far enough away. My father returned only for brief visits, his long hair falling down the back of his black silk shirt, hundred-dollar bills folded in half and clipped in his pocket. "Your father seems to have done well for himself in Toronto," people said, their admiration ending in a question mark. "He's in the music industry," my brother and I learned to say, "he's a promoter." But my grandfather was not impressed. "Working in goddamn barrooms. Would have been foreman by now." Toronto meant nothing to my grandfather, and he would not allow us to visit there when we were children. Traveling was something you did because you had to—if you got a job in another city, a real job, not in the music industry, but, say, as a dentist, my grandfather's dream profession—"Look at the Miller boy," he kept saying, "he's making money hand over fist." Traveling was not something you did for fun or experience or love. "Waste of money, that's all it is," my grandfather said. It had taken quite a bit of work just to convince him to allow me to leave home to go to university, first in Ottawa and later in Toronto. And now I wanted to go to the Third World. The Third World! It was preposterous! It was for the birds!

"And what about Robert?" my grandfather demanded. "I thought you were getting married. What does Robert have to say about all of this?" My grandfather liked Robert: he was smart and dependable. I had met him at university. My grandfather said Robert was blue-chip stock.

"I'm coming *back,* Grandpa. And Robert thinks it'll be a great experience." I didn't say that Robert's initial enthusiasm was declining now that I'd actually applied. "I've never been anywhere," I said. "This may be the only chance I'll ever get to do something like this."

"I've never been anywhere either and it hasn't hurt me," he said. "It's just plain foolishness. Don't take chances. Prepare for your future and forget about going Over There."

"Well, I've only applied. Maybe I won't be accepted," I said, hoping to erase the fret lines from between his eyes, if only temporarily. I hated to worry and disappoint him but I could not lie outright and promise not to go.

The World University Service of Canada (WUSC) called me for an interview. The two interviewers, neither of whom had been to Bhutan, gave a short introduction to the program there. When secular education began in the country thirty years ago, with the help of a

Canadian Jesuit named Father Mackey, the Bhutanese government chose English as the medium of instruction. On Bhutan's northern border, Tibet had been annexed by China and the world had not even blinked. Bhutan did not want to suffer a similar fate; it was time to end its policy of official isolation and enter the modern world. The Royal Government proceeded cautiously, however, and the pace of development was kept deliberately slow. The education system, still in its early stages, was suffering from a severe shortage of teaching staff, which made it necessary to recruit foreign teachers. Although the vast majority came from neighboring India, there were about seventy teachers from volunteer agencies such as WUSC and the British organization VSO at schools and institutes throughout the country. WUSC had a total of fifteen Canadian teachers there, all placed in eastern Bhutan, where Father Mackey had helped start the first English-medium schools in the 1960s. These teachers were provided with accommodations and paid local salaries. Work terms were for two years, although teachers could and often did extend their contracts.

Conditions were very basic, sometimes in fact quite difficult, the interviewers said. Life at the college posting for which I had applied was a bit more comfortable, but it was by no means luxurious. There were few roads in Bhutan, and most of them would be closed during the heavy summer rain and the winter snow. There would be other Canadians, yes, but I would be several hours away from most of them. Basically, I would be cut off, immersed—how did I feel about that? How would I fill up my time? Did I have a boyfriend? How did he feel about my decision to leave him for two years? Did I realize that there were no phones in the eastern part of Bhutan? That most Bhutanese lived in villages and hamlets dotted across one of the most difficult terrains in the world? They proposed several situations—a serious argument with the principal, discipline problems in class, illness, cultural misunderstandings, an accident: what would I do? I constructed answers as best I could, trying to sound sensible and good-humored, ignoring the voice in my head that kept asking, "But what would you *really* do?"

Afterward, I went back to the library and flipped through the books again, studying the pictures, trying to place myself in them. I had a strange feeling in the pit of my stomach, like I was standing at the edge of a cliff.

The letter of acceptance from WUSC came in September of 1988, along with a Briefing Kit, a spiral-bound book of information on travel, health concerns, culture shock, and a list of things I should bring. I shoved my incomplete applications to Ph.D. programs into a file folder, restored several tomes of literary criticism to the university library and turned my attention to the list. The List! I could recite it in my sleep. I returned from daily excursions to hardware stores, sports stores, electronics stores, drug stores, grocery stores, mountain-equipment stores and the Tropical Diseases Institute, to count and organize items on the bedroom floor. There were piles of Warm Clothing (thermal underwear, flannel shirts in dark colors—winters would be cold, the Briefing Kit said, and the houses would be unheated); Medicines (Gravol, antibiotics, delousing shampoo); Equipment (hand-held water filter, Swiss Army knife, assorted tiny tools, $50 high-tech flashlight with a five-year warranty); Other Useful Items (vegetarian cookbook, plastic containers with lids, Ziploc bags, lighters, packets of dried food).

Robert stood in the middle of the room, staring at the piles. "Surely you don't have to take all this," he said.

"I do," I said, stuffing woolen socks, tampons, and *The Norton Anthology of English Literature* into a hockey bag. "It's like preparing for a two-year camping trip."

"It looks more like you're preparing for a natural disaster. What kind of place are they sending you?" he asked, reading the instructions on the delousing shampoo.

"It's a remote posting, Robert."

"Well, maybe it's too remote," he said. "After all, you haven't really been anywhere before. Couldn't they send you to an easier posting? What about—"

I put my hands over my ears. "I don't want to hear it, Robert," I said. "I am *going* to Bhutan." I was suddenly overwhelmed by a desire not to go.

Robert spoke my fears aloud. "It's just so far away, and for so long. Two years—I won't even be able to phone you."

"You could apply too," I said. "We could go together." We had talked about this possibility before, but I knew that Robert had other plans for his life now. He had been a professional musician before I met him, but it hadn't paid off, and he'd given it up to return to university. It had been a sad and troublesome choice, to give up the thing he loved best, the music in his head, in order to have something more tangible, a degree in his hand, a guaranteed job in teaching or administration. My grandfather wholly approved, but secretly, I sympathized with the part of Robert that missed his music. He was rebuilding now, he said, putting the pieces in place, he wanted to have something when he finished. This was not a time to go anywhere.

I could call up the office in Ottawa, I thought, and tell them I can't go. I could cite personal reasons. I could still apply to graduate school. I could take a year to think about it. Two years was a long time to be apart—I *should* think about it. But I knew that if I didn't go now, I never would. And lots of people had relationships over long distances, I told myself. We knew several couples who had survived long separations.

I went back to the List. I would take my portable keyboard and lots of batteries, and books I'd always wanted to read: a collection of Buddhist readings, *Lost Horizon*, the *Tibetan Book of the Dead.* I selected photos of Robert, my family and friends, a few postcards to stick on the walls of my new home, a miniature blue teacup I'd had since I was a child. My luggage grew heavier; I bought another hockey bag. This comforted me. I wasn't going out there with nothing. In between the shopping and packing, I argued endlessly with my grandfather on the phone. We debated travel v. academic qualifications, the first world v. the third world, challenge v. goddamn stupidity, the chances of contracting dengue fever on the other side of the planet v. the chances of being run down by a milk truck outside one's childhood home, for the experience v. for the birds. Another letter came, fixing the departure date for February 16, 1989, several weeks away. I called my friends to say this is it, yes, I am going, goodbye.

A few days later, I got a phone call from the head office in Ottawa. The principal of the college in Bhutan, a Canadian Jesuit, had rejected my application. He wanted someone older, with more experience. Apparently, he was uncomfortable with the fact that I would be the same age as some of the students. The man on the phone was very sorry, but . . .

But nothing! I thought. I'm packed, I'm ready, I am *going*. I said, "I'm all ready to go."

The voice said yes, but . . . and I said yes, but . . . and this went on for several minutes until he asked if I would be willing to teach in a junior high school. Junior high meaning grades one through eight. In a more remote posting. There was still one position open, although it was, uh, quite different from the one I'd applied for. There was no electricity, for one thing.

"Yes, fine, grade eight in a more remote posting," I said.

"Well, you'll probably be assigned to grade two."

"Fine, fine," I said. Grade two in a more remote posting. Kindergarten on the Tibetan border. I didn't care. I was going.

"Jesus Christ, Jamie Lynne! I hope you know what the hell you're getting yourself into," my grandfather kept saying.

I said I knew. I had been to the library, I said, I had looked things up. I had seen the maps. I knew how far away I was going.

In truth, I had no idea.

People kept asking *why* I was going, and I gave the entire range of possible answers. For the experience, I said. I've never been anywhere. I'm tired of school. I want to learn about development, the Himalayas, Buddhism. I want to do something different. I want to travel. I don't want to be a tourist. It sounds fascinating. I don't know. I knew I seemed a fairly unlikely candidate for an adventure into the unknown. And secretly I doubted that I had what it took, whatever it took, to head off alone to a country most people had never heard of. In light of this, my determination to go puzzled me. It was more than just growing up under the smoke stacks, dreaming the small-town dream of escape like my parents before me. And it was more than feeling that I was going to wake up one morning soon trapped in my future. For all my years of study, I wasn't sure I had actually learned anything. I had gained intellectual skills and tools, yes, but what did I know? I wanted to throw myself into an experience that was too big for me and learn in a way that cost me something.

I spent my last night in Canada with Robert, trying to forget that I was leaving the next day. I held his hand tightly long after he had fallen asleep, the names running through my head—Paro, Thimphu, Pema Gatshel, Bhutan Bhutan Bhutan.

He took me to the airport in the morning. We held hands, we kissed goodbye. It was only two years, we told each other, and we would be together again at Christmas. We would write. It wouldn't be easy but we would stay connected, because we loved each other, because we wanted to get married, because I was coming back. But on the other side of the security check, I sat and cried. I loved Robert. I didn't know why on earth I was leaving him.

Mountains all around, climbing up to peaks, rolling into valleys, again and again. Bhutan is all and only mountains. I know the technical explanation for the landscape, landmass meeting landmass, the Indian subcontinent colliding into Asia thirty or forty million years ago, but I cannot imagine it. It is easier to picture a giant child gathering earth in great armfuls, piling up rock, pinching mud into ridges and sharp peaks, knuckling out little valleys and gorges, poking holes for water to fall through.

It is my first night in Thimphu, the capital, a ninety-minute drive from the airport in Paro. It took five different flights over four days to get here, from Toronto to Montreal to Amsterdam to New Delhi to Calcutta to Paro. I am exhausted, but I cannot sleep. From my simple, pine-paneled room at the Druk Sherig hotel, I watch mountains rise to meet the moon. I used to wonder what was on the other side of mountains, how the landscape resolved itself beyond the immediate wall in front of you. Flying in from the baked-brown plains of India this morning, I found out: on the other side of mountains are mountains, more mountains and mountains again. The entire earth below us was a convulsion of crests and gorges and wind-sharpened pinnacles. Just past Everest, I caught a glimpse of the Tibetan plateau, the edge of a frozen desert 4,500 meters above sea level. Thimphu's altitude is about half that, but even here, the winter air is thin and dry and very cold.

The next morning, I share a breakfast of instant coffee, powdered milk, plasticky white bread and flavorless red jam in the hotel with two other Canadians who have signed on to teach in Bhutan for two years. Lorna has golden brown hair, freckles, and a no-nonsense, home-on-the-farm demeanor that is frequently shattered by her ringing laughter and stories of the wild characters that populate her life in Saskatchewan. Sasha from British Columbia is slight and dark, with an impish smile. After breakfast, we have a brief meeting with Gordon, the field director of the WUSC program in Bhutan, and then walk along the main road of Thimphu. Both Lorna and Sasha have traveled extensively; Lorna trekked all over Europe and northern Africa, and Sasha worked for a year in an orphanage in Bombay. They are both ecstatic about Bhutan so far, and I stay close to them, hoping to pick up some of their enthusiasm.

Although Thimphu's official population is 20,000, it seems even smaller. It doesn't even have traffic lights. Blue-suited policemen stationed at two intersections along the main street direct the occasional truck or landcruiser using incomprehensible but graceful hand gestures. The buildings all have the same pitched roofs, trefoil windows, and heavy beams painted with lotus flowers, jewels and clouds. One-storied shops with wooden-shuttered windows open onto the street. They seem to be selling the same things: onions, rice, tea, milk powder, dried fish, plastic buckets and metal plates, quilts and packages of stale, soft cookies from India—Bourbon Biscuits, Coconut Crunchies, and the hideously colored Orange Cream Biscuits. There are more signs of the outside world than I had expected: teenagers in acid-washed jeans, Willie Nelson's greatest hits after the news in English on the Bhutan Broadcasting Service, a Rambo poster in a bar. Overall, these signs of cultural infiltration are few, but they are startling against the Bhutanese-ness of everything else.

The town itself looks very old, with cracked sidewalks and faded paintwork, but Gordon told us that it didn't exist thirty-odd years ago. Before the sixties, when the third king decided to make it the capital, it was nothing but rice paddies, a few farmhouses, and a *dzong*—one of the fortresses that are scattered throughout the country. Thimphu is actually new. "Thimphu will look like New York to you when you come back after a year in the east," he said.

At the end of the main road is Tashichho Dzong, the seat of the Royal Government of Bhutan, a grand, whitewashed, red-roofed, golden-tipped fortress, built in the traditional way, without blueprints or nails. Beyond, hamlets are connected by footpaths, and terraced fields, barren now, climb steadily from the river and merge into forest. Thimphu will never look like New York to me, I think.

The Bhutanese are a very handsome people, "the best built race of men I ever saw," wrote emissary George Bogle on his way to Tibet in 1774, and I find I agree. Of medium height and sturdily built, they have beautiful aristocratic faces with dark, almond-shaped eyes, high cheekbones and gentle smiles. Both men and women wear their black hair short. The women wear a *kira,* a brightly striped, ankle-length dress, and the men a *gho,* a knee-length robe that resembles a kimono, except that the top part is especially voluminous. The Bhutanese of Nepali origin tend to be taller, with sharper features and darker complexions. They too wear the gho and kira. People look at us curiously, but they do not seem surprised at our presence. Although we see few other foreigners in town, we know they are here. Gordon said something this morning about Thimphu's small but friendly "ex-pat" community.

When we stop to ask for directions at a hotel, the young man behind the counter walks with us to the street, pointing out the way, explaining politely in impeccable English. I search for the right word to describe the people, for the quality that impresses me most—dignity, unselfconsciousness, good humor, grace—but can find no single word to hold all of my impressions.

In Thimphu, we attend a week-long orientation session with twelve other Irish, British, Australian and New Zealand teachers new to Bhutan. Our first lessons, in Bhutanese history, are the most interesting. Historical records show that waves of Tibetan immigrants settled in Bhutan sometime before the tenth century, but the area is thought to have been inhabited long before that. In the eighth century, the Indian saint Padmasambhava brought Buddhism to the area, where it absorbed many elements of Bon, the indigenous shamanist religion. The new religion took hold but was not a unifying force. The area remained a collection of isolated valleys, each ruled by its own king. When the Tibetan lama Ngawang Namgyel arrived in 1616, he set about unifying the valleys under one central authority and gave the country the name Druk Yul, meaning Land of the Thunder Dragon. Earlier names for Bhutan are just as beautiful—the Tibetans knew the country as the Southern Land of Medicinal Herbs and the South Sandalwood Country. Districts within Bhutan were even more felicitously named: Rainbow District of Desires, Lotus Grove of the Gods, Blooming Valley of Luxuriant Fruits, the Land of Longing and Silver Pines. Bhutan, the name by which the country became known to the outside world, is thought to be derived from *Bhotanta,* meaning the "end of Tibet" or from the Sanskrit *Bhu-uttan,* meaning "highlands."

While the rest of Asia was being overrun by Europeans of varying hue but similar cry, only a handful of Westerners found their way into Bhutan. Two Portuguese Jesuits came to call in 1627, and six British missions paid brief but cordial visits from the late 1700s until the middle of the next century. Relations with the British took a nasty turn during the disastrous visit of Ashley Eden in 1864. Eden, who had gone to sort out the small problem of Bhutanese raids on British territory, had his back slapped, his hair pulled, and his face rubbed with wet dough, and was then forced to sign an outrageous treaty that led to a brief war between the British and the Bhutanese. Considering the consolidated British empire in the south, and the Great Game being played out in the north between the colonial powers, Bhutan's preservation of its independence was remarkable. I am full of admiration for this small country that has managed to look after itself so well.

Sessions follow on Buddhism, Bhutanese Customs and Etiquette, the Education System, Village Life, Health and Emergencies. I take notes frantically, filling up page after page: *visiting someone for first time, always bring small gift, biscuits or juice, always refuse whatever is offered a few times before accepting. Visitors will do same in your house so keep insisting until they accept. Cup will be refilled three times.* Arra = *rice-based alcohol.* Puja = *religious ceremony.* Lhakhang/gompa = *temple. Never cross your legs in front of high official (bottom of foot considered disrespectful).* La/Lasso La = *respectful addition to end of sentence. Eat well-cooked meat only (pork = tapeworm, trichinosis).*

Buddhism considers all life sacred, therefore do not kill insects or rodents in your home in front of Bhutanese. Prayer flags usually found in high places or over water, wind carries prayers to heaven. Bacterial dysentery = diarrhea with blood & fever. Amoebic dysentery and giardia = diarrhea with mucus, no fever. Languages of Bhutan: Dzongkha, Sharchhop (east), Nepali. English = medium of instruction in school. Many other dialects throughout country. Very hierarchical society. Discuss everything with your headmaster first, do not go over his head, always go through the Proper Channels.

Someone asks about relationships. The group leader says that the Bhutanese are very relaxed about sex, especially the eastern Bhutanese. Usually, people get married by moving in together. They get divorced by moving out. There is no stigma attached to divorce or having children out of wedlock. "Now, out in eastern Bhutan," she tells us, "you may hear the term night-hunting. This refers to the practice of sneaking into a girl's house at night, which is a lot more difficult than you would imagine, considering that in most houses, the whole family sleeps in one room. Generally, the idea is, if you're still there in the morning, you're married." We all laugh. She goes on. "You'll find that if you do have a relationship with a Bhutanese, the village will be quite accepting of the whole thing. Just remember, they say there are no secrets in Bhutan, especially in eastern Bhutan, so you can expect everyone to know about it by the next day."

She clears her throat. "Just don't have a relationship with any of your students," she says, looking straight at me. I glance around—no, she is definitely looking at me. I raise my eyebrows at her. "Are you the young lady going to the college?" she asks.

"No, I'm going to Pema Gatshel. Grade *two*," I answer indignantly, thinking, well, now I know the whole story there. Too young indeed! The Jesuit principal thought I'd run off with a student.

We move on to other concerns. If you fall seriously ill, go to the nearest hospital. If there's no hospital, go to a basic health unit. Send a wireless message to your field director. There are stories about teachers who had to be carried down mountains on makeshift stretchers by their students. Our field director says they've been fairly lucky, though; they've had very few emergency evacuations. He reminds us what is meant by emergency evacuation: getting down from your village to a road, finding a vehicle, making the two- or three-day journey back to Thimphu. Someone asks, "So basically, if my appendix bursts out there in Tashi Yangtse, I'm a goner?"

"Well, yes," our field director says, and smiles apologetically. "Sorry, but it's not like you can call a helicopter." Everyone nods. Of course you can't.

I do not ask about those little yellow dial-a-copter cards that WUSC gave us in Canada with a phone number for medical evacuation. I carry mine with me, tucked into my passport. I seem to be the only one who actually believed I could call 1-800-GET-ME-OUT.

The other teachers, many of whom have taught in other developing countries, do not seem the least bit alarmed. Quite the contrary, they are having a wonderful time. Everything is funny to them. The power blackouts, the icy hotel rooms, the coxcomb in someone's chicken curry. They call the orientation itself "disorientation," the health session is dubbed "From Scabies to Rabies." The stinking local bus is the "Vomit Comet," the dubious-looking dumplings we eat at lunch are "Dysentery Danishes." Instead of a copy of *Where There Is No Doctor*, they call for copies of "Where There Is No Body Shop." They tell horror stories with glee. The man who loses all his bottom teeth after getting a simple filling. A woman with tapeworm cysts in her brain. Leeches in various orifices. A Canadian in Tashigang cracked up and was found running around the prayer wheel in the center of town, naked; he was taken out in handcuffs. Typhoid, paratyphoid, hepatitis A, B and C, TB, meningitis, Japanese encephalitis. They make up a little song. I try to join in but my laughter sounds loud and empty in my ears; I am steps away from a prolonged, hysterical outburst.

There are frequent power failures in the evening. We go to bed early, because it is too cold to do anything else, and there is nothing else to do anyway. I read my book of Buddhist teachings by candlelight. My first exposure to Buddhism came through Robert, who had practiced

Zen meditation in his days as a musician. I had never been at ease in the Catholicism in which I had been raised; it left too many false notes and dead ends in my head. The basic teachings of Buddhism stretch and trouble me, but they also ring clear and true. According to my book, this is the first of four degrees of faith: a feeling of mental clarity when hearing the Dharma—Buddhist teachings.

The historical Buddha was born a prince, Siddhartha Gautama, in northern India, in the sixth century BC. A sage predicted that he would either become a great monarch or abandon worldly power altogether and seek enlightenment. Alarmed at the prophecy, Siddhartha's father created a world of rich comfort in the palace so that the boy would not be bothered by spiritual questions. At the age of twenty-nine, however, the young prince managed to get out of the palace, and was shocked at the suffering he found outside the walls. He was especially disturbed by the sight of an old man, a sick man, a corpse, and a mendicant. Realizing that his life was also subject to decay and death, he decided to leave the palace and seek the true meaning of existence. For seven years, he practiced rigorous asceticism until his body collapsed. Practice was no longer physically possible, and he still had not reached enlightenment. He understood then the truth of the middle way—that neither extreme of self-indulgence nor self-denial could lead to the realization he was seeking. After bathing in a river and drinking a bowl of milk offered to him by a village maiden, he sat under a Bodhi tree to meditate, and as a full moon rose, he came to understand the true nature of reality, and the way out of suffering.

The first of the Four Noble Truths taught by the Buddha claims that life is suffering. The second truth explains why. We suffer because the self desires, grasps, clings, is never satisfied, never happy, never free of its many illusions; we desire what we don't have, and when we get it, we desire to hold on to it, and when we are sure we have it, we lose interest in it and desire something new. In our constant, blind striving for something more, something better, something new, something secure and permanent, we act in ways that hurt ourselves and others, and create bad karma, which leads to rebirth and therefore more suffering. Even if we manage to be content with what we have, we are still subject to old age, sickness and death, and so are our loved ones. The third truth says that we must end this ceaseless wanting and grasping if we want to end suffering. The final truth explains how—through the Noble Eightfold Path of Right Understanding, Right Thought, Right Speech, Right Action, Right Livelihood, Right Effort, Right Mindfulness, Right Concentration.

The Buddha did not claim to be a deity. When asked about the creation of the universe and the existence of God, he refused to speculate. He was not offering a new religion but a way of seeing and living in the world. For me, though, one of the most interesting things about Buddhism is not that there is no all-powerful God who we must fall down and worship, but that there is no permanent self, no essence of self. It isn't even clear among scholars if Buddhism accepts the idea of a soul, an immortal individual spirit. Separateness is an illusion. Nothing exists inherently on its own, independently of everything else, and a separate, permanent, inherently existing self is the biggest illusion of all. There is nothing we can point to and say, yes, this is the self. It is not the body or the mind, but a combination of conditions and circumstances and facilities. At the moment of death, these conditions and facilities break down, and only the karma generated by that life remains, determining the circumstances of the next rebirth.

This is a principal tenet of Buddhism, but the Buddha tells his disciples not to take his word for it. They are to analyze and search and test what he says for themselves. On his deathbed, he reminds them, "Decay is inherent in all compound things. Work out your own salvation with diligence." I am struck by this spirit of independent inquiry, by the fact that enlightenment is available to all, not through a priest or a church or divine intervention but through attention to the mind. In Buddhism, there is no devil, no external dark force—there is only your mind, and you must take responsibility for what you want and how you choose to get it.

I read until my eyes burn and my head hurts, until I fall asleep. But my sleep is punctured by the barking of dogs and frequent nightmares. I wake several times a night, and some nights merely float on the surface of sleep and anxiety, wondering if the other new teachers feel the same way, wondering what those goddamn dogs are still barking at, wishing for earplugs, wishing for Robert, wishing for home. I wake up exhausted. Even Lorna and Sasha, who have been completely unfazed by everything so far, complain of restless sleep and strange dreams. Someone says it is the altitude.

I send telegrams to my grandfather and Robert to say that I have arrived safely. What I do not say is that my body has arrived but the rest of me is lost, perhaps in transit. In my dreams at night, I have lost my luggage, my wallet, my passport. I cannot find a taxi, I miss the bus, I drive past the airport again and again. I have brought the wrong ticket, I must make a phone call but I cannot find a quarter. My suitcase is full of toilet paper, full of ants, full of Orange Cream Biscuits. In my dreams, I do not know where I am going: am I coming here or going home? It is more than just the altitude.

On Saturday morning, I go with Lorna and Sasha to the open-air vegetable market. Under roofed stalls, farmers preside over piles of potatoes, skinny green chilies, dried fish, unidentifiable roots and bulbs. Several varieties of rice, including Bhutan's own "red" rice, which turns a pinkish-brown when cooked, baskets of rice crisps, buckwheat, barley. Strings of dried cheese cubes, pungent balls of raw cheese, dried mushrooms and apples and fierce red chili powder measured out in blackened tin cups. The odor of the cheese mixes with the caustic smell of betel nut and the lime paste it is chewed with, and sends us scurrying away. In the handicraft section, we find religious books and ritual objects—little brass bowls, chalices, long musical horns, incense. Bamboo baskets and mats, twig brooms, a black yak-hair blanket. I run my hand over it and shudder at the scabrous texture.

At one end of the market is the meat department. Men with axes hack apart carcasses, hang up strips of red flesh. Legs and hoofs in one pile, intestines in another. "I grew up on a farm," Lorna tells us. "This doesn't bother me." It bothers me, but I maintain a grim silence. I'm trying to appear as imperturbable as the others. Three pigs, the color of old wax, lie side by side, eyes frozen open. A man brushes past us, hoisting a bloody leg of something over his shoulder. "Yes, madam?" calls a boy with an axe in his hand. "Anything?" We shake our heads and move on.

On the way out, we pass religious men with prayer beads, chanting prayers, telling fortunes with handlettered cards and dice. One man has a miniature three-storied temple, called a *tashi-go-mang,* its myriad tiny doors open to reveal statues and intricate paintings of deities. People touch coins and bills to their foreheads and then press them into the doorways for luck and blessings. "Do you want your fortune told?" Lorna asks. I shake my head vehemently. That's all I would need—confirmation of my grandfather's predictions.

At the market, we see a few tourists for the first time, distinguishable from the resident expatriates by the cameras around their necks; the expats are carrying jute bags loaded with tomatoes and onions. Tourism is carefully regulated, we learned during orientation, so that Bhutan can preserve its culture. The number of annual visitors is kept low by a daily tariff of two hundred U.S. dollars.

After the market, we go to the bank to cash travelers' checks into *ngultrum,* the Bhutanese currency. I feel I have walked into a scene from Dickens. In the gloom inside, dozens of clerks behind wire-mesh walls labor over massive, dusty ledgers, writing figures with leaky fountain pens, counting stacks of money, tying up sheaves of yellowed paper, seemingly ignoring the customers who are pressed up against the counter, waving slips of paper. I am required to sign my name an inordinate number of times before I am given a brass token and told to wait "that side." I head in the direction of "that side" and wait for an hour, folded into the crowd at the counter, standing on tiptoe to see what the clerk in the cage is doing, straining to hear my number, irritated with the whole disorderly, inexplicable process. There's no sign telling me where I should be, there's no line, people push and press and squeeze in front of me, and the clerk is ignoring us all as he chats to a blue-uniformed guard with an ancient, rusted rifle. Do these people have all the time in the world *or what?* This is something I have already thought a good number of times, waiting for breakfast in the hotel, standing at the counter in shops or offices, stuck behind a truck blocking a lane, wondering why the bakery isn't open yet when the sign says clearly OPEN 8 AM and it's already 8:20. Everything seems to take up more time, and the more time things take up, the more time people seem to have. "Doesn't this just make you crazy?" I ask Lorna.

She shrugs. "It's not like we have to *be* anywhere," she says. It's true. We aren't going anywhere. What is my problem? I have all the time in the world, and I am more impatient than ever.

After the orientation session, we begin a week of language lessons. For a small country, Bhutan has an extraordinary number of languages and dialects; at least eighteen have been recognized, some confined to a single village. Lorna, Sasha and I are to learn Sharchhog-pa-kha, which means "eastern-staying people's tongue," the main language of eastern Bhutan. Chuni, the pretty, soft-spoken young woman who is to be our teacher, says we can call both the people and the language "Sharchhop" for short.

Sharchhop has no script. We cannot hear the difference between b and bh, d and dh. I cannot pronounce *tshe* or *nga*. The grammar is incomprehensible, the verb must dangle its legs off the end of the sentence, and our progress is slow. After two weeks, I can count to eight, ask *where are you going,* and have two possible answers to *are you a cowherd: no, I am a teacher; no, I am a nun.*

I am learning another language as well: lateral road, hi-lux, land-cruiser; out-of-station, off-the-road, in-the-field; expat, consultant, volunteer; United Nations Development Program, Food and Agricultural Organization, World Food Program. *Are you a consultant? No, I am a volunteer. Where are you going? I am going to the field. Are you taking the Vomit Comet? No, I have a ride in the FAO hi-lux.*

I have stopped eating meat. I don't know if it was the trip to the market or the story of tapeworm cysts. In fact, I cannot eat much at all. I use bottled water to brush my teeth and wipe the droplets of unboiled, unfiltered water out of my glass before filling it. Sasha frowns. "I don't think we have to be *that* careful," she says.

"You never know," I shrug. Anything can happen. You can't be too careful. Better safe than sorry. Prevention is better than a cure. I have turned into my grandfather. Jesus Christ, Jamie Lynne!

Chuni tells us stories when we get tired of Sharchhop grammar. "This is a true story," she begins, "this really happened," and tells us of cloud fairies, wicked stepmothers, lamas who change into birds, prophetic dreams, a talking raven. A holy man throws his seven sons into the river to find out which ones are demons, and three turn into black dogs. "Be careful of poison villages," she warns us. "Some villages are poison, especially in the east, Tashigang-side. You should never eat or drink anything there." I want to get this straight, especially since we are all going "Tashigang-side," but she has already begun the next story. Witches, a yeti, battles won by throwing hailstones back. All her stories have markers in the physical world. It happened there, at the rock by the river, she says. That is how the place got its name. You can still see the imprint his body left, the ruins of the castle, the burnt tree, it's on the way to Paro, it's near a rocky outcrop in Lhuntse, not even birds go there now.

Gordon drives us back to the Paro valley one afternoon for a picnic of bread, cucumbers and tasteless tinned cheese, past the airport, at a sunny clearing near the river, where we stop beside a *chorten,* a monument made out of whitewashed stones with a square base, a globular middle, and pointed top. Chortens are complex Buddhist symbols representing the body of Buddha, Gordon tells us. Inside there are precious stones, written prayers, relics. In Nepal, most chortens have been desecrated and robbed, but, in Bhutan, this is extremely rare. The Bhutanese still believe in the sanctity of these monuments, and would expect divine retribution if they disturbed one.

Across the river, hanging from a cliff is the monastery of Taktsang, the tiger's nest, where Padmasambhava and his flying tigress landed. The flying tigress does not seem half as incredible as the monastery itself, which looks as if it has been glued to the cliff face. "Imagine," Sasha says, "hauling up all the stones and wood, and then actually building it up there. A few people must have fallen to their deaths."

Gordon says the only death he knows of is recent: a tourist supposedly fell trying to get a good picture.

Afterward, we drive to Drukgyal Dzong, built in 1647 to celebrate the victory of Bhutanese troops over invading Tibetans. In 1951, a fire started by a butter lamp consumed most of the fortress and now the dzong stands in ruins. The road loops around a stone marker and continues back to Thimphu. Lorna is singing some twangy country song about "the end of the road." But the end of the road is the beginning of a wide footpath that disappears around the green bulk of a mountain. Beyond is a snow peak, the sacred mountain Jomolhari, home of the goddess Jomo, over seven thousand meters above sea level. Years ago, the Royal Government gave an international climbing team permission to ascend the mountain under the condition that they not disturb the goddess, and the team apparently kept their promise and did not set foot on the actual peak.

A man passes us, leading three ponies laden with sacks and bamboo baskets, their bells singing softly as they step carefully off the tarmacked road, onto the other, older road. Watching the ponies pass, I feel for a moment that I am an illusion, standing in jeans and a sweatshirt outside a landcruiser, a camera dangling against my leg. What are you doing here, the landscape asks me. I don't know yet.

I begin to wonder what is happening beyond these mountains. I want the eleven o'clock news, the *Globe and Mail,* I want this program to be interrupted by a special bulletin. In Bhutan, news seems to be all word-of-mouth, what someone heard from someone else two days or two weeks ago, rumor and gossip and travelers' tales. News of the road conditions, for example, fluctuates wildly. We are told that the passes are blocked with snow, we will not be going to our postings for a while. But someone heard that the passes are clear. No, two passes are cleared, we can get to Bumthang. The passes are partially clear, the road is open to light vehicles, someone came through last night from the east. The passes are clear but there is no petrol. There is petrol but no diesel. No, there is petrol *and* diesel but all passes are blocked, all roads are closed. We will leave tomorrow, we will leave next month.

Lorna and Sasha and I are drinking Golden Eagle beer with Rita, a British teacher who has already been here for a year, and Wayne, an Australian engineer, in Benez, a little restaurant that draws a mixed crowd of foreign teachers and young Bhutanese in Western dress. Country music is leaking out of a speaker. Rita and Wayne are discussing various ways to walk from Tashi Yangtse in eastern Bhutan to Paro, a walk of more than thirty days. Lorna, Sasha and I have spent the day shopping for national dress and learning to put it on. The kira is actually a long rectangle of cloth wrapped around the body and belted, with an inner blouse and a jacket over top. The belt must be tight, or the whole ensemble begins to unravel. Lorna has been making us laugh all day with her down-home Saskatchewan expressions. She has one for every occasion. Coyote-ugly. It's as hot in the city as it is in the summer. "Doncha just hate getting gowned up?" she'd asked when we were dressed and standing stiffly in our kiras, trying to breathe. Now she overfills her glass and beer bubbles up and runs off the table onto the floor. "Wherever you go, there you are," she says, shaking her head.

We are tired of discussing the roads, the snow, the passes, our possible date of departure, our postings and what is available there, our nearest Canadian neighbors. I will be able to visit them if I can get on a truck carrying gypsum from the mine at the bottom of the Pema Gatshel valley and then a ride from the Pema Gatshel junction up the road five hours to Tashigang. Sasha will have electricity, Lorna and I will not. Sasha will be on the main road, I on a feeder road, Lorna will be off-the-road and will have to walk three hours up a mountain to get to her new home. Rita, who is posted off-the-road in Mongar District, has to walk six hours. Next year, she says, she wants to go to an even more remote place, three days off the road, deep into central Bhutan. I privately think that Rita is displaying alarming symptoms of dementia.

We order supper—*thukpa,* a noodle soup for me and Sasha, rice and chicken curry for Lorna, and for Rita, *ema datsi,* the national dish, a blistering stew of chilies and cheese. Wayne is drawing a map on the back of an envelope. The Eagles are singing "Hotel California." We order more beer. And I think, sometimes it all makes sense: you are sitting in a restaurant with your companions. It could be a restaurant anywhere, it could be Sault Ste. Marie. Other times it makes no sense whatsoever. I don't know how this relates to the rest of my life. There is no link between my life on the other side of the planet, all those dark miles and starry oceans away, and me sitting at this table, tearing my beer label off in strips, no connection at all. Except for myself: I myself must bridge the gap, I am the bridge—although I feel more like the gap. All the experiences and achievements that defined me at home are irrelevant and insignificant here. There is just me, here, now. *Wherever you go, there you are.*

We are told to buy supplies in Thimphu, because "things" are not available outside the capital. I walk through the tiny shops. Things are not so available in the capital, either. We buy kerosene stoves, jerry cans, pressure cookers and hot-water flasks, noodles, cocoa powder, peanut butter. The shopkeepers wrap our purchases neatly in newspaper, and we carry them in our new *jholas,* handwoven cloth shoulder-bags. Sasha, an artist and a vegetarian, goes off in search of sketch paper and dried beans. We both buy large square tins with lids against the rats. I spend the last day in Thimphu packing and repacking my luggage, transferring my most precious supplies from home—chocolate bars, raisins, and a sample bottle of Cointreau—into the square tin. But in the morning, we are told the passes are blocked again (or still) with snow and we will be not be leaving "for some time." We will have more orientation in Thimphu, we will visit the temples, the National Library.

I do not want to have more orientation. I want to go home. I tell Sasha I am coming down with something, and lie in bed and wish for things: a *Cosmopolitan* magazine, a bagel and cream cheese, a grocery store, the Eaton Centre two days before Christmas.

The Lateral Road—Bash on Regardless

The passes are open and we are driving across the lateral road in a hi-lux, Lorna, Sasha, Rita, me, and Dorji, a driver from the Department of Education. After a three-week delay because of snow-blocked passes, we are finally on our way to our postings. "So what do you think so far?" Rita asks when we stop at Dochu La, a pass forty-five minutes out of Thimphu, from where we have an unobstructed view of the northern border: a row of impossible snow-peaks rising up from blue mountains. "Look, that tiny white speck is Gasa Dzong," she says. "It's a two- or three-day walk from here." She knows the names of the peaks—Tsheringma, Table Mountain, Kula Kangri. "This must be one of the best views in the world," she says. "I always feel so happy to be able to see so far." Behind us, dozens of tattered prayer flags are flapping in a cold wind. I glance at Rita: she does look ridiculously happy to be here. It seems to be a consensus among all the other Western teachers we have met. They all love their villages, their schools, their kids, their particular hardships—rats or crazy headmasters or the landslides that close the road during the summer monsoon. Every expat teacher we met in Thimphu returning from holidays in Thailand or Nepal kept sighing and saying, it's so good to be back, so good to be home.

From Dochu La, we descend through mossy fir trees to a forest of shiny-leaved oak and rhododendron in bloom, some trees so crowded with scarlet flowers I almost laugh. Cartoon trees! Impossible trees! I like the magnolia better, the simple white flowers stark against black branches. "I read somewhere that the magnolia is one of the oldest flowers in the world," Sasha says when we stop to take a photograph. This is something I would like to look up. In an encyclopedia, in a library. "Do any of the school libraries have encyclopedias?" I ask Rita.

"The college in Kanglung has," she says.

"But not our schools?"

"Where you guys are going, you'll be lucky if there's even a library."

There are a thousand new things from the orientation course I want to find out about: how reincarnate lamas are discovered, the characteristics of the Tibeto-Burman language group, who Francis Younghusband was. And all the things I've been meaning to look up for the past several years come back to me with renewed urgency: the meaning of "phylogenetic," the origin of the Mafia, whirling dervishes. And then there are all the things I wish I could look up: why I have exiled myself to such a faraway place, and if I will forget everything I know in the valleys of eastern Bhutan, and who I will be when I come out.

The road twists and writhes and burrows through forests. Rita says there are an average of seventeen curves per kilometer on the roads of Bhutan. Someone once counted. At an average speed of thirty kilometers per hour, it will take us three days to drive the 550-odd kilometers to Tashigang District. I eat crackers and Gravol to calm my stomach. The hi-lux grinds its way up to passes eerie with snow and silent white mist lying over the withered trees and the drip drip of water on black rocks, then descends into valleys, tangled green and warm. Monkeys scatter as we turn a corner. Grey langurs, someone says. We pass through tiny villages, hamlets of three or four houses. The country seems almost empty to me. So much unmarked, unmarred wilderness.

The two- or three-story houses have ground-floor walls made out of whitewashed stone or mud, and upper levels of mud and wood. The narrow windows with their scalloped tops have sliding wooden slats to let in light and shut out the rain or the cold. The exterior walls are decorated with elaborate paintings, in faded blues and reds, of lotus flowers, deer, birds, and giant stylized phalluses ("to ward off evil spirits," Rita says). Ladder steps lead to heavy wooden doors with irregular latches and locks. The roofs are covered with stone slates, or wooden shingles held down by large stones. Newer houses have roofs of corrugated iron sheeting. In the crawl space under the eaves, wooden barrels and boxes are stored, leathery items I cannot identify, earthen gourds and coils of frayed rope. Women weave at looms set up in the pale winter sunlight, and children, their cheeks dark red with cold, wave at us solemnly as we pass.

The scenery changes almost every time we turn a corner. Shadowy pine, sunlit oak and beech, dry, hot groves of subtropical pine, called "chir pine" according to Rita, dense, moist jungly forests. Sometimes the mountains roar up, steep and black and haughty. Other times they are more gentle, sprawling, spreading, dissolving into haze. In these I can trace profiles, a smooth forehead, an aquiline nose, a stubborn chin. Whenever we stop and climb out of the vehicle, I am struck by the silence. It is particularly deep and strong higher up. At the passes, when the wind drops suddenly, the silence almost hums, and I can feel the weight of the earth beneath me, intensified by the emptiness between this solid piece of ground and the nearest ridge, a short flight away. It becomes a strange mental gravity. If I stand too long, I begin to feel rooted.

We stop in the town of Tongsa, dominated by Tongsa Dzong, a massive, magnificent fortress. Rita takes us to a restaurant she knows, where the proprietor, a grave and beautiful Tibetan woman, leads us into the warm kitchen overlooking the dzong. We sip hot tea, studying the temple roofs and towers of the dzong, the ladder steps and turrets, the golden spires. Sasha makes a quick sketch. Once again, I have the feeling that I am an aberration in the face of something immense and very old. "The land that time forgot," I say but Lorna makes a face. "The last Shangri-La. That's starting to bug me," she says.

"But it *does* seem like that," I say. "Like all those stories about stepping backwards in time."

She chews the inside of her lip. "I just think if I lived here, I'd hate to have a bunch of foreigners telling me this was Shangri-La. Especially if they came from a nice cushy life in a wealthy country."

In late afternoon, we come over a pass into the Bumthang valley in central Bhutan, wide and gentle, full of pale gold grass and surrounded by dark pine-covered slopes. The Swiss Guest House, which Rita has promised will have pine-paneled rooms, wood-burning stoves called *bukharis,* a hot shower, and toast for breakfast, is full, so we stay instead at a tourist hotel, where the cabins have bukharis but no wood to burn in them, and the taps in the bathroom remain disappointingly dry after much-promising gurgling.

Rita corrects our pronunciation of Bumthang. "Bum—thang!" she drawls, laughing. "What is that, a disorder of the backside?" Bumthang, pronounced boom-tahng, is also called Jakar, which means place of the white bird. Jakar Dzong, looking stern and remote on a knoll above the town, started out as a monastery in the sixteenth century. Construction of the building had already begun at a different site when a white bird was seen circling the knoll. This was taken as an omen, and the monastery was moved. The valleys of Bumthang, Rita tells us at dinner, are considered very holy, full of monasteries and temples and pilgrimage places. No animals may be slaughtered in the valley, and smoking is banned. This is where Padmasambhava, also known as Guru Rimpoché, arrived in the eighth century to help a king who had fallen gravely ill after offending a local deity. Through meditation, Guru Rimpoché subdued the deity, turning it into a fierce protector of the Dharma, and the king was restored to health. The cave where Guru Rimpoché meditated still bears the imprint of his body. Rita says that Guru Rimpoché is worshiped in Tibet and Bhutan as the second Buddha. "The Buddha apparently predicted he would return to teach a more evolved form of Buddhism," she says. "Guru Rimpoché is seen as that incarnation, and any place where he meditated is considered extremely sacred."

Bumthang is also the birthplace of the *terton* Pema Lingpa, who dove into a lake in the next valley with a burning lamp and emerged with religious treasures and the lamp still lit. I want to hear more about the hidden treasures, but this is all Rita knows: that *terma,* religious treasures—scriptures, scrolls, statues, ritual objects—were hidden by Guru Rimpoché, to be discovered centuries later by *tertons,* treasure-finders. Another thing on the List of Things to Look Up.

We are woken in the early morning by the rusty call of crows. The sun has not yet risen over the ridge, and a cold mist hangs over the valley. The dzong of the white bird lies in shadow. It looks like the Bhutan of long, long ago, I think, remembering Rita's history lessons. An older, colder, forbidding Bhutan. Our breath makes frosty clouds as we shiver and squirm into our clothes, which are stiff and cold. There is still no water, and we brush our teeth without it, outside under a stubby pine tree. We drive up to the Swiss Guest House for breakfast, and it does include toast and honey, just as Rita promised. "This is the last time you'll eat toast in a while," Rita says, "unless you can bake bread." She begins an elaborate explanation of how to bake using some ridiculous pot-in-a-pot-on-a-kerosene-stove method. Lorna and Sasha write it all down. "It's too complicated for me," I say. "Anyway, maybe they sell bread in Pema Gatshel." Rita lifts her eyebrows at this but says nothing. The sun has hoisted itself over the rim of the mountains and the mist in the valley turns gold as it breaks up and floats away, but we are reluctant to leave the warm, pine-scented room, and order more toast and coffee.

On the way out of the valley, we stop at a shop to buy cheese and apple juice, produced in local factories started by the Swiss twenty years ago. The air smells of woodsmoke. Dorji returns from the petrol pump looking grim. There is no diesel in Bumthang, he reports.

"Do we have enough to get to Mongar?" Rita asks.

"Mongar also no diesel," he says. "Maybe Tashigang."

Even I know we don't have enough to get all the way to Tashigang, almost two hundred kilometers away. I am about to suggest that we return to the Swiss Guest House to see if there are any rooms available, *instead* of getting back into the vehicle, why is everyone getting *back* into a vehicle that doesn't have enough fuel to get us to the next petrol pump which is at any rate *empty*, do people want to be stranded on the top of some godforsaken mountain in the snow and mist where we would freeze or die of starvation before anyone would even think to look for us? It is too late. Everyone is back in the hi-lux already, and they are waiting for me. *I don't understand,* I want to wail. But I climb in.

This morning we are on our way up to Trumseng La, the highest pass we will have to cross, almost four thousand meters above sea level. Patches of old snow begin to appear along the road, becoming fresher and deeper as we ascend until we are toiling through winter. Dorji slows the hi-lux down to ten, fifteen kilometers per hour, honking at every corner. We stop when we reach the top, climb out, shivering in the cold and ghostly mist under wind-blasted trees, to read the sign erected by the Public Works Department: "You have reached Trumseng La, Bhutan's highest road pass. Check Your Brakes. Bash On Regardless. Thank you."

On the other side of the pass, we are surprised by an enormous truck parked close to the mountain wall. The driver has lit a fire under the fuel tank. "The diesel freezes," Rita explains. I ask her why this method of thawing the fuel doesn't blow the entire truck off the side of the mountain, but she says she doesn't know.

Shortly after Trumseng La, Dorji slows down again and points ahead. The whole mountainside collapsed there last year, Rita informs us, the cliff falling away suddenly, killing 247 road workers who were camped at the site. It looks as if someone has taken a very large, very sharp knife and sliced off the side of the mountain, leaving only a narrow ledge, like decorative trim, on the rock face. Surely we aren't going to drive across that, I think. There's no *road*. The whole thing will fall away under the weight of the truck and we will end up dead at the bottom of the ravine. This is just plain foolishness! This is for the birds! But no, we are to bash on regardless. We cross it very, very slowly. This gives us ample time to study the details of the catastrophe, the deep cracks in the raw, naked rock above, the slide of stone and mud and tree roots straight down a thousand, thousand meters into the ravine below.

I feel worse, somehow, when we are over it. Now there is *that* between me and Thimphu. Why didn't I ask to be posted in Thimphu? At least you can't fall off the road there, at least it has hotels, hot running water, the bakery. Why can't I live in a hotel in Thimphu for two years? Thimphu is only an hour and a half away from the airport. From

Thimphu, I could get to Calcutta, to international airline offices. From Thimphu, I could get home. But every kilometer takes me farther away. Farther and further, I sing myself to sleep, farther and further on a nearly empty tank.

I wake when my sweater slips to the floor and I bang my head on the window. We have stopped outside a collection of windowless bamboo huts. Dorji disappears inside. "He's asking for diesel," Rita tells me. Oh yes, of course, I think sourly. They'll obviously have some in there. Rita is clapping. "He got some!" Everyone is clapping, and Dorji grins as he holds up a jerry can. I clap too, especially loudly.

We stop at a shack made of planks, woven bamboo mats, tin sheets and plastic. FOODINGS AND LODGINGS the sign says. We climb out, stretch and yawn. Inside, from blackened pots on a mud stove, a women serves plates of steaming rice and tiny bowls of bones in broth. "Aren't you going to eat?" the others ask. I shake my head and sip bottled water. They exchange glances. I know what they are thinking. They are thinking I won't make it. I won't last two months, let alone two years. Later, when I have gone home, they will tell stories about me. Remember that girl from Sault Ste. Marie, what was her name, she'd never been anywhere in her life? She was afraid of everything, remember? Is that the one who only ate crackers? What was she thinking when she decided to come?

We spend the second night in Mongar at the Hospital Guest House, which belongs to the Norwegian Leprosy Mission. It is a treacherous walk down from the narrow bazaar in the dark, after a dinner of instant Maggi noodles in the Karma Hotel with syrupy tea for dessert and a shot of Dragon Rum "brewed and bottled," the label claims, "by the Army Welfare Project, Samdrup Jongkhar." Not a very glamorous name for a brewery, but the rum is quite good. The crowing of roosters wakes me from a warm and happy dream in which I am walking from the university library to meet Robert for coffee and croissants. My breakfast in Mongar is water and crackers. We say goodbye to Rita, who will now begin her six-hour walk to her school, and get back into the hi-lux for the three-hour drive to Tashigang.

Sasha is the first to be dropped off, at a village between Mongar and Tashigang. We help her unload her luggage, two suitcases, one large, one small, her tin box and hot-water flask. A young man appears, introduces himself as the headmaster, and leads us to his house, where we sit stiffly on hard benches. A small boy brings a wooden bowl of rice crisps and three cups of tepid tea. "Do you think the water was boiled properly for this?" I whisper to Sasha. She downs her tea in one long swallow in answer. Then we are taken to her quarters, a two-room cottage, its rough mud walls streaked with fresh whitewash. Inside there is a wooden bed frame, a desk, a chair. We stand at the doorway, peering in. Even Sasha looks unsettled. It is so starkly empty and far from home. A rooster crows outside, and I have to fight hard not to weep, overwhelmed at the thought of leaving Sasha here by herself, in this shack that is to be her home. I can't imagine how she will survive, how any of us will. "What a great view," Lorna says from the window, and my voice returns, false and bright and strained. "We'll all visit each other," I say. "We'll only be a few hours apart when you think about it." When I think about it, I realize I have a whole new meaning for "the middle of nowhere."

We get back into the hi-lux and I turn to wave goodbye, but Sasha has gone inside and the door is firmly closed.

Subtropical, warm even now in early March, Tashigang is wedged into the crook of a mountain. Bougainvillea erupts over doorways and races along the top of stone walls, and tall, elegant eucalyptus sway over the stream that runs down from the mountain and through the middle of town. Tashigang reminds me of a medieval town, pictures from a high-school history book, the narrow crooked streets and three-storied, Tudor-style buildings with tiny balconies tacked on. The "lower market" is a row of shops along the road to the dzong; the "upper market" is a circle of shops around an enormous prayer wheel. Prayer wheels are cylinders inscribed with mantras, ranging from hand-held to room-sized. Spun around in a clockwise motion by the devout, they operate on the same principle as prayer flags: when set in motion, the printed mantras multiply the prayers being sent out for the benefit of all sentient beings. We sit on a bench outside a shop in the upper market and watch the traffic—horses carrying sacks of rice, two old women chatting beside the prayer wheel, children chasing a dog with a string of red chilies around its neck. Parked outside a shop, beside a blue UNDP jeep, is a battered bus with telltale streaks marring the Bhutan Government Transport Service sign painted across its side. "That must be the Vomit Comet," Lorna says. "And look over there, that must be the fire station." She points to four red, dented metal buckets hanging from a pole.

A white woman in a kira emerges from a shop. "Well, hello," she says. "You must be the new Canadians. I'm Nancy. I expected you here three weeks ago but then the roads closed. What to do." She shepherds us into the Puen Soom Hotel, a tiny restaurant in the corner of the market, and orders tea. There is a poster of the Canadian Rockies on the wall, and a miniature Canadian flag propped up among the bottles of whiskey behind the bar—signs of other Canadians in eastern Bhutan who use Tashigang as a meeting place. Nancy has a hangover, from a farewell party the night before. She is on her way out, her contract has finished, and she is returning to Canada. She has to be in Ottawa in three weeks, for an interview, for a job teaching in the Arctic, she tells us.

It must be something in the water, I think: no one here is content with a moderately difficult life. They all want to be four days off the road, and then, when they have served their time and can go back home to a nice warm apartment with a bus stop around the corner, they go teach in the Arctic!

"Is there diesel in Tashigang?" Lorna asks.

Nancy looks up, surprised. "You mean you were sent out here without any spare diesel?"

"The driver managed to find some along the way, but there's none in Bumthang or Mongar."

"Well, there's none here either," Nancy says, sighing. "We'll have to go ask *Dasho Dzongda* for help this afternoon." The Dzongda is the district administrator, and Dasho is a title, like Sir, conferred by the King.

Lorna sighs, too. "I guess we have to get gowned up, then," she says.

We finish the tea, and Lorna and I walk up the ridge behind the town and sit under some prayer flags, looking out across the narrow river valley. The hillsides nearby are brown and dry and detailed with shrubs and rocky outcrops and zigzagging paths, but in the distance, the mountains become insubstantial in the haze. Tashigang Dzong is on a lower spur to our right, above the turquoise river. Across the river and up behind the ridges is Bidung, Lorna's new home. Somewhere south is Pema Gatshel. Somewhere west is Thimphu. And beyond Thimphu—but no, I am too tired to retrace the journey mentally. I want to just click my heels three times and be home.

After more tea at the Puen Soom, we struggle into our kiras and walk through the lower market with Nancy to the dzong. A policeman stands at the gate, beside a jumble of worn rubber flip-flops and plastic sandals. "You have to wear shoes *and* socks into a dzong," Nancy explains, "or else go in barefoot." We step into the cool inner courtyard. Directly across from us is the massive stone wall of the dzong's three-storied temple. On either side of the courtyard are offices with thick wooden doors. Handlettered signs pasted on the lintels announce the DISTRICT EDU-CATION OFFICER, DISTRICT ANIMAL HUSBANDRY OFFICER, DISTRICT AGRICULTURE OFFICER. Very young, freshly shorn monks peer down at us from the wooden balconies above, and giggle when we wave to them. We are led into the Dzongda's chamber, where we sit on a bench under the window and are served tea and more Orange Cream Biscuits. I remember not to cross my legs and to wait for the Dzongda to begin drinking his tea before I touch mine. "Please have," he says, gesturing to our teacups. "Thank you, Dasho," Nancy says, and then explains who we are and where we are trying to go without diesel and why in very respectful tones. The Dzongda listens, nodding, and then rings a bell. A clerk appears, bent forward in a bow, and the Dzongda barks a long order in Dzongkha. The clerk murmurs over and over the honorific word for "all right." "*Lasso la, lass, lass, lass.*" The Dzongda has ordered a release of diesel from an emergency store. He says that the District Education Officer will arrange for horses and porters to transport

Lorna's things to Bidung, I can leave tomorrow in the hi-lux, which will drop me off in Pema Gatshel and return to Tashigang to take Nancy to Thimphu. It is all settled.

Out in the courtyard, we pass a regal-looking monk with a cat-o'-nine-tails. The small monks scatter at his approach. "The *Kudung*," Nancy says, "the Disciplinarian."

"They sure take authority seriously here," Lorna remarks.

We spend the night in a guest house, a stark, unwelcoming wooden cabin above the town. I lay awake for hours, listening to the dogs barking hysterically in the alley below. I can find nothing to throw at them except the batteries from my walkman: I fling them out into the night, and the barking continues uninterrupted.

The next morning, it is just Dorji and me on the winding road from Tashigang to the Pema Gatshel junction. Thirty minutes outside of Tashigang, we pass a cluster of immaculate white buildings spread over a green plateau. "Kanglung College," Dorji reports. I look longingly at the neat lawns and gardens, the basketball court, the wooden clock tower that declares the wrong time in four directions. This could have been my posting, I think sadly, noticing the tidy cottages, the electricity wires, a tall young man with the most beautiful face I have ever seen, reading a book under a flowering tree.

Just outside of Kanglung, a coy road sign informs us IF YOU LIKE MY CURVES, I HAVE MANY. Another admonishes BE GENTLE ON MY CURVES. An hour later, the driver announces, "Khaling," as we drive through a heavily misted town. An hour after that, we stop in Wamrong for lunch. I have seen no hint of the Canadian teachers already posted here and in Khaling, Leon and Tony, whom I met briefly in Thimphu. I sit on a retaining wall and nibble biscuits, looking out over the cloud-filled valley below. Two young boys stop throwing stones at a grotesquely deformed dog, to stare at me, pointing and whispering "*phillingpa*"—foreigner. "*Kuzu zangpo*," I greet them. They bump into each other, laughing, embarrassed, trying to scramble away.

When we reach the Pema Gatshel junction, the late-afternoon sun is already slanting over the hills. "Where is Tshelingkhor?" I ask Dorji.

In Thimphu, someone said there was a village at the junction. Dorji points to two bamboo shacks at the roadside. "Shop-cum-bar," I read. "Tshelingkhor."

The hi-lux turns off the main road.

"Can a village be two houses?" I ask Dorji.

"Village can be one house also," he says.

We bounce along the deeply gouged road, through a dense forest of gnarled oak, passing waterfalls and landslides. Suddenly, the forest opens and Pema Gatshel is below us, a deep, green, leafy salad bowl of a valley. Dorji points out the roof of the hospital, the dzong, a temple high on a hilltop. We drive through the bazaar, a straggling row of unpromising-looking shops. "Pema Gatshel Junior High School is there," Dorji says, gesturing ahead. I see a metal roof, a barbed-wire fence, cement walls.

"My new home," I think, but I do not believe it.

What to Do?

It is the third day of school, and I am standing in front of class II C. There is a blackboard but no chalk. There are no books, no crayons, no syllabus. There are, however, five students. The rest are "coming, miss." They have been coming, miss, for three days. The headmaster, a young man with a wispy mustache and a brilliant smile, says it will take a week for all the teachers and students to arrive. It is always like this at the beginning of the new school year each spring, he says.

"And the books?" I ask.

"After some time," he says, smiling. "We ordered them, but . . . what to do."

I certainly don't know. I have five students who spring to their feet each morning and shout, "Good morning, miss." I don't know what to begin teaching, whether to begin teaching or wait until the others come, how to keep them occupied until the others come. I don't even know their names yet.

This is how it has gone so far. First day: I am given a register and list of names and am told to take attendance. "My name is Jamie," I tell the members of class II C, three boys and two girls who could be any age between four and eleven. "The first thing I would like to do is learn all of your names, so I'd like you to all stand up one by one and introduce yourselves." This cheery speech is met by an exchange of bewildered glances but when the faces turn back to me, they are still smiling. "Does everyone understand?" I ask.

"Yes, miss," they chorus.

"Okay, you first," I say, pointing to a boy in the first row with standing-up hair. He looks like the oldest of the five.

"Yes, miss," he says, rising to his feet. I wait. He waits. I smile. He smiles back.

"Yes?" I say gently.

"Yes, miss?" he repeats politely.

"Go ahead," I say.

"Yes, miss." He sits back down.

"What is your name!" I finally exclaim, exasperated. He leaps to his feet again and shouts back, "My name is Song Sing!"

"Song Sing?" I repeat incredulously. He looks doubtful but says, "Yes, miss." I run through the list of names. There is no Song Sing among them. "Can you come and show me your name?" I ask. "Come and show me where your name is here."

He points to one. "This my name. My name is Tshewang Tshering."

"Tsay-wong Tse-ring," I repeat slowly. He looks relieved.

It takes most of the morning to get through the rest of the names. Phuntsho Wangmo. Sangay Chhoden. Karma Ngawang Dorji. Ugyen Tshering Dorji.

"Are you two brothers?" I ask the last two. "Brothers? Brothers?" They shake their heads shyly, giggling. Later, when I ask the headmaster, he looks equally confused. "Brothers? I don't think so."

"They have the same last name," I say.

"Oh! We don't have last names here," he says. "Just two names, which a lama gives. It can be Dorji Wangchuk, Wangchuk Dorji. Karma Dorji, Dorji Wangmo. Only the Royal Family has one last name. And the southern Bhutanese, they are Nepali, they have last names. Sharma, Bhattarai, Thapa."

"But how do you know who is related without last names?" I ask.

"Just like that only," he shrugs.

Day Two with Class Two. I practice saying their names, and they practice saying, "Yes, miss." No matter what I ask them, they smile and say, "Yes, miss." Do you understand? Yes, miss. Am I saying your name right? Yes, miss. Where are you going? Yes, miss.

Maybe I am talking too fast. "Do you have, any, books?" I ask very slowly, and am elated when they say, "No, miss." We smile at each other for some time. This gives me courage to try to fill in the complicated form the headmaster gave me this morning—student's name, father's name, mother's name, village, *gewog*, student's date of birth. We try it orally first, but I cannot even begin to spell their parents' names, and what is a *gewog*? I give them each a piece of paper. "Write down," I say slowly, "your name. Are you all writing your names?"

"Yes, miss."

"Good. Is everyone finished? Okay. Now, write down your birthday. Okay? Your birthday? Under your name."

They are still looking up at me. "Your birthday. Date of birth. When you were born," I repeat.

There is a prolonged silence, and then a conference begins in Sharchhop with Tshewang Tshering, the tallest, explaining, and Ugyen Tshering Dorji, the smallest, disagreeing. "You go first," I tell Tshewang. "When is your birthday?" He picks up his pencil and writes very carefully while the others watch. Over his shoulder I read, "It is rice and pork."

"Never mind," I say weakly. "We'll do it another time. You can go out now and play." They tumble out of their seats and burst out of the classroom, shrieking, as if it were the last day of school.

The classroom is furnished with long, narrow tables and benches. The teacher's desk is at the front of the room, its plain wooden top ink-stained, its two drawers empty. The blackboard is extremely small, but it doesn't matter because the stubs of soft chalk I found make no impression on it whatsoever.

In the staff room today, I meet several teachers who have just arrived from India. Everyone is very friendly, shaking my hand, asking me my "good name," welcoming me to the school on behalf of their colleagues and on their own behalf. Everyone asks me if I have "settled myself up" yet, and when did I come, and did I come across the top road, and am I knowing the Canadians who were here before me, Sir Dave and Mrs. Barb, except Mrs. Joy, from southern India, who asks if I am Christian. I am taken aback by this and stammer something about being raised a Christian but no longer, uh, something or other. The lines on her face deepen and she shakes her greying head; this is obviously the wrong answer.

Every second sentence is punctuated with the phrase "isn't it." Mr. Sharma asks me if I have met Mr. Iyya yet. I say no. "Oh, you will be having much in common with Mr. Iyya, isn't it," he informs me. "Mr. Iyya is always reading English novels and writing poetries. Mr. Iyya is a tip-top poet." He asks what my qualifications are, and before I can answer, tells me his: B.A., M.A., M.Ed., M.Sc. Actually, he confides, he is overqualified for this place, isn't it, but what to do.

Mrs. Joy asks me why I am wearing "that dress." I look down at my kira. "You don't have to wear their dress," she says grimly. She is wearing a brown synthetic sari and a grey sweater.

"But I want to," I say.

"It doesn't look nice on you," she tells me and I begin to ponder the irony of her name. The bell rings for lunch, and I excuse myself.

The school is a cold, concrete edifice, its cement walls discolored, crumbling in places, waterstained. Behind are the girls' and boys' hostels, off to one side is the dining hall. The front yard, a large, bald, dusty rectangle, is also the "playing field," where I send class II C each day after attendance to play until the bell rings for lunch. The whole compound is surrounded by a barbed wire fence. Across the road is a long, low ramshackle row of staff quarters, and a somewhat less dilapidated, two-story concrete apartment building, where I live. I mount the steep ladder steps to my flat on the second floor and let myself in, not wanting to be in any of the five dank rooms but not knowing where else to go. The cement walls are dark with smoke and grease and handprints, and I remind myself to find out who the landlord is. Maybe it wouldn't be such a bad place with a couple of coats of paint, a carpet of some sort, some real chairs instead of those punitive wooden benches. There is an abundance of wildlife, mice or rats, black beetles with pincers from the tool department of a hardware store, moths and ants and fleas, and today, an enormous hairy spider. Are there tarantulas in Bhutan? I beat it with a broom and sweep it out the door; it resurrects itself on the step and scuttles off.

I turn on all the taps, but there is still no water. I really must speak to the landlord. I have not unpacked. I cannot unpack until I clean, but I don't know how to begin to tackle the thick layer of damp and dust and decay that lays over everything. I have not had a bath since I left Thimphu, because there is rarely water in the taps, and when there is, it is numbingly cold and I am too afraid of the kerosene stove to try heating it. The stove, which has to be pumped before it is lit, hisses and splutters alarmingly, and I am sure that I will die in a massive kerosene explosion. I am almost out of crackers. The teachers downstairs, Mr. and Mrs. Sharma, from Orissa in eastern India, have invited me for supper twice. "Please, it is no problem for us," they said. "We have to cook for ourselves anyway, isn't it." But I cannot find the energy to go, to sit stiffly with strangers, nodding and smiling, trying to find things to talk about. Standing at the bedroom window, I look out over the verdant confusion of the Pema Gatshel valley. It makes my head hurt, looking down the green steepness, looking up into the empty sky. There are long moments when I cannot remember where I am. I feel completely unfamiliar to myself, almost unreal, as if parts of me have dissolved, are dissolving. The Buddhist view that there is no real self seems completely accurate. I have crossed a threshold of exhaustion and strangeness and am suspended in a new inner place.

It is dark by 6:30 in the evening, an absolute unbroken darkness, and crushingly silent. I light the kerosene lamps, fiddling with the wicks to stop them from smoking, and finally blow them out and light candles. I flip through my Sharchhop language notebook to the heading "School"—*sit down! stand up! don't shout! go outside! the teacher is angry! do you understand?*—but find nothing to help me communicate better with class II C. I try to write letters home even though the headmaster says that another landslide has blocked the lateral road and there is a *bandh,* a strike, in Assam. It will take a week or three to clear the road, and no one knows for sure about the strike, the last one went on for one hundred days. Writing will put things in order, or in sentences at least. I begin but cannot get beyond the first lines. After that, I fall into an abyss, sit blankly, blinking, staring.

A thick white mist moves into the valley one afternoon, bringing a cold, solemn rain. It rains all night, and at dawn the roof begins to leak, directly above my bed, directly, in fact, on my head. I get up and push the bed to the far wall. The sound of rain on the metal roof is the saddest thing I have ever heard. Outside, mist lies in deep drifts over everything. All around, the mountains sleep, blankets of cloud drawn up to their shoulders, over their heads. The teachers in the flats below have set buckets under the eaves and have strung up a clothesline in the stairwell. Mr. Sharma whistles as he hauls his buckets of rainwater in. I resolve to stop feeling sorry for myself. I, too, will set out buckets to collect water; I will snap out of this sorry state.

I walk to the bazaar, skirting the deep puddles along the road, stepping gingerly over cow dung. Children come out of the shops to stare at me. "English, English," they call shyly, and when I wave at them, they giggle and hide. Shopkeepers emerge from their shops to watch me pass. I feel a spectacle, and turn hastily into the nearest doorway. Inside, I point to what I want, a box of milk powder, two boxes of biscuits—no, *not* Orange Cream—okay, okay, Orange Cream, a jar of instant coffee. I am smiling painfully and nodding at the shopkeeper's questions. I don't know what he is asking. "*Gila,*" I say, which means "yes, it is." He looks at me quizzically. It is not the right answer. What was the question? I cannot live here if I don't speak the language.

Back out on the road, I contemplate visiting a few more shops, just to see what is available. Out of the corner of my eye, I see a blur. A dog growls, and there is a sharp pain in my ankle. I look down and see a tiny puncture, a spot of blood. But *why* did it bite me, I whine to myself, and then I realize. Oh god, oh god, I've been bitten by a rabid dog. I've come all the way across the world to die of rabies. I have to identify the dog. Yes, yes, the health lecture is coming back to me: confine the dog immediately and watch it for ten days for signs of rabies. But which of the twenty dogs milling around was it? I rush back into the shop.

"*Khu,*" I say breathlessly. Khu is dog. "Khu—" and I make a biting motion with my hand and show my ankle. The shopkeeper clucks sympathetically, but shows no alarm.

I have to ask if he knows the dog, if he thinks the dog is rabid. How do you say rabid in Sharchhop? I am thinking frantically. Mad. I could ask, is the dog mad? But I don't even know the word for "mad." I use the closest thing. "*Rotsigpa?*" I ask. Was the dog angry? The shopkeeper stares at me. He thinks *I'm* crazy. I can just hear him telling people, "What could I say? I *guess* it was angry. It bit her, didn't it?"

I flee to the hospital, where the tiny puncture wound is washed with hot water and antiseptic soap. The Norwegian doctor there listens to my story and goes up to the bazaar. He and his family have been in eastern Bhutan for several years, and speak fluent Sharchhop. While he is gone, I eat marzipan cake and drink black coffee brought by Liv, the Norwegian nurse. How is this cake possible, I want to know. And will I get more of it before my throat closes up and I have to be tied to a stake like Old Yeller? When the doctor returns, he tells me he doesn't think the dog is rabid. "There is a brown dog in the bazaar who is always biting people," he says. "Was it a brown dog that bit you?"

"Yes," I say. "No. I don't know. Maybe I should go to Thimphu for rabies injections." Or Canada.

The doctor reassures me. "No, no," he says. "I am sure that is not necessary. We've had no reports of rabies in Pema Gatshel recently."

"I guess you're right." I certainly *hope* he's right.

"You're staying in the building across from the school?" the doctor asks. "Where the other Canadians used to stay?"

"Yes. I need to see the landlord, actually," I say. "The roof leaks, there's hardly ever any water, and the whole place needs to be painted."

"Oh, I think the landlord lives in Thimphu," he says. "Water is very much a problem here, especially in the monsoon: too much outside, not enough inside. But what to do?"

What to do, what to do. I'm beginning to see that "what to do" means "absolutely nothing at all can be done." Back in my flat, I begin to unpack, swallowing hard periodically, checking my throat for pain or other signs of hydrophobia. The apartment has no cupboards or closets, so I lay things out on tables and windowsills, all my medicine and tools and batteries, I line my shoes neatly up beside the door and drape a few shirts over a clothesline the former tenants have strung across the bedroom. I leave my portable keyboard in its case on a bench, and stack my books on the little bedside table. There doesn't seem to be much else. How have I come with so little? I have left everything behind.

The Way to Tsebar

T he mist is at war with the mountains, and winning. It creeps like a disease, withering green trees, eroding ridges, diminishing the massive bulk of the mountains, turning solid rock to shadow. Everything looks long-deserted, haunted, like the last day of time. At night, it rains heavily. I have never seen so much rain. It's only March, not even the monsoon yet. I imagine the massive landslide on the lateral road, the rest of the mountain being washed away. It will take months, maybe years to fix. I feel besieged.

I walk around the school compound after class, watching the clouds moving over the mountains. Sometimes they fall from the sky in great swaths into the valley below, or are torn in strips that trail behind the main cloud body, dragged through forests and over ridges. My attempt at free-lance phonics was an astounding failure in class II C today, as was spelling dictation. Some of the kids can write passably well, others can barely hold a pencil. We spent the rest of the day drawing pictures. Later, in the staff room, talking with the other teachers, I felt acutely the edges and corners of myself which do not fit in here. I am too casual, too blunt, no one laughs at my jokes. I find myself speaking more slowly and formally, answering in complete sentences, standing almost at attention. I am afraid of making a mistake, saying the wrong thing, giving offense. I don't know why it is so difficult and there is no one I can talk to about it in my own language, my own inflections.

I give myself a good talking to: you said you wanted to come for the experience. Well, here it is, the experience. It's culture shock, it will pass. There's a whole page on it in the Briefing Kit, with a chart. Anyway, you only have to stay a year, you can go home at Christmas and not come back. You can always go home now, if things don't get better, if you hate it.

I hate it.

But I don't have the courage to ask to be sent back. I want divine intervention, I want to be absolved of blame and responsibility. I wish for an urgent message from home, an ultimatum from Robert, come home right now or it's all over between us, a serious but not too terrible illness, easily treated with tablets and bedrest at the Toronto General Hospital.

I sit at the table until it is dark, fiddling with my shortwave radio, which seems to have direct access to Radio Beijing. Everything else is noise—fading orchestras, electronic bleeps and blips and squelches. I turn it off. Outside, the dogs begin to bark. Hark, hark, I say aloud, and eat a cracker, an Orange Cream Biscuit, another cracker. I wish for cappuccino, I wish for baked potatoes, I wish for raspberry cheesecake. I wish to go to sleep and wake up in Canada. My legs are covered in flea bites which calamine lotion does absolutely nothing to help, and I scratch them until they bleed. I can't believe I volunteered for this. Am I going to cry? Then I remember the tin. The tin, the tin, how have I forgotten the square tin with the round lid, the rat-proof tin, the treasure box, the Christmas chest, the store of all goodness. I pry open the top, reach in and pull out a cellophane package of dried beans. Lentils. Split peas. A package of origami paper. It is Sasha's box. I have Sasha's split peas and origami paper and she has my chocolate. Life is suffering! Now I *am* going to cry. I sit on the floor and cry and cry, and when I have finished, I have decided: I will go home in the morning. I have made a mistake, a terrible terrible mistake, but it can be rectified. I will send a wireless message to Thimphu. I will say I am sick. I will lie, I will cry, I will beg. I will throw myself on the floor and scream. They cannot make me stay here! They cannot make me stay!

But the next day, the mist is gone and the sky is a clean, clear, dazzling blue. I can see every curve and contour of the mountains all around, edges and lines are hard and bright in the sharp morning light. At school, there is a letter for me. It has come from Tsebar, a village across the valley and up the next mountain, from Jane, a British teacher. *I heard you were there,* she writes. *Why don't you come and visit this weekend? I'd walk across but I hurt my ankle washing clothes in the creek.* She has drawn a map. *It's only a three- or four-hour walk.* Only!

I decide to go. I cannot go back home until the roadblock is cleared anyway. I will go to visit this Jane across the valley, and on my way back, I will go home. I will pass this house and the fields and the school, I will pass the gate, the crooked shops, the little white temple, I will keep going, straight home. At home, I will go to the library, I will reread *The History of Literary Criticism.* I will make notes, a reading list, a study schedule. I will not make this mistake again.

I take my sleeping bag, my high-tech flashlight, a bottle of water, a mini medical kit and my copy of *Where There Is No Doctor.* Down the valley path I go, stumbling under the hot afternoon sun against rocks and the roots and bones of trees. In some places, the path descends so steeply that I must clutch wildly at overhanging branches and nearby shrubs to hold myself upright. The path finally levels out, and I find myself in front of three shops. I can see the gypsum mine further downhill. Funded by the Government of India, Bhutan's principal aid partner, the mine is an immense, ugly white scar in the lush greenery. Parked on the roadside, loaded with chunks of gypsum, is a huge orange truck, its front and sides garishly painted with eyes and elephants, its windshield garlanded with tinsel and plastic flowers.

I continue on to the river, which zigzags wildly across the valley floor. I have to cross it six times, over sodden logs laid across large flat rocks. The sun is even hotter down here, and I am soaked with sweat by the time the path enters the forest and begins to ascend. Too bad I'm not staying, I think: I'd really be in good shape after two years of this.

I stop, panting, at a stream. How much farther up is it? Shouldn't I be there by now? Is this the right way? Why is my backpack so heavy?

You shouldn't have brought *Where There Is No Doctor.*

What if something happens out here? I'll need it.

The only thing that's going to happen is you're going to collapse under the weight of it.

You can't be too careful.

Yes, you can. You can be careful unto craziness.

Caution is not crazy. Singing a song about tapeworm cysts in the cerebellum is crazy. Carrying a medical book into the jungle is not crazy. Coming here in the first place was crazy. Look at this narrow little path. This path is crazy. What if I get lost?

You won't get lost, you have a map.

No, I don't, I left it on the table with Sasha's kidney beans.

You don't need a map. This is the path, you just have to follow it. Keep going.

I keep going. The sun has disappeared and there is no sign of Tsebar. There is no sign of anything. I am already exhausted, and my water is finished. I practice my Sharchhop in my head. *Where are you going? I am going to Tsebar. Are you a nun? No, I am a teacher.* Shadowy thoughts of wild animals begin to solidify, taking the shape of bears. There are bears in Bhutan, I read it in a library book. *The Himalayan black bear: fierce black bear with characteristic white V on its chest.*

Are you a teacher? No, I am a coward.

The way up grows even steeper, and my legs ache and burn and shake. I stop, gasping, and rub my stinging eyes. The path bifurcates around an enormous mango tree, one route continuing sharply up, another leveling off into a dense forest. It levels off because it leads to a village, I reason, and take it. Forty-five minutes later, it plunges into a pool of stagnant water and does not come out on the other side. I sit on an exposed tree root and stare into the shadows, trying to determine the most reasonable thing to do. Everything seems reasonable. I should go back to the mango tree. I should go back to Pema Gatshel. I should spend the night here. I should go on and look for the other end of the path. I should scream for help.

Everything seems possible: I will find the path, I will find a village, I will find Tsebar, someone will find me, no one will find me, I will be lost in the bush and die of starvation. My stomach feels like a huge, hollow, echoing drum, and I have run out of thoughts. I have reached the end of something, but I do not know what it is.

Twigs snap behind me and there is a cow. A reddish-brown bulk with a bell. Another cow, black with a bent horn. A calf. A boy with a stick. He seems surprised to see me. A man bent under a load of wood and a woman with a basket come up behind him. The cows drink from the green pool, and the man and woman stare at me.

"Where you is going, miss?" the boy asks me.

"I'm going to Tsebar."

The boy looks troubled. "But, miss," he says. "Tsebar is not this way."

"Which way is Tsebar?"

He gestures. Back and up.

"Thank you," I say. "I'm a teacher at Pema Gatshel. Across the valley. Do you know Pema Gatshel?"

"Miss," he says with great patience. "I am in your class."

Karma Dorji is also going to Tsebar with his aunt and uncle. I follow them back to where the path splits, and we sit under the mango tree. It is almost dark now, but I feel strangely light. I came to the end of something and passed through it. I do not know what it was. "Tsebar is not far," Karma Dorji says. "We is always taking rest here." He pours clear water from a cloudy jerry can into my empty water bottle. The aunt and uncle unwrap three multicolored round baskets. They pass one to me, and Karma Dorji helps me pull it open. Inside large chunks of meat, red chilies and onions are embedded in a mound of rice.

Karma Dorji and his uncle are going to share a basket. They are waiting for me. His aunt is saying something.

"She is telling our food is not that very good, please don't mind," Karma Dorji translates. "She is telling please eat."

"Thank you," I say, and eat the meat. It is delicious.

Entrance

Quand un étranger
arrive . . . il éprouve,
sans pouvoir s'en
rendre compte, un
sentiment de gaieté
et de bien-être qui
persiste jusqu'au
départ.

—Ibn Khurdadba

Anyone Can Live Anywhere

A vast and silent darkness settles over Tsebar as we approach, and my flashlight cuts a bright wide beam through the blackness. Karma Dorji points to the dark shape of Jane's house a few yards away. The wooden slats that cover the windows are rimmed in warm yellow light. Jane opens the door before I knock. "You made it," she smiles. I turn to thank Karma Dorji's aunt and uncle again, but they wave off my thanks and disappear.

"I didn't think you were coming," Jane says. She is wearing a dark blue kira that falls smoothly to the floor, and her straight blonde hair is tied neatly back. Everything about her is elegant and serene. How is it possible, I wonder, to wash clothes in a creek and still look like that?

"I got lost," I gasp, wriggling out of my backpack. I am afraid to sit down. My knees will not bend, and if they bend, surely they will never again unbend. I stand inside the door, looking around. At one end of the room is a kitchen; the low stove is made out of mud, with two holes in the top for pots and another in the base for the wood. Pots and plates are stacked tidily on shelves above a screened cabinet. At the other end is a sitting area with benches and a low, wooden table. The floor is covered with a straw mat, and the rough mud and stone walls look freshly whitewashed. There are candles everywhere, jam jars of flowers, blue-covered cushions on the wooden benches. In one shadowy corner, there is a skinny chicken. I blink several times but it does not vanish. Is it a pet? Is it dinner?

Through the door to the other room, I can see a thick quilt spread over a wooden bed, a stack of books and a kerosene lamp on a bedside table, a shuttered window.

"What a lovely house," I say. Jane laughs but I mean it. It feels like a real home, except perhaps for that chicken. I tell myself that I will also transform that horrid place in Pema Gatshel. I will have blue-covered cushions and jam jars of flowers when I go back. And then I remember: I am not going back to Pema Gatshel. I am going home.

"How is your foot?" I ask. I notice she is limping slightly.

"Okay but not great," Jane says. "I'm supposed to go across to Pema Gatshel next week for our health course—it should be better by then."

"*Our* health course?"

"It's run by the Norwegian doctors at the Pema Gatshel hospital for all the teachers assigned to morning clinic. Do you mean you haven't been assigned to morning clinic yet?"

I shake my head.

"You will be," she promises, taking down tin plates and spoons from the shelves. I start to say that I have already eaten but realize I am hungry again. "My landlord and his wife are coming for dinner. In fact, they are bringing dinner. Pema is an excellent cook," Jane says. "Now, tell me, how is everything over there at Pema Gatshel? How do you like it?"

I hate it, I want to say. Pema Gatshel is awful, my students don't understand a word I say, I got bitten by a dog, my apartment is hideous and, anyway, I'm going home right after this visit. But the door opens and a man and woman come in. Jane introduces them: Jangchuk, her landlord, a thin wiry man in a dark-red gho, and his wife, Pema, plump and apple-cheeked. We smile crazily at each other, and then Pema begins to unpack several bottles and pots from her bag.

"*Bangchang* and arra before dinner," Jane says. "Can you drink?"

"I haven't had arra yet. What's bangchang?"

"It's a kind of barley beer. It's delicious."

We sit in a semicircle around the mudstove. Jangchuk has taken a small wooden bowl out of his gho and is wiping it with a piece of cloth. Jane and Pema have their own wooden bowls; I am given an enormous tin mug. Pema stirs and strains and ladles and finally fills our cups. I sip at mine gingerly and am pleasantly surprised. The bangchang is warm and mild, sweet and salty. "It's good," I say. "How do you say delicious in Sharchhop?"

"*Zhim-poo la,*" Jane says.

"Zhim-poo la," I repeat, and Jangchuk and Pema laugh. Pema ladles more bangchang into my cup.

"Zhé, zhé," she says.

"She's telling you to drink up," Jane says. I take a slightly bigger sip. It must be safe, I think, if Jane is drinking it, and it really is good. Pema adds more bangchang to our cups and exhorts me to drink. I begin to feel warm and sleepy. When the ladle swings my way again, I keep my hand firmly over my cup and do a ridiculous mime of a drunken, dizzy me. Pema nods and puts her ladle back in the pot, but as soon as I move my hand away, her arm shoots over and my cup is full. "An old Sharchhop trick," Jane laughs. I am relieved when the pot is empty, but Jane says, "Now comes the arra."

Pema fills my cup with what looks like water. I take a tiny sip of the sharp, bitter liquid and shudder.

"Zhimpoo la?" she asks.

I nod helplessly.

"It's more of an acquired taste," Jane says, draining her bowl. "It reminds me of saké."

It reminds me of lighter fluid, but by the fourth or fifth tiny sip, it's not quite so bad, and by the second cup, I am sure that it is improving my comprehension of Sharchhop. Dinner is mountains of rice and large chunks of potato cooked with chilies, followed by a final cup of arra, called *zim-chang,* the good-night drink. "If you were staying with Pema, you'd get *zheng-chang,*" Jane tells me. "Wake-up arra, served at dawn." Pema tries to make me eat and drink more but I collapse on the floor in protest. "This is Bhutanese hospitality," Jane says. "They fill you up until you can't move and then say sorry, we have nothing to give you."

I volunteer to wash the dishes, but Jane doesn't have running water inside the house. We will wash them tomorrow outside. Out in the latrine, squatting in the malodorous darkness, I realize what a luxury my indoor plumbing is, even if the running water doesn't run very often. Back inside, Pema and Jangchuk and I say many goodbyes and then they are gone. Jane puts cushions on the floor under the window and I unroll my sleeping bag over them and climb in, fully dressed. My feet and shoulders ache, my face is rough and gritty, and my brain feels like it is sloshing around inside my skull. Jane sets a candle on the low table. "Now, there are just two things I have to tell you about before you go to sleep."

I am already asleep. I do not want to hear two things.

"If you hear things falling off the shelves in the night, it's just the rats. And in the morning, could you just reach behind you and slide open that window to let the chicken out?"

"The chicken?" I had forgotten about the chicken. I struggle to sit up. There it is, sleeping in a nook near the stove. "Do you get fresh eggs every morning?" I ask Jane.

"Well, that's why I got it, but it doesn't lay eggs for some reason," Jane says. "Good night."

I blow out the candle and push myself down deep into the sleeping bag. Do not think about the rats, I tell myself. Do not, do not. I lie there, hoping that sleep comes before the rats, but it does not. And it's not just rats, it's the Rat Olympics. I can hear them sprinting across the floor, vaulting from shelf to shelf, somersaulting over pots and plates. On the sidelines, spectator rats cheer them on. Something falls with a crash and the crowds go wild. I sit up, gasping.

"They knock that same tin off every night," Jane calls from the next room.

I find my flashlight and aim a spot of light at the kitchen. There is a moment of silence and then they begin again. I burrow deeper into my bed and concentrate on the gentle ringing of a horse's bell outside. Eventually, I fall asleep and dream I am walking. All night I walk up and down hillsides, over streams, through forests. I have a dim idea that I am trying to walk out of Bhutan, but Bhutan never ends. I awake, exhausted, to cool grey light and the sound of clucking. The chicken is heading my way. I fumble with the wooden slat above my head, but the chicken is not interested in the window. It is interested in my flashlight, which it hops and clucks around until the flashlight falls to the floor with a suspicious little ping! I retrieve it and turn it on. I take the batteries out and put them back in. Nothing. The chicken throws itself out the window with a shriek of satisfaction. I lie back down, composing a letter in my head to the manufacturers. *Dear Sirs: Your $50 high-tech flashlight guaranteed to last five years has been broken by a barren chicken.*

We sit outside on the step, eating oatmeal with powdered milk for breakfast. Sunlight pours down thickly and the whole green world shimmers. Jane is talking about how hard it was when she first arrived. She hadn't quite realized . . . how hard it would be. But then, she got to know people, Jangchuk and Pema befriended her, she learned a little Sharchhop. And she started teaching and that made up for everything else. The kids make it all worthwhile, she says. They are bright and unaffected and responsive. She loves them.

I say maybe I've made a mistake, maybe Bhutan is not for me.

Jane nods. "I felt that way at first. But you know what they say about these overseas postings: anyone can live anywhere. You think you can't in the beginning, but then you do."

After breakfast, we go to collect water, each of us carrying a plastic bucket. A group of children follows us, shouting "Good morning, miss!"

"Good morning Kezang, good morning Nidup, good morning Karma," Jane calls back. The village tap is a black standpipe in the center of the village. Several people are there with an assortment of buckets, bamboo containers, jerry cans and tin pots. Jane knows everyone. "*Pema Gatshel lopen,*" she tells them, pointing to me. *Lopen* means teacher. We fill the buckets and haul them back. I slop most of my water onto my ankles and shoes. Jane washes the plates and pots on her front step, scrubbing them with a gritty powder first and stacking them up in grey soapy piles, rinsing each item carefully so that no water is wasted. The kettle on the kerosene stove is steaming, and I pour the water into a Chinese thermos. There is no shop in Tsebar: kerosene and all other manufactured goods have to be carried across the valley from Pema Gatshel. Jane cooks on the mudstove in the evening, and only uses the kerosene stove in the morning, to cook breakfast and boil water. Her stove uses wicks and is easier to light than my "pump and explode" type. "Oh those things," Jane says. "They terrify me. I don't know how you manage." I like the sound of that word, *manage*. *How is she doing? Oh, well, it's difficult but she's managing.* I do not tell Jane that I manage by not cooking.

Now she collects the buckets again: she is going to the creek to wash clothes, and I go with her. We walk through the village, several stone and mud houses scattered around a temple. Groves of ancient mango and oak trees crowd close around the village. With its tarmacked road and gypsum trucks and shops, Pema Gatshel suddenly looks like a big town in comparison. I ask where the path goes to after Tsebar and Jane says that India is only a few ridges away. I stand and turn, taking in the view: 360 degrees of mountains folded into one another, ridges running down into unseen valleys and rising again, this geography repeating itself over and over. It is hard to imagine the plains of India from here. It is hard to imagine anything at all beyond these mountains, and I have the strangest feeling that I have been here forever, that I have dreamed up that other life in Canada.

We turn off the main path and hobble down a slope to the creek, where Jane immerses her clothes in the shallow water, and I sit on a rock in the shade. She tells me about Jangchuk and Pema, how they took care of her in the beginning, bringing her dinner every night until she could manage for herself. Jangchuk is a *gomchen*, Jane says, a lay priest and the caretaker of the temple. Gomchens usually belong to the Nyingma sect of Tibetan Buddhism (slightly different from the Drukpa Kargyue sect, which is the official religion of Bhutan); they are allowed to marry; they do not wear the robes of a fully ordained monk, but their ghos are longer, worn calf-length instead of knee-length, and they often keep their hair long. People go to them for all sorts of religious ceremonies, for blessings, horoscopes, births, deaths, illness.

"Don't people go to the hospital in Pema Gatshel?" I ask.

"Mmm, they'd almost always go to a lama first, because illness is usually seen as having a spiritual cause. If the lama is unable to do anything they might go to the hospital, but by then it's often too late, and if the person dies in the hospital, people blame the foreign medicine."

"Is traditional Bhutanese medicine herbal?"

"Some of it is," Jane says. "But most of the treatment here consists of particular prayers and pujas. They also do a couple of other things, like blood-letting. Tiny incisions are made at a certain place on the body. The worst thing I've ever seen was the searing. I didn't actually see it, only the scars on Pema. They burn the skin with a heated metal rod." She draws thick rectangles on her arm with her thumb and forefinger to show me.

She tells me about another treatment which Pema underwent for her chronic stomach pain. After some prayers, she said, Jangchuk had taken a cow's horn with a hole in the tip and applied the base to Pema's stomach. He sucked on the tip and then lifted the horn—there on Pema's stomach was a black clot, which Jangchuk hastily threw out. Jane said he hadn't made an incision; she had been watching carefully, and there was no sign of bleeding. "What was it, do you think?" I ask. Jane shrugs. "I don't know. Jangchuk said it was the thing that was making her sick, and sure enough, she got better shortly afterward."

I do not answer. I am thinking about magician's techniques, sleight-of-hand, a false-bottomed horn. "Do you think it could have been a trick?" I ask Jane.

She says she considered this, but why would he trick his own wife?

"Maybe it was psychological," I said. "A placebo."

But Jane shakes her head. "No," she says. "Jangchuk believes in his medicine. You know, in the beginning, people would tell me so-and-so was sick because he'd seen a ghost or a black snake, or he hadn't made an offering to his guardian deity, and I'd just shake my head. But now, I'm not so sure."

"But do you believe that people really get sick because they've seen a ghost?" I ask.

"I can't say anymore. So many things happen here that you just can't explain, and I don't know enough of the language to understand the whole picture. I ask the older students but I think a lot gets lost in the translation. They say 'ghost' or 'black magic' but who knows exactly what that means? We're seeing just the tip of a whole belief system. Faith makes things real."

"But only psychologically," I say. "Not physically real, right?"

"With ghosts and black magic, what's the difference?"

I watch her soap and pound her clothes on the rock, wring them out and drop them into her bucket. Laughter floats down from the groups of other women washing their clothes upstream. We climb back up to the main path. Jane goes home to hang up her clothes, and I go to the temple, where Jane says there will be a puja, a religious ceremony, held regularly in honor of Guru Rimpoché.

The temple is surrounded by a stone wall. In the flagstone courtyard, prayer flags hang limply in the warm air. The whitewashed walls of the main building taper slightly as they rise to the gently pitched roof. Around the top, under the eaves, is the broad band of dark red paint that indicates a religious structure. Inside, under the window where the light falls in, men wearing maroon scarves over their ghos sit in a row, their musical instruments in front of them: bronze and silver horns, some very long, a drum held upright on a carved wooden handle, cymbals, a bell. Prayer books, consisting of long narrow sheets of unbound paper between thin wooden covers, lie open in front of them. I remember to take off my shoes and stand hesitantly in the doorway until Jangchuk sees me and gestures for me to come in. Sitting cross-legged on the polished wooden floor, I study the frescos on the walls, the carved pillars, and the elaborate altar, which is laden with butter lamps, bowls of water, offerings of rice, fruit, flowers, incense, packages of biscuits. The paintings on the walls show dozens of Buddhas and other figures I do not recognize; the paint has faded, and the walls are smoke-blackened, but the faces of the Buddhas are serene and gentle, smiling down. Behind the altar is an enormous Buddha, gold painted, with black eyes and dark blue hair and the same kind smile.

The prayers begin softly, rhythmically, partly chanted partly sung. I close my eyes and try to think about nothing, but I cannot keep my mind empty, or even quiet. Thoughts roll in, pulling me along. Suddenly the horns are blown and I am so startled I nearly leap to my feet. The sound is long, clear, trilling, mournful, something between music and a cry. From the longer horns, low notes blurt out. A drum begins to beat. I can feel the music at the base of my spine, in my stomach, my throat. The chanting begins again and the bell stitches bright silver notes into the droning voices. A sudden, short silence, followed by a prayer sung in a minor key, and I struggle to keep the melody in my head, but it is driven out by the cries of the horns and the renewed beating of the drum. I cannot think because my head is full of the sound. It is beautiful, it is not beautiful, it is discordant and stark, it is frightening, yes but it is also somehow comforting, it is music for great unroofed spaces, it is, what is it? It is convincing, I think finally. It is the closest word I can find. I close my eyes and now it is easy to think of nothing.

When I open my eyes again, I am not sure where I've been. Jangchuk and the others are standing up and filing out into the courtyard, and they motion for me to follow. Outside, we are served plates of rice, vegetable curry, dahl and ema datsi with bowls of arra, and I am exhorted to eat more, drink more. When I finally stand up to go, I feel lightheaded. Also strangely light.

At Jane's house, I fall into a warm and dreamless sleep. When I wake up, it is dark outside, and Jane is picking through a basket of rice by candlelight. Tomorrow I will walk back to Pema Gatshel. The thought does not make me as unhappy as I expected. Anyone can live anywhere. We will see. . . . I search for my flashlight to take to the latrine and then remember that it is broken. I take a candle instead, which I somehow manage to drop into the hole. I remind myself to ask Jane why she just doesn't eat that chicken.

For Your Kind Information and Necessary Action, Please

I am in a drugstore. The aisles seem unusually long, it is some kind of superstore, and everything gleams under the overhead lights. I push my cart slowly, studying the shelves carefully. What do I need? Look, here's this bath gel new and improved with a flip-top lid. The drugstore leads into a grocery store. I stand in the cereal section, considering deeply: Shreddies or Fruit Loops? The store will close soon, I have to hurry. "Shoppers," a glad voice says, "visit our ladies' department for unbelievable savings." I wake up, blinking: I am in Pema Gatshel. I must push back against the dark disorientation this realization causes if I am to get out of bed, and it seems I must get out of bed: someone is knocking on the door.

On the doorstep are two of my students. Karma Dorji, who rescued me on the way to Tsebar, is short and sturdy, with a round, cherubic face, nut-brown skin, and a distinctive cowlick. Norbu is taller, with a crooked little grin and a perpetually runny nose. Their ghos are faded, and on their feet they wear rubber sandals. Silently they offer their presents: a bundle of spinach, a cloth bag of potatoes, a handful of spring onions. Karma Dorji reaches inside his gho and removes a small brown egg. "Thank you!" I say. "Thank you very much!" They look embarrassed at my effusive thanks.

"My mother is giving," Norbu says.

"Please tell your mother thank you," I say, wondering if I should be paying for these things.

"Yes, miss." They leap down the ladder-like stairs and bound across the playing field.

Back inside, I hear water sputtering from a tap. This means I must fill every bucket, basin, pot, pan, bottle, kettle, jug, mug and cup right now, before the water disappears. In the kitchen, I pump up the kerosene stove until it is hissing steadily, throw a lit match at it and run into the bedroom, waiting for the explosion. When none comes, I creep back to the kitchen and put a pot of water on the blue flame. It immediately dies, and I have to repeat the process.

In the bathroom, the water has stopped. I have one full bucket. I can either bathe or wash my clothes. The drain is partially blocked, and although I have stuck a variety of implements down there—thick branches, thin willow wands, a piece of barbed wire—there is always a swamp in the middle of the bathroom. Gritting my teeth, I squat next to the bucket, and begin to pour the cold water over myself with a plastic jug. By the time I have finished, I am shivering violently and have to climb back into bed for several minutes before I can begin my daily kira ritual, a series of physical and mental contortions as I swathe and pin and belt the length of cloth around me. Sometimes, I stop, exasperated, holding some unexplained end, trying to figure out how it got free and where I should put it, and I wonder if I shouldn't just give up and wear a skirt and sweater. No, I will not give Mrs. Joy the satisfaction. Yesterday in the bazaar, an old woman stopped me and began to tuck in various parts of my kira, pulling the skirt down as she yanked the top up. Stepping back, she studied her adjustments critically. "*Dikpé?*" I asked. Okay? She shook her head and waved me on: it was still wrong, but it was the best she could do with me.

With the egg Norbu has brought me, I make a pancake, which I eat with Bhutan's own Mixed Fruit Jam, and then I leave for school, descending the steep staircase slowly, backwards, clutching the rails.

At school, I sit in the staff room with the other teachers, watching the students in the playing field. Many of them did not start school until they were eight or nine, which means that most of the class VIII kids are in their late teens. They all wear the school uniform, grey-blue ghos and kiras. Some of the smaller kids wear hand-me-downs, faded and splotched and miles too big for them. Pema Gatshel has both boarders and day students, and many of the day students walk for one or two or three hours to school each morning and evening. When it rains, they arrive at school soaked, and sit in their wet uniforms the whole day.

When the bell rings, we stand on the steps for morning assembly. The students stand in front of us at the edge of the playing field, in lines according to gender and class. The number of female students decreases steadily from preprimary to class VIII. The school captain, a class VIII boy named Tshering, leads the morning prayer and national anthem. From where I am standing, I can see the tip of a snow peak shining above a row of dark blue mountains in the northwest. I like to think that I am facing home, and wonder what Robert is doing right now, half the world away. It is yesterday evening there, and I picture him, with perfect clarity, in his apartment, reading the paper in his armchair, playing his guitar, cooking dinner. I wonder if he is thinking of me at the exact moment I am thinking about him. There is no way to find out. I am a million billion trillion miles away. Sometimes during morning assembly, my throat closes up and it hurts to breathe. Sometimes, though, I remember my book of Buddhist readings: feelings, desires, sorrows are all created by the mind. Everything in fact is "mind." If I remember this, I simply turn my attention back to the slow and stately singing, and the sadness drains away.

After the national anthem, a senior student gives a short speech in English or Dzongkha on an assigned topic: punctuality, honesty, respect for dear parents and teachers. Every English speech ends with the same breathless rush: ". . . and so my dear friends, I sincerely hope you all will be punctual/honest/respectful to your dear parents and teachers." The headmaster then makes a speech in Dzongkha; I know only the first word, *dari,* which means "today."

Dari, after the assembly, the headmaster informs me that I have been assigned to morning clinic, and will have to attend the first-aid course at the hospital starting on Monday. I have also been assigned to the library, he says, and gives me the key. I have already been to the library, a poorly lit room with a few very tattered picture books, abridged editions of *The Red Badge of Courage* and *Heidi,* and a great many Canadian readers published in the mid-1970s. How these came to be here, no one seems to know.

I like the headmaster and his wife, who has just given birth to twins. At first, I think he is very young to be a headmaster, but I change my mind when I see him with the students. He is sternly and completely in control. It is not so much his character as the Bhutanese way of being in authority, I think, remembering the officials we met in Thimphu, the Dzongda in Tashigang. Whatever it is, it elicits a fearful, unquestioning obedience from the students. With the staff, he is more relaxed, but I sense an undercurrent of tension between him and the Indian staff. The Indian teachers freely admit they are here because they could not find jobs in India, and they almost seem to resent the fact that they have to take orders from the Bhutanese. Last week, in the staff room, Mr. Sharma commented loudly on the uselessness of attending morning assembly if it's going to be in a language he doesn't understand. "Half the staff doesn't understand Dzongkha," he said.

"Well, half the staff does," the headmaster replied levelly. "Dzongkha is our national language." Mrs. Joy tried to give me a whispered account of "the problem with these people," meaning the Bhutanese, but I pulled away. I do not want to be a part of whatever factionalism is developing here.

Outside the door of my classroom, I pause briefly, listening to the clatter and chatter inside. It stops abruptly as I swing open the door. This is my favorite part of the day. "Good morning, Class Two C," I say. The entire class leaps up and sings out, "Good morn-ing, miss!" Twenty-three faces are smiling at me. Sometimes they shout it with so much conviction that I laugh.

I have a syllabus now, and the students have textbooks and thick notebooks, and pencils which they sharpen with razor blades. I haven't mastered this skill yet, and have to ask one of the kids to sharpen my pencils for me. Sharpening miss's pencil has become a somewhat prestigious task, but they were puzzled the first time, watching me almost slice off my fingers, and there was much whispered consultation in

Sharchhop. "Where did they find this one?" I imagined them saying. "She can't even sharpen a pencil."

I teach English, math and science in the mornings, and in the afternoon, the Dzongkha lopen comes in to teach the national language. From the other classrooms I can hear the drone of students spelling or reading and reciting in unison: "h-o-u-s-e, house, c-a-r-r-y, carry, g-o-i-n-g, going." In the other classrooms, the teacher says something and the students say it back, over and over and over. I cannot think what good this rote learning is doing anyone. I ask the students to read out loud individually and they look at me as if I have lost my mind.

Often, attendance is the only thing we manage to accomplish in class II C. There are a thousand interruptions. A woman knocks at the window and holds up a cloth bag. The entire class rushes over. "Class Two C," I say, "sit down. There's no need for all of you to be at that window." Actually, there's no need for any of them to be at that window. "Who is it?" I ask.

"It is Sangay Jamtsho's mother," they answer.

"What does she want?"

"Sangay Jamtsho forgot his jhola."

"Sangay Jamtsho, go and get your jhola," I say. The entire class rolls toward the door, like ball bearings, but I am there first. "I said Sangay Jamtsho. Sit back down, the rest of you."

Sangay Chhoden comes up to my desk. Beneath her thick thatch of hair, her delicate features are screwed up in concentration. "Miss," she says so softly I can barely hear. "House going."

"What do you mean, Sangay?"

"Yes, miss."

I start again. "House going?"

"Yes, miss."

"Your house?"

"Yes, miss, my house going!"

"Now?"

"Yes, miss. House going now, miss."

"But why, Sangay? Why house going now? Now is school. Are you sick?"

"No, miss. House going now."

I sigh, exasperated. "Are you coming back?"

"Yes, miss. Coming."

"Okay, go."

Dorji Wangdi, the office assistant, tea-maker, and general all-round helper whose official title is "peon," knocks at the door. "Chit from Headmaster, Sir," he says, handing me a notice. It has been noticed that some teachers are "biasedly motivated" and all staff are kindly requested to follow the rules and regulations of the school and to attend to each and every duty including morning assembly without prejudice to their utmost ability for the smooth functioning of the school. This notice is for our "kind information and necessary action, please."

Sangay Dorji puts up his hand. His "stomach is paining," can he go to the toilet? Norbu's hand shoots up. His stomach is also paining. So is Sonam's! So is Phuntsho's! I tell them to wait until Sangay Dorji comes back, but Sangay Dorji does not come back. I am so intent on explaining the difference between long 'a' and short 'a' that I do not notice until another student calls out, "Miss! Sangay Dorji is playing outside!" I look out the window, and yes indeed, there is Sangay Dorji, playing outside.

I send Karma Dorji to get Sangay, and we get all the way to long 'o' before I look out the window to see Sangay *and* Karma playing outside.

Mr. Iyya, Pema Gatshel's self-proclaimed bard, knocks at my class-room door. Originally from Madras, Mr. Iyya has been at the school for more than ten years. His curly black hair is slicked back with hair-oil, and he sometimes wears a spotted cravat. His everyday speech is a garbled mess of malapropisms, misquotations, and flights of fancy, and his poetry, which he pastes on the school bulletin board, is even worse. He is in charge of all English extracurricular activities—the school magazine, debates and plays. Underneath the genteel-poet guise, though, he has a terrible temper. Yesterday, I was horrified to see him break a stick on a class III boy's hand.

"Yes, Mr. Iyya?" I ask.

He bows deeply and says he would like to apologize to my ladyship for this untimeless interruption but he would like to most humbly request me to borrow him my cane as he has the gravest misfortune of a broken one.

"My what?" I ask.

"Your ladyship's cane."

I stare at him. Mr. Iyya is definitely unhinged. I turn to class II C. "He wants one stick for beating, miss," one of them informs me.

"I do not use a cane in my classroom," I tell Mr. Iyya coldly, and close the door with a bang.

Dorji Wangdi knocks at the door. Another chit for my kind information and necessary action. There will be a puja at the school in a few weeks for the benefit of all sentient beings. All teachers are invited to attend.

Mr. Tandin, the class VIII history teacher and Store-In-Charge, comes to tell me that the School Store will be open for one half-hour. I go up to the Store and bring back twenty-three boxes of crayons. Class II C falls silent at the sight of them, and then erupts in a cheer. "Miss, I am very happy to you!" Sonam Phuntsho crows jubilantly. The crayons are magic. Class II C is very quiet as I explain that these are their own crayons, and they have to look after them, as it is highly unlikely that I will be able to persuade Mr. Tandin to release twenty-three boxes of crayons from his paltry store ever again. I tell them I will read them a story and then they will draw me a picture of the part they liked most. "Once a long time ago there was a mouse," I begin, but there is another knock at the door.

After school, I go up to the library and fling open the window. Everything is covered with a fine white dust. I begin to pull books off the shelves in an attempt to impose some sort of classification system, but there is hardly enough material to classify. I ponder various systems, but the most appropriate one seems to be: unreadably tattered, moderately tattered, and untouched (all the Canadian readers fall into this category). I lock the door and go home to find three students sitting at the top of my stairs, their ghos splotched with mud from an after-school soccer game. Karma Dorji and Norbu are back, and they have brought Tshewang Tshering, whose standing-up hair has recently been shaved off. "Are you waiting for me?" I ask stupidly. Of course they are. My Australian neighbor on the other side of the building, some sort of sheep or cow or horse insemination expert, has been out-of-station since I arrived. "May-I-come-in-miss?" they chorus as I open the door. Once inside, they stand uneasily. I usher them into the sitting room. They sit in a row on a bench, looking around, smiling at each other, dangling their bare, dirty feet above the floor. Finally, Tshewang Tshering asks me, "Miss, you have snaps?"

"Snaps?"

"Yes, miss. We looking snaps."

Snaps? I feel my face creasing up into a hundred lines of bewilderment as I try to guess what "snaps" could possibly mean. I have an insane idea that they want ginger snaps.

"Miss," Tshewang Tshering says. "Snaps. Mother, father, sister, brother."

"Oh, you want to see pictures! Snapshots!"

"Yes, miss!" They are nodding vigorously.

Oh hurray! I understand! I hurry off to the bedroom and pull out a Ziploc bag of photographs.

"This is my mother," I say, handing out the pictures which they seize eagerly. "My father. My father's house."

"This your sister?" Karma Dorji asks, holding up a picture of my brother, Jason.

"No, that's my brother."

"Your brother, miss?"

"Yes, Karma."

"He is lama!"

"A lama? No . . ."

"Why—why he is having long hairs?"

"Oh, because—because, hmmm," I search for an answer. "Just like that only," I finally say, and they nod.

Tshewang Tshering is looking at a postcard of the Toronto skyline. "Miss, this your house?"

"No, that's a bank."

"This your house?"

"No, that's an office. All offices."

"This one your house?"

"No, no! That's the CN tower."

Another postcard, of Yonge Street. "This your village, miss?"

"Yes. Toronto."

"Who is this?" Tshewang Tshering asks, pointing to some tourists on the postcard.

"I don't know," I say, bewildered by the question. "Just some people." And then I understand. I explain that there are two million people in Toronto, more people in this city than in all of Bhutan.

"*Yallama!*" they say softly, the Bhutanese expression for surprise or disbelief.

Karma Dorji is flipping through a stack of magazines and music books. "Miss, this your mother?"

I get up to look and almost fall down laughing. "No, that is not my mother!" It is Johann Sebastian Bach.

Finally, I ask them if they would like some tea. "No, miss," they say. But I know this is a Bhutanese no, so I go into the kitchen. They follow. Karma Dorji takes the pot from me. "We is making tea for miss," he says.

"Oh no, that's okay," I say. "I'll make it." I try to prize the pot away from Karma Dorji, but he won't let go. "You're too young to be making tea by yourself," I explain. "My kerosene stove is very dangerous." They are reluctant to go, and stand in the kitchen doorway, watching as I pump up the stove. "Back, back," I tell them, gesturing wildly as I throw a match at the stove and push them out of the kitchen. They think this is hilarious. They have to hold each other up, they are laughing so hard.

"Not funny," I say crossly. "Dangerous. You boys wait in the other room."

74

"Miss, I am doing now," Karma Dorji tells me when he manages to stop laughing. "I am knowing this one. My house is having same-same stove." And before I can stop him, he is pumping up the stove. When it begins to hiss, he lights a match and deftly applies the flame to the stove. A strong blue light appears. I stand openmouthed as Tshewang Tshering fills a pot with water. Norbu is rummaging through the kitchen, pulling out packages of tea, milk powder and sugar. Karma Dorji shakes the cuff of his gho out and wraps the length of it around the pot handle. He pours the steaming tea into the mugs. I follow them into the sitting room with a packet of biscuits. Karma tells me that he does the cooking at home when his parents and older sisters are working outside.

"What do you know how to cook?" I ask.

"I am cooking food, miss."

"What kind of food?"

"Food, miss," he says again. "Miss is not eating food?"

"Of course I eat food," I say. "What do you think I eat?"

"Miss is only eating biscuits, my father is telling."

"How does your father know?"

"My auntie is having one shop. She is telling miss is not buying food, only biscuits."

"Aren't biscuits food?" I ask, a little miffed that my eating habits have become news.

"No, miss. Food is rice."

"Ah," I say. "Rice. Well, in my village, in Canada, we do not eat very much rice, so I don't know how to cook it."

They obviously find this hard to believe. "What people is eating then in your village?"

"Oh, potatoes, bread, noodles."

"Miss," Karma Dorji says, his mouth full of biscuit, "I am teaching you how to cook rice. Just now, miss. You have rice?"

"Yes, but —"

All three of them are back in the kitchen. Tshewang Tshering is washing out the teacups. Karma Dorji has found the rice, which he pours onto a tin plate and picks through. I watch helplessly. Within minutes, the rice has been cleaned, rinsed and put into a pressure cooker on the stove.

"Miss." Karma Dorji is looking around the kitchen critically.

"Yes, Karma?"

"You is having onion and chili? I am making *momshaba.*"

"Now wait a minute, Karma. The rice is enough."

Karma Dorji begins to chop up onions and chilies. Norbu is separating the spinach leaves he brought this morning and washing them in the sink. The pressure cooker whistles suddenly, sending me scurrying out of the kitchen. "What does that mean?" I ask from the doorway.

"Not finished," Karma Dorji says. "Three times then finished."

After the third whistle, they remove the pressure cooker and Karma Dorji fries the onions and chilies, and then adds the spinach leaves and some tomato slices. Tshewang Tshering pulls the little weighted knob off the pressure cooker lid and steam shoots out to the ceiling. I flutter around the kitchen, issuing unnecessary warnings—be careful, that's sharp, watch out, you'll get a steam burn. When everything is ready, I tell them that they must stay and eat. They protest, but I insist until finally they pull their tin lunch plates from inside their ghos. I am always amazed at what the upper portions of these ghos can hold: books, plates, cloth bags, a bottle of arra for me, rice crisps, dried apples, a cucumber, a handful of chilies to eat in class. Karma Dorji serves the food and we eat in silence. I cannot believe how good everything is, the rice sweet and unsticky, the spinach perfectly cooked, although extremely hot. I ask how many chilies are in this dish. Karma says ten.

"Ten! *Yallama,*" I say, wiping my eyes and nose. "How old are you, Karma?"

"Eight," he says and plops another serving of rice onto my plate. "Now miss is knowing," he says. "Now miss is eating food."

When they have gone, I write in my journal: "Anyone can live anywhere, even you. This is for your kind information and necessary action, please."

Morning Clinic, Day Duty, Evening Walk

Jane arrives for the health course with presents for me from Jangchuk and Pema: a basket of plums, a bottle of arra, a ball of raw cheese and a lump of fresh butter wrapped in a banana leaf. She stays with me, and for a week we sit with teachers from all over the district in an airless hospital classroom, taking notes. The course is taught by the Norwegian medical staff. We learn first about traditional beliefs regarding common illnesses: diarrhea is believed to be the result of too much water in the system; an inflammation anywhere on the body may have been caused by invisible arrows fired by certain forest spirits; mixing Western medicine and Bhutanese medicine can kill the patient. We move on to common childhood diseases: scabies, lice, parasites, conjunctivitis. Tuberculosis, leprosy, malaria. At the end of the week, we are given a box of medicine to take back to our schools: packets of Oral Rehydration Solution, acetaminophen, tall tankers of benzyl benzoate for scabies, deworming tablets, waxy capsules of antibiotic eye ointment, gentian violet powder, gauze. Jane packs up her rucksack with luxuries from the Pema Gatshel shops—jam, biscuits and coffee. I refill Pema's basket with packets of tea and sugar—it is inauspicious in Bhutan to return a container empty—and send it back with Jane.

Maya, a vivacious teacher from southern Bhutan, is my clinic partner. On the first morning after the course, we open the staff room doors to a dismally long lineup of customers. The most common complaints are: stomach paining, head paining, cough-and-cold, and diarrhea. There are various forms of diarrhea: water diarrhea, burning diarrhea, gassing diarrhea and, my personal favorite, shooting diarrhea. Students often end up in my apartment or at Maya's, infected hand or foot soaking in a bucket of hot salt water. A boy brings a slightly swollen finger to my house before I am dressed one morning. I can find no wound and send him away. Two days later he is back, his finger swollen grotesquely to the size of a small cucumber. I send him to the hospital, where his finger is lanced and drained. I vow to be more careful.

One morning before school, Karma Dorji brings two red-eyed children to my doorstep. They are holding copies of Canadian news magazines and sniffling. Karma Dorji pushes them into the room.

"Yes, Karma?"

"Miss, you is knowing these two girls? Class II B."

"Yes, I know. They came to visit me yesterday."

"See, miss. They is taking these magazines yesterday. Stealing!"

"Hmmm." I had not noticed the magazines were missing. "Well, I'm sure they were going to bring them back."

"See, miss, their eyes? All red."

Their eyes are indeed red and inflamed. An obvious case of conjunctivitis, I think, and tell the girls to come to morning clinic for ointment. But Karma Dorji has another explanation. "No, miss. They is reading stolen books and their eyes is all coming red." No wonder there is so little crime in Bhutan, I think when I hear this. People still expect karmic retribution even if they escape punishment.

Before school, after school, Saturday afternoon, Sunday morning. There is always someone at my door and it is making me crazy. Sick kids, fighting kids, kids with boils, scrapes and gashes; kids offering potatoes, garlic, enormous bitter white radish; kids wanting to see snaps, play the keyboard, listen to the Walkman, look at things ("Miss! What is these?" they ask, holding up sunglasses, a nail file, a box of tampons). Kids wanting just to come in ("May I come in, miss?"). Big kids wanting help with English homework, wanting to help me with my housework or cooking or shopping, if miss is ever needing anything, they can help. Fellow teachers, coming for tea, coming to chat, have I settled myself up, do I have a boyfriend at home, why did I come here actually, and do I want to sell my camera. Mr. Iyya, trying to get me to agree that Lord Tennyson was the greatest poet who ever lived, a man at the zenith of his glory, isn't it, and would I mind reading this small something he has inscribed of late, a poor plain wordly offering to the muses. Men and women from the village coming to ask if I want to buy cloth, handwoven kiras, belts, bags, do I want balls of cheese or butter, a bottle of milk or arra, anything at all? *Hang rang tshaspé,* they ask. What do I need? They will find it, they will bring it.

I need to be alone. After a full day of talking, smiling, listening, showing, nodding, translating, I want to be alone. I want simply to come home, close the door, and sit in silence, gathering up the bits of myself that have come loose. I want to think, or not think. I want to rest.

But no, this is not to be. They feel sorry for me because I am here alone. Miss, poor miss, she lives all alone. Cooks alone, eats alone, sleeps alone. They shake their heads at the thought of it, and they want to help. I think of the Bhutanese houses I have been in—a kitchen, an altar room, and the main room where parents and grandparents and children and any other relatives eat and work and sleep—and I understand. People in Bhutan are rarely alone.

I decide to go for a walk every day, out of town, along the curve of the mountain to the waterfall and back, *alone.* The first day, I lock my door—not because I fear theft, but because I know from experience that if I leave it unlocked, I will have a houseful of people waiting for me when I come back—and walk quickly through the bazaar. Sangay Chhoden comes running out of her mother's shop as I walk by. "Miss!" Even when she shouts, her voice is just audible. "Miss, where going?"

"*Korbé,*" I say. Roaming.

"I coming, miss?" she asks, pushing her heavy bangs out of her eyes and smiling shyly, and I cannot say no. Soon we are joined by Phuntsho Wangmo. Sangay and Phuntsho practice English, I Sharchhop. What is this? This is a road, a rock, a tree. That is a house, a cow, a chicken. Big dog, little dog. Where do you live? This is the temple, that is the school.

The next day, several more students join us. Soon, half my class is waiting for me after school. They insist on carrying my jhola because "in Bhutan student is always carrying lopen's things," and we continue our lessons. I learn about the intricacies of Bhutanese names. Although most are used interchangeably for boys and girls, there are a few which indicate gender. Wangmo, Chhoden, Lhamo, and Yuden are girl's names. Wangdi is always a boy's name. Phuntsho Wangmo would definitely be a girl, Phuntsho Wangdi a boy, but Phuntsho Tshering could be either. All the names have religious or natural meanings. Karma means star, Sangay means the Buddha, Pema is lotus, Tshering is long life. The combinations can be surprisingly poetic: Pema Gatshel, lotus of happiness, Karma Jamtsho, lake of stars.

The kids try to teach me the name of every tree and shrub and plant but I only retain the name for the marijuana which grows wild everywhere: it is called pakpa nam, pig food, because it is given to the pigs. We move on to adjectives and human traits, and I learn that it is okay to be poor if you are kind, it is even okay to be lazy if you are generous, but the very worst thing to be is arrogant. "Showing proud," the kids tell me, their faces wrinkled in disgust. "Like a high shot. This is very very bad." I ask them to describe various people. The school captain is proud. Mrs. Joy is angry. The headmaster is strict. "Mr. Iyya?" I ask. He is *nyospa*. They tap their foreheads to show me. Mr. Iyya is mad. We are shaken by a fit of conspiratorial giggles.

I begin to string together longer sentences, and my students are pleased with my progress.

One evening after my walk, I find Mr. Om Nath, the Bhutanese science teacher, waiting for me on the doorstep. Over tea, he says that he has come to explain about "day duty," which each staff member takes turns doing. Tomorrow will be my turn to supervise morning study for the senior students (six a.m.), an hour of social work (seven a.m.), breakfast (eight a.m.), lunch (noon), dinner (six p.m.), evening study (seven p.m.), and lights out (nine p.m.). At the end of the day, the duty officer must record his or her comments in the duty register.

For me, day duty will also include morning clinic (8:15 a.m.), classes (8:30 a.m. to 3:30 p.m.) and library duty (four p.m.).

Mr. Om Nath tells me I don't have to worry about the girls. Miss Maya is the girls' matron; she looks after the girls. He says this rather darkly, nodding at me knowingly. I nod back knowingly. I haven't the faintest idea what he's going on about, but I think I've taken in enough for today.

The next morning, I plod across the playing field at dawn, listening to the children's voices droning morning prayers. In the silvery light, the world feels like a large, cool temple. I sit bleary-eyed in a classroom while the students murmur over their open books; it is the longest, coldest, slowest hour of my life. At seven o'clock, I wander around the school compound, watching students clear drains, sweep walkways, pick up garbage. There are no janitors here: in Bhutan, the students are responsible for school maintenance. This is called social work, and it is officially part of the curriculum. At breakfast, I look on uselessly as the students line up for a breakfast of boiled bulgur served from cooking pots large enough to bathe in. There is actually no need for a teacher to supervise, I think, flipping through the duty register during evening study. The students are exquisitely well-behaved. What am I supposed to write? I begin to read:

March 15. Not enough dahl at lunch time. Smaller students did not get. (Signed) Mr. Om Nath.

March 17. Class II C students very noisy at lunch time. (What! Well, of course they're noisy at lunch time. Kids are supposed to be noisy at lunch time! How dare someone write about my kids in the duty register? I am outraged.) Scolded class VIII girls for reading library books during evening study. (Signed) Mrs. Joy.

I skim through the entries. Sangay Dorji (class V B) went to toilet during evening study, did not return. Cooks adding too much water to dahl. No water today, students could not wash. Class VIII boys sent to fix latrine. Petromax lamp broken, evening study canceled. Sonam Wangmo, class VII A, caught writing love letter to Sangay Dorji, class

VI B (Mrs. Joy again). Window in girls' hostel broken. Mr. Sharma did not show up for evening study duty. And then I find this:

> Night came striding with her strident strides,
> Ere gloried flowers blosoom'd, now shadow loom'd,
> And the hoary hand of abysmal darkness o'er the darkling land did boast,
> And the Lord said, "Let there be light,"
> And Lo! There was no light.

From this, I surmise that the Petromax lamps were broken again. Mr. Iyya has signed his entry with a flourish.

Hidden Valleys

The strike has lifted in Assam: there is no mail from home, but fresh supplies of fruit, vegetables and staples have arrived in the market. I walk home with two bulging bags, down the road from the bazaar, past the row of teachers' quarters. A man with a mean, swollen face is leaning on the verandah of Mrs. Joy's place in an undershirt and a towel, smoking a cigarette. This is my first glimpse of the infamous Mr. Joy. Maya has told me that Mrs. Joy's husband is a drunk. He used to teach, too, but was fired after passing out in the classroom. Mrs. Joy never comes to staff parties, Maya said, because Mr. Joy gets drunk and becomes "too nasty." The man leers at me as I go by. Poor Mrs. Joy, I think. Her name seems painfully ironic now.

Outside my door, a woman with reddish gold hair and vividly blue eyes is sitting beside a box of groceries. She is Lesley, she tells me, a British teacher, she is visiting various friends and teachers in eastern Bhutan, she will go to Tsebar tomorrow to visit Jane but she'll have to spend the night here if that's okay with me, she is sorry to barge in like this without warning but what to do, that's Bhutan for you, she has brought these things up from Samdrup Jongkhar for me, she's very glad to meet me by the way, and who is that awful lecherous man in the undershirt a few doors down?

Lesley has been in Bhutan for three years. Her first posting was a village in the high, cold, subalpine district of Bumthang, where she lived for two years in a room in the temple and learned to speak Bumthap, the language of central Bhutan. She extended her contract for another year, and her next posting was one thousand meters lower, in the warm, wet jungles of Kheng, where she learned to speak

Khengkha. She *walked* from one posting to the other, a journey of three days.

It is immediately apparent that Lesley has an encyclopedic knowledge of Bhutan. I cannot let her complete a sentence without interrupting with another question, and later, when we settle down to write letters, I take out my journal and make notes:

Reincarnations of lamas. Usually, the dying lama will leave instructions, indicating a time or place or some other clue. His followers begin to look for him about two years after his death, using the clues and sometimes in consultation with an oracle. They may hear about a child who is acting rather strangely—saying that he wants to go to his real home, perhaps describing his former monastery. For the first two or three years of life, the child retains some knowledge of his former life, but it usually fades after that. The dead lama's disciples bring his belongings, mixed up with other similar items, to the child, and ask the child to identify his former things as proof of his identity. The belief is that a high lama has learned to control his mind even after death and therefore can direct his mind into its next rebirth.

Ghost-catchers. Elaborate sculptures made of dough, thin sticks and colored thread, called lue. *Used in certain pujas to draw away any negative influences, spirits, bad luck, and yes, ghosts as well.*

Hidden valleys, called beyul. *Secluded places that have been blessed and sealed by Guru Rimpoché for followers of Buddhism in times of difficulty. There is some disagreement as to whether these are actual valleys hidden away in the mountains, or mythical places, or places in some other dimension that you can only get to through spiritual practice. Only people with the right karma can enter them. "Lost Horizon" is supposedly based on Shambhala, the most famous hidden valley. There are supposed to be several such valleys in Bhutan, in Gasa and Lhuntse, here they're real places with physical coordinates as well as being spiritual places in some non-physical dimension. The one in Lhuntse is sealed to outsiders from the time of rice planting to the time of harvesting. Not even Bhutanese from outside the valley can enter during this time.*

I don't know if my List of Things to Look Up is now shorter or longer.

Lesley suggests tea and *momos* in the bazaar. I tell her that Pema Gatshel has no restaurant.

"There must be at least one tea stall," she says. "Let's go look."

The sun has disappeared behind glossy green mountains, and a thin banner of pink-and-gold cloud stretches across the darkening sky. In the market, Lesley turns into a rather shaky-looking hut. Behind the counter, a young mother is playing with her baby. Behind her on the wall is a curling poster of Phoebe Cates, and I wonder where it came from.

"*Momo cha?*" Lesley asks the woman.

She nods and goes into a back room. We sit at one of the wooden tables. "So you speak Sharchhop too?" I ask Lesley. She says, "About five words." The woman comes out with two plates of steamed dumplings garnished with chili sauce and two glasses of tea. I open one of the dumplings and study the minced meat and onions inside, feeling the old familiar fear rise up. Lesley looks up suddenly. "These are certainly well-cooked," she says intuitively. "They're like rubber. The only thing we'll get from these is indigestion." I eat the momos, while Lesley and the woman behind the counter have a conversation in Sharchhop, English, and sign language about our respective ages, marital status, number of children, brothers, sisters.

We walk back home in the dark, using Lesley's flashlight. I am still not used to nightfall in Bhutan, the way it really does *fall,* suddenly and completely, and am always unconsciously waiting for the lights to come back on. Lesley makes a bed on the floor of the sitting room. In my own room, I sit at the table. I have not managed to make my place as charming as Jane's, but in the candlelight, with a few jars of wildflowers around me, I am not displeased with my home.

I have an idea that I will write in my journal, but I do not. I sit, listening. The night is full of crickets. I am thinking about how Lesley was not afraid to walk into an unknown hut in an unfamiliar town and order dinner, how she is not afraid to talk to people even if she knows five words of their language. I would have never thought to look into that place on my own, let alone go inside and order a meal. I would have never started a conversation with the woman behind the counter. I remember that first breaking of fear when I ate with Karma Dorji's family on the way to Tsebar, the feeling of relief and freedom, a bodily lightness. I have done nothing but worry since I arrived in Bhutan, two and a half months ago. Will the road be open, will the strike really last one hundred days, will I run out of food, will I get sick, will my mail get through, will there be water in the taps, will those dumplings give me amoebic dysentery. Large parts of me have been shut down: inside whole rooms are in darkness, doors closed, curtains drawn, sheets thrown over the furniture. I live in a tiny cramped room of what-if. I must stop being afraid, I think as I get into bed.

An hour later, the rumble of thunder wakes me up. From the bed I can see the storm approaching in one window, lightning illuminating swollen storm clouds. From the other window the sky is still starry and clear. I fall asleep when both windows are full of rain, and I dream that Lesley and I find a hidden valley in Pema Gatshel. Between the school and the hospital, we follow a barely perceptible path and emerge from a grove of trees into a grassy, steep-sided ravine with a silver stream singing through it. "It was here all along," I say happily, and awake to see that both windows are filled again with stars.

Lesley leaves the next morning for Tsebar, and I hurry off to school to find the students and monks carrying items up and down the stairs—buckets of water, trays, bowls of rice, flowers, freshly cut pine branches, books, religious instruments, folding chairs. The Bhutanese teachers are shouting orders. Today there will be a puja, the students tell me, to chase away the ghosts. The headmaster laughs at this. Not exactly ghosts, he says. Pujas are held regularly in temples, but they are also held elsewhere for hundreds of other reasons—for the birth of a child, a wedding, promotion, or cremation, to ensure the success of a new project or a journey, to protect a household from harm. This puja, he explains, is being held to clear away any bad karma, obstacles, or harmful thoughts left over from last year that might hamper the success of this school year.

After morning assembly, the teachers are called upstairs to a classroom which has been cleared out. Red-robed monks sit in rows, chanting prayers. The Bhutanese teachers prostrate in front of an altar laden with offerings of food and water, butter lamps and incense. The Indian teachers bow, some deeply, some stiffly. Mrs. Joy merely nods her head. The headmaster tells me that I can do whatever I wish, it is up to me. I prostrate in front of the altar, because it is holy and beautiful, and then linger, listening to the prayers and the music, the same horns and bells and drums I heard in Tsebar. Back outside, we are served salty butter tea called *suja* and rice crisps. Someone pinches my arm, hard, and I almost drop my cup. It is Mrs. Joy. "Why did you bow down up there?" she hisses. "It is worshiping idols."

I try to explain that an altar is an altar, a god is a god. "It's all pretty much the same to me," I tell her.

She shakes her head angrily. "You broke the First Commandment!"

I cannot remember what the First Commandment is. I consider telling her to mind her own goddamn business, but then I think of Mr. Joy, leaning on the railing in a cloud of cigarette smoke, smiling nastily, and I say nothing. "May all sentient beings have happiness and the causes of happiness," I think wearily. It is the only Buddhist prayer I know so far.

At lunch, I mail a hastily scrawled note to Lorna. *My kids think I'm an idiot, one of the teachers addresses me as "your ladyship," I have fifty-three flea bites, and my blackboard doesn't work. How are you?*

A week later, Lorna writes back: *Ha! I have fifty flea bites on one leg alone! Your kids are right. What is a blackboard?*

Royal Visit

Mr. Iyya rushes into the staff room during morning clinic. "Have you heard the Good News?" he asks, wringing his hands.

For a moment, I think Mrs. Joy has got to him, but no—the good news is that the King is coming to Pema Gatshel! He will be here today! This very afternoon!

"Really?" I ask, painting Yeshey Dorji's infected chin with gentian violet. "Will he come to the school? Will we get to meet him?"

Mr. Iyya assures me that he will, and we will. He has met the King before, he says. The King is knowing Mr. Iyya very well, yes very well. He stops abruptly, looking stricken. "What is it, Mr. Iyya?" I ask. He says he must write a poem for the visit of His Majesty to our humble valley. "An epic poem!" he exclaims. "In the style of Homer!"

He'd better get moving, I think to myself, if he's going to finish it by this afternoon.

The headmaster comes in. Yes, he says, the King is on tour and will come to Pema Gatshel, no one knows for sure when, but classes are canceled in order to prepare.

From the class VIII history book, which I have been reading during library duty, I know that the King, Jigme Singye Wangchuck, assumed the throne upon the death of his father in 1972. He was seventeen, the youngest ruling monarch in the world. Throughout his reign, he has made frequent tours of the country to explain government policy and discuss development plans, and is by all accounts a well-loved ruler.

The history of Bhutan before the monarchy is extremely difficult to follow. Before the 1600s, there was no central authority in Bhutan. Each valley was ruled by its own king or clan leader. In 1616, Ngawang

Namgyel, a Tibetan abbot, was engaged in a serious clerical dispute in his monastery when the protective deity of Bhutan appeared to him in a dream in the form of a raven flying south. The abbot left Tibet and crossed the high Himalayan passes into northwestern Bhutan, where he quickly established himself as an extraordinary leader. After defeating various invading Tibetan armies and unifying the valleys of Bhutan under one central administration, Ngawang Namgyel became the supreme ruler of the country, and assumed the title of *Shabdrung,* which means "at whose feet one submits." His legacy is evident everywhere in Bhutan today, from the country's legal code to its many dzongs, fortress-monasteries which represented a combination of political and religious power.

Before his death, the Shabdrung devised a dual system of government to look after both secular and spiritual affairs. The country's monastic body was governed by an elected leader called the *Jé Khenpo,* and administrative and political affairs were managed by a temporal ruler, known as the *Desi,* with a number of local governors, called *penlops,* working under him. The Shabdrung's reincarnations were supposed to be the supreme head of both systems.

Over the years, however, this system floundered. The penlops became all-powerful, appointing and dismissing Desis and Jé Khenpos as they wished, and political rivalries led to great internal instability. The history book lists a series of conflicts, ranging from court intrigue (one of the most interesting cases involved a smallpox-infested silk gho sent as a present to a political rival), dzong-burnings and kidnappings (especially of wives), to multiple assassinations and outright civil war. Then, at the end of the nineteenth century, one person, Ugyen Wangchuck, the Tongsa Penlop, emerged out of this turmoil as a powerful figure, bringing the penlops under his increasingly centralized authority. In 1907, penlops, lamas, and people's representatives gathered at Punakha and voted to establish a hereditary monarchy, electing Ugyen Wangchuck "Druk Gyalpo," the Precious King of the Dragon People.

Strangely, the Shabdrung's reincarnations disappear from the history text shortly after this without a word of explanation. When I asked Mr. Dorji, the history teacher, about this several weeks ago, he looked uncomfortable for a moment, and then said that the Shabdrung's current incarnation lives in India. "Was he born there?" I asked. Mr. Dorji shook his head. "He was born here, but now . . . he lives there." It was clear that I was not going to get any more out of him.

Preparations for the royal visit are exhaustive. I am asked to help Mr. Sharma supervise the cleaning of the yard. Mr. Sharma walks back and forth with a stick, shouting incoherently as the kids converge on the playing field, picking up paper, twigs, leaves, bits of cloth. He comes rushing over to me. "No. NO!" he says, gesturing for me to drop the litter I have picked up. "They will do it!"

"I'll help them," I tell him. "Then it will get done faster."

This does not go over well with Mr. Sharma. "It sets a bad example," he says.

"Really? I think it demonstrates the dignity of labor."

This offends Mr. Sharma, who says that he is a Brahmin, and this is not his work.

Elsewhere, the straggly flower garden in front of the school is being weeded and lined with stones and the stones themselves are being whitewashed. Some teachers are putting together a wall magazine of students' essays and drawings. Classrooms and hostels are swept out, water is poured over steps, branches are lopped off trees. The tip-top poet is nowhere to be seen.

Jane appears with a group of selected teachers and students from the other villages of the district for the royal visit. We go to the tea stall for momos and sit there all evening, talking quietly in the candlelight. Jane explains protocol to me: the entire village will line up along the road, and when the royal convoy passes, everyone will bow. The Bhutanese are not supposed to look directly at the King, and will keep their eyes lowered in deference. "Can we look at him?" I ask. I have seen pictures: every shop and house has one, draped with a white scarf. He is a handsome man. Jane thinks it is okay to sneak in a few looks.

We order a "peg" each of Bhutanese whiskey and orange squash, a sickeningly sweet syrup, and the combination turns out to be so awful that we have to dilute it with water from the plastic jug on the table. "Let's just hope the whiskey will kill whatever else is in the water," Jane says. I stare down at my cup: for once, I hadn't thought about germs.

Several drinks later, we hear thunder rumble in the next valley. Jane tells me that Bhutan is called Land of the Thunder Dragon after the Drukpa Kargyue branch of Buddhism practiced here. When the religion was established in the twelfth century, the founder heard the thunder dragon roar, and named his school Druk—dragon. We listen to the dragon approach. It climbs a ridge in the south, the thunder becoming sharper as it gets closer. Suddenly the storm is above us, breaking open, pouring down. Neither of us has an umbrella or a flashlight. "Let's wait it out," I suggest. "The storms here are always over so quickly." We wait and wait and wait, but the dragon stays right here, thunder cracking over our heads, rain roaring on the tin roof. Karma, the woman behind the counter, is falling asleep. We decide to go. Outside, we are soaked instantly. Jane says she is just waiting to step off the mountain and go sliding down to Gypsum. I say I am just waiting for lightning to strike us both dead. We slip in the mud and cling to each other, laughing hysterically. Jane says she is just waiting to see me open that Canadian combination lock in the dark. Somehow I do and we fall into the apartment, shivering, hiccuping, laughing still, and drink hot, weak tea. My skin feels cool and clean when I crawl into bed, and I fall asleep listening to the storm fade into the next valley.

I wake up with nausea and a bloated stomach. A hangover, I think, but when I sit up, I belch and taste rotten eggs. "Jane, are you sick?" I call out.

"What, you mean a hangover?" she calls back.

"No . . ."

She opens the bedroom door. "You look awful. Does it taste like eggs gone bad?"

"Yes."

"Then it's giardia. Do you feel well enough to get up?"

I do not, but I am not going to miss the King's visit.

I wear a kira purchased from a woman who came to my door last week, a series of brilliantly colored stripes worked in wool on a cotton background. Jane reminds me to bring my *raichu,* the narrow, red ceremonial scarf that women wear over their left shoulders when meeting a high-ranking official. Men wear a *kabney,* a broad scarf of cream-colored raw silk, draped diagonally across the body. At the school, the students are gathered on the playing field, ghos and kiras neat, hair sleeked back with water, faces shining. The class VIII girls come to adjust our kiras and help us fold our raichus properly. They show us how to bow when the King passes. The higher the rank, they explain, the lower the bow. For a Dzongda, you would touch your knee with the fringed end of your raichu or kabney. "For our His Majesty, you must touch the ground," they say. This is very important. This is called *driglam namzha.* They bow gracefully. Jane and I need more practice. I hope I do not fall on my face in front of the King.

An hour later, we are still standing around outside. Preparations are still not complete, and the headmaster looks grim as he checks the school compound. Then the Dzongda shows up and the activity intensifies. He asks the headmaster why there is no gate. The headmaster says he was told not to make a gate. The Dzongda says of course they have to make a gate! Now! Class VIII boys! Hurry! Bamboo poles are brought from somewhere and tied together, and slowly the skeleton of a gate materializes at the entrance of the school. The students bring armloads of pine branches to drape over the frame. The rest of the school is lined up, practicing driglam namzha. I ask Jane what this term means exactly, and she says she doesn't think it can be directly translated. "Some people say etiquette, some people say rules and regulations, or discipline, or law. From what I understand, it's a collection of rules governing behavior and social interaction. How to serve tea to your superiors, how to sit or stand in the presence of royalty, the proper way to wear national dress, that kind of thing." I sit on the school steps, exhausted already, listening to my insides rumbling and heaving; I put my head down on my knees and fall into a thin, unhappy sleep.

When I open my eyes again, teachers are shouting contradictory orders at the students who are rushing to and fro, colliding into each other in a farcical attempt to obey each new command. All students line up on the playing field! All students return to your hostels! All students assemble in the dining hall! You, class VIII girls, bring water and clean these stairs! Class VIII girls, stay where you are! Class VIII girls, why you are just standing there? Go to the road! Where are you going? Who told you to go to the road? Go to the road, we are walking down to Gypsum!

This last order is reinforced by the Dzongda. Yes, we will go to Gypsum. We will all walk down, everyone, now! I go inside to use the staff toilet, and on my way out, stop to look at the wall magazine. I particularly like a poem by a class VIII student describing the temporary beauty of life:

Despite all these colorful sceneries, wonders,
Nothing remains,
No matter the floodgates of our joy.

One board, set apart, contains Mr. Iyya's epic poem. It begins with the sun rising to the zenith of its glory and continues through vales and dales of peace and happiness, with many a rushing river and gamboling lamb, until it reaches this, our humble valley, where "the King's golden face shone like the purple sun yonder over these eastern hills! O! Bridal Bower of Bliss." I am still laughing weakly when Jane comes to find me, and we set off down the road to Gypsum, arguing over the reference to the bridal bower of bliss. Jane says that Mr. Iyya is making an allusion to the King's marriage last year to four sisters. I say Mr. Iyya is insane and therefore it is best to make no connections between the poem and the external world.

At Gypsum, we are given Gold Spot pop. "No Natural Ingredients!" the bottle proudly proclaims. The fizz settles my stomach. Then a truck pulls up and we are told to get in. We have been called back up to Pema Gatshel. "What on earth," I mutter to Jane.

She laughs. "I don't know! But let's not miss the ride up."

At the school, the gate is being dismantled. I don't even bother to ask why. Someone shouts, and everyone rushes to line up. There is a glint of silver on the road above town—a vehicle! No, it is nothing. After thirty minutes, the lines begin to dissolve, and everyone goes back to milling around in the school yard. At 4:30, we are called again. A vehicle, the pilot jeep, is coming down the road. I stand nervously with Jane, fretting with my raichu, squirming in my kira. The pilot vehicle approaches. We can see several other cars behind it, mostly dark blue landcruisers. Horns and drums sound from the dzong, and I am excited. The pilot car drives by, and suddenly I am looking down and bowing deeply like everyone else. When I straighten up, I see the last of the cars disappearing down the road to Gypsum. And then, after a full day of preparing, putting up and taking down gates and practicing to meet the King, we are sent home.

The next day, we sit in a large tent made out of heavy white canvas with blue lotus flowers painted on the roof. Jane and I are in the second row. The air is hot, heavy, and motionless but I am glad to be sitting down after another full morning of lining up, falling out, milling around, standing about. A man in military dress enters the tent, signaling everyone to rise. The King walks to the front of the tent, followed by an entourage of government officials and bodyguards. He is taller than the average Bhutanese, and as handsome as his pictures, with sculpted cheekbones and a Cupid's-bow mouth; he is wearing a simple checked gho and traditional felt boots. I glance around furtively: everyone's head is bowed. The King takes his seat in front of a low carved table. We sit, and he begins to speak in Dzongkha in a stern, sober voice.

My stomach is still in motion, and I press my hands over it. Please God do not let me have to get up in the middle of his speech. I look sideways at Jane, who is looking up, so I look up, too. We are caught, staring outright, and lower our eyes again. A great wave of sleepiness settles over me. When I wake up, I am looking at the roof. My head is thrown back and my mouth is open. How long have I been asleep? I am mortified.

Students stand to ask carefully rehearsed questions, which the King answers, and then the meeting is over. "Jane," I whisper, "I fell asleep!"

"I know," she says.

"Did I snore?" I ask.

"Well, not exactly," she says. What the hell does that mean? Either I was snoring in front of the King of Bhutan or I was not! There is no time to discuss it. We are served suja and *desi,* sweet, saffron-colored rice with raisins and bits of cashews, and then the teachers are called outside.

The King thanks the staff in English for our work, assuring us that it is of utmost importance because Bhutan's future depends on the education of her children. The Bhutanese teachers look awed, almost rigid with veneration. For the last two days, I have wanted to laugh at the frantic preparations, but now I see this is no laughing matter for the Bhutanese. This is their *King.* I don't even know what that means. Although the monarchy is less than a century old, the culture of obedience, hierarchy and loyalty is much older (take the Shabdrung's name, for example—"at whose feet one submits"). Centuries of history have gone into forming the reverence on the faces of my Bhutanese colleagues. Having been raised in a culture in which authority is always suspect, I am a stranger here where it is still considered sacred.

On his way out, the King stops in front of Jane and me and shakes our hands. He asks in a kindly voice if everything is all right and if we are enjoying our time in Bhutan. We tell him we are. Then he is gone. We see the convoy of cars winding its way up and out of the Pema Gatshel valley. The King's license plate says BHUTAN.

Back at the school, I find the headmaster and the Dzongkha lopens shaking their heads in dismay. The headmaster explains: "His Majesty asked me if Mr. Iyya understood Dzongkha, and I said no. I didn't know why he was asking. Now Lopen here is telling that Iyya was looking at His Majesty all through the speech! Smiling and nodding through the whole speech as if he understood!"

I do not mention my own serious breach of protocol. "Did His Majesty have time to read Mr. Iyya's poem?" I ask.

The headmaster smacks his hand to his forehead. "I hope not," he says, and we both break into laughter.

Entrance

Just off the headmaster's office is a closet which contains the school's ancient, manual ditto machine. Using it is almost as much trouble as copying everything by hand: the copy fluid leaks, the machine chews the paper and swallows it, the handle jams after every third copy. I tried to operate it myself this morning, and now Dorji Wangdi is pulling out shreds of wet, inky paper from the machine's jaws. I stand around uselessly in the headmaster's office which contains a desk, a heavy, old, oily typewriter, grey metal filing cabinets, and a globe. I put one finger on Bhutan and another on Lake Superior, amazed at how far away I am from home, half the world away. I have come as far as I can. In fact, if I go any farther, I will be on my way back.

Dorji emerges from the ditto room, hands smudged black. "Sorry, sir," he tells me. "Today no."

"Oh well," I shrug. "What to do?"

I shouldn't have tried to do it myself, but I was feeling particularly able after fixing my leaking roof. Yesterday, I had climbed into the rafters and placed an empty coffee can over every waterstain on the wooden beams. Early this morning, when it began to rain, I sat up in bed, listening with great satisfaction to the sound of water dripping into tin. The day before that, I had taken a few planks and bricks from a pile of building materials behind the school and built a low platform in the bathroom. I wasn't able to fix the drain, but at least I no longer have to stand in dirty water to bathe.

After school, I go up to the market to get my daily half-bottle of milk and a ball of cheese from Tshering, the woman who owns the last shop at the end of the road. The cow, a silent black and white bulk, is tethered to a pole just outside the shop. Today I give it a tentative pat.

My kids find my fear of cows extremely funny. "Miss, you is not having cows at your village?" they ask when they see me making feeble shooing motions at cows on the road. "No, I am not having cows at my village," I say crossly. "Shoo! Shoo, cow, shoo!" They come to my rescue, swatting the cow's flank with a stick and hissing "Shhhht!"

The shop smells warmly of grass and manure and fresh milk. Tshering removes the bamboo covering from the metal bucket and fills my bottle with a hand-carved wooden ladle. Today I have to tell her that I cannot pay her. Once again, my salary has not come. The other teachers line up outside the headmaster's office on the last day of the month to receive their salaries in cash, but now, for the second time the headmaster says that my name is not on the payment list. The Education Department has not received my posting order yet, and the headmaster has no money to pay me. He has sent a message to Thimphu, he says, but it will take some time. I have finished the last of my ngultrum and yesterday went to the Bank of Bhutan (Pema Gatshel Branch) to cash a traveler's check. The sole bank employee in the bare room took the check and studied it, back and front, for a long moment, before shaking his head gravely and handing it back to me. I owe money for milk and cheese, and I need rice, coffee, chilies, soap, kerosene, everything.

"*Ama* Tshering," I say. "*Tiru mala.*" No money.

The woman shrugs. "*Dikpé, dikpé,*" she says. "*Omé bilé.*" You can give it later. I go down to Sangay Chhoden's shop, where I tell her mother my story and she nods sympathetically and gives me tea and the same answer. She doesn't even bother to write down the amount I owe her. I walk back home, partly relieved, partly still worried. Even though no one seems particularly alarmed or surprised that I have no money, I feel terrible buying things on credit here. I know that my students think I am immeasurably wealthy. Miss, how many cars your mother is having? How much money your father is making? *Zai! Yallama!* Miss, you is very very rich. I try to explain: in Canada, that is not rich. In Canada, my family is an average family, like your family. But this is an obscene lie. I am appallingly rich in comparison.

I am also appallingly wasteful. Last weekend, they came to visit while I was cleaning up, and watched anxiously as I piled garbage into a box until Karma Dorji finally burst out, "Miss! You is throwing?" Yes, I said, looking down at the empty beer bottles and scrap paper. "Miss, we are taking, okay?" he asked. I said of course they could take it, and remembered the roomful of stuff left behind by the last Canadians. I had not yet figured out how to dispose of the bottles, plastic containers, and tin cans in there. It took me several weeks just to figure out how to take care of my own garbage, after realizing with a shock one morning that no one was going to come along with a truck to clear it away. I had to go through my overflowing bucket and separate what could be burned, what could be composted, what could not be thrown out after all. The more complex and developed a society becomes, I think, the less responsibility individuals have to take for their actions. As long as I could lug my garbage out to the curb two mornings a week in Toronto, what did I care what happened to it? But here, we are made to see the consequences of our consumption.

"Most of it's rubbish," I told the kids, leading them into the room off the kitchen. Except I could see right away it wasn't. The bottles could be stopped with cloth plugs, the empty tins could be measuring cups and plant holders, the lengths of string and wire, the paper, the cardboard boxes, the torn plastic sheeting—all of it was useful, valuable. I felt ashamed, watching them pulling open the boxes excitedly, jubilantly waving a plastic jug with a broken handle, a squashed soccer ball, an empty shampoo bottle. They quarreled over a French-English board game with all its cards and pieces missing. "Miss, you is throwing?" they asked in disbelief. I nodded. What would they do with it? With the squashed soccer ball? They looked so pleased when they left, telling me over and over, "Miss, I am very happy to you," that I wanted to cry.

It occurs to me now that in Sharchhop, the same word is used for both "thrown out" and "lost," and there is no distinction between "to need" and "to desire." If something is thrown out, it is lost to further use, and if you want something here, you probably also need it. When

I study my Sharchhop book, I wonder who is richer, who poorer. English has so many words that do not exist in Sharchhop, but they are mostly nouns, mostly things: machine, airplane, wristwatch. Sharchhop, on the other hand, reveals a culture of material economy but abundant, intricate familial ties and social relations. People cannot afford to make a distinction between need and desire, but they have separate words for older brother, younger sister, father's brother's sons, mother's sister's daughters. And there are two sets of words: a common set for everyday use and an honorific one to show respect. There are three words for gift: a gift given to a person higher in rank, a gift to someone lower, and a gift between equals.

In the village, few written records are kept, but everyone knows who is related to whom, why that person left the village, what inauspicious signs shone down as they set out, what illnesses and misfortunes befell them after, what offerings were made, what consolation followed. Here the world is still small enough that knowledge is possible without surnames, records, certificates of birth and death. The world is that small, and yet it seems vaster to me, bigger and older and more complex than my world in Canada, where there is an official version of every life and death, and history is lopped and fitted and trimmed into chapters, and we read it once or twice and forget. It is written down; there is no need to remember. There is no need to remember, hence we forget. Whereas here history is told so that it can be remembered, it is remembered because it is told. The Sharchhop word for "history" translates into "to tell the old stories."

Back at home, I collect my two buckets of rainwater from below the eaves. The tap water has been off for two days, but the rain has been plentiful. I am managing. In the evening, I am surprised by the sound of a vehicle outside my window. A white hi-lux has wedged itself in front of the building, and boxes, crates and tins are being unloaded onto the muddy ground. My Australian neighbor, I think, and it is. He knocks on the door later, a man with tufts of greying hair standing on end and a big grin. He introduces himself as Trevor and starts handing things over. He has brought my tin and a note from Sasha, bread from Thimphu, Swiss-made cheese from Bumthang, peaches and plums from Tashigang, and letters from home that ended up at the field office. I start to help him cart his luggage up the stairs but he waves me away. "Go read your mail," he says kindly. I tear open the envelopes and read hungrily. Then I put my groceries away, arranging things carefully on the shelves. I feel immensely rich and unaccountably lucky, as if I had just won a lottery.

At my desk, I start a letter to Robert about the difference between arrival and entrance. Arrival is physical and happens all at once. The train pulls in, the plane touches down, you get out of the taxi with all your luggage. You can arrive in a place and never really enter it; you get there, look around, take a few pictures, make a few notes, send postcards home. When you travel like this, you think you know where you are, but, in fact, you have never left home. Entering takes longer. You cross over slowly, in bits and pieces. You begin to despair: will you ever get over? It is like awakening slowly, over a period of weeks. And then one morning, you open your eyes and you are finally here, really and truly here. You are just beginning to know where you are.

I write about all the things I have learned. Mustard oil must be heated until it smokes before you fry anything in it. Climbing a mudslide is easier barefoot. Water has a lower boiling point at high altitudes. Now I am knowing, as my students would say. All my former knowledge and accomplishments seem useless to me now—all the critical jargon I carry around in my head, tropes and modes and traces, thirteen definitions of irony, the death of the author, the anxiety of influence, there is nothing outside the text. So what? That doesn't help me in the least now. Let Jacques Derrida come here, I think. Let him stay up half the night scratching flea bites and then deconstruct the kerosene stove before breakfast. I have had to learn everything all over again, how to walk without falling headlong into bushes, how to clean rice, how to chop chilies without rubbing my hand in my eye and blinding myself. Eight year olds have had to take care of me. My ignorance amazes me.

Now when I long for the small comforts of my Canadian life, I remind myself that someday I will be home, longing perhaps for the misted view of mountains from my bedroom window, the smell of woodsmoke, a room lit by candlelight, the sound of rain moving into the valley. The rain has stopped, and the clouds are shifting to reveal a sharp, thin crescent moon and one bright star. It's the kind of moon you can climb into, a silver boat, a rocking chair. Robert, I write, I am just beginning to realize where I am.

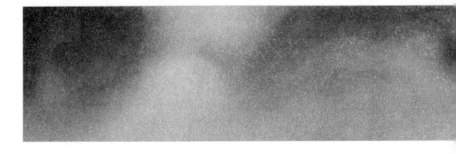

Movement Order

*Early in June, the
rains set in, and
were so constant
that . . . there
generally fell a
shower in some part
or other of the
twenty-four hours,
and the tops of the
hills were constantly
involved in clouds.*

—Samuel Davis

in Bhutan, 1783

Rangthangwoong

The start of a three-day holiday, and I have a list of things to do:
get rid of the rat in the kitchen without the aid of the trap that
so horrified my students (oh miss, they told me, you is killing this rat,
then you is coming back as rat for many lifes), fix the screens that let
in a thousand flies a day (the same karmic rule applies to killing flies),
bake bread using the old pot-in-the-pot-on-the-kerosene-stove
method. But then Trevor knocks on my door to say that he is going
up to Tashigang for the weekend and do I want to go. I stuff a tooth-
brush and a clean tee shirt into my jhola and race down the stairs to
where the hi-lux is coughing up a cloud of gritty smoke.

Tashigang has grown somehow in two months, I think, as we pull
into the center of town between a bus that is disgorging an endless
stream of stiff-limbed, dazed passengers and a truck loaded with crates.
It seemed so small and medieval when we drove through in March. I
took no account then of the tarmacked roads, the electricity wires, the
number of buildings—bank, hospital, telephone exchange, barber,
tailor, post office, hydropower cell, wireless station, school, police
headquarters, petrol station, bars, bars-cum-hotels. I didn't notice the
hand-drawn AIDS poster on a shop wall. I didn't notice you could buy
shoes in Tashigang. And shoe polish, playing cards, colored markers,
curtain rings and hair dye. I didn't notice you could buy so many things
you didn't actually need.

Two Westerners are sitting on a bench outside the Puen Soom, and
although it has been months since I met them in Thimphu, I recognize
them instantly. Leon, posted in Wamrong, and Tony from Khaling, are
in the second year of their contracts. They are both tall and blond and
very thin, but in their faded cotton clothes and rubber flip-flops, with

colorful jholas at their feet, they do not seem out of place. They are reading and sipping glasses of murky liquid. Mud puppies, they inform me, sweet tea with a shot of Dragon Rum. Tomorrow they are going to visit Catherine, the Canadian teacher in Rangthangwoong, and they invite me to come along. I hesitate. I don't want to miss my ride back to Pema Gatshel with Trevor tomorrow, but when will I get another chance to go to what-was-it-called again? I decide to go.

Leon and Tony are staying with Kevin, another Canadian teacher posted in Tashigang. "Is there room for me, or should I stay in a hotel?" I ask.

"Which hotel would that be?" Leon asks, gesturing grandly at the bazaar. "Bedbug Inn? The Flea Seasons?"

"This is eastern Bhutan," Tony says. "Where there's a floor, there's room."

On the way up to Kevin's house, we stop at a bakery to buy soft, flat rounds of Tibetan bread. On one wall are somber, black-and-white photographs of the four kings of Bhutan and a religious calendar from last year, the Year of the Earth Dragon. On the wall opposite is a poster of a scarlet-lipped, dagger-nailed Joan Collins. No one seems to mind the incongruity.

Kevin lives in a concrete block of a house furnished with the usual wooden benches and stiff chairs. We sit in the kitchen, drinking beer, peeling vegetables for dinner and sharing reports on the lateral road, the mail situation, and the state of everyone's health—who got what from where and what they did about it. I laugh until my throat hurts. A leech up the nose wouldn't have seemed so funny three months ago.

Outside, shadows collect under the eucalyptus trees and the air is filled with birdsong and the whistling of pressure cookers as neighbors prepare their evening meals. Inside, I find the electric lights harsh and strangely wasteful. I am used to having a circle of warm light only where I need it; I feel out of sync with the growing twilight outside and keep checking my watch. Leon and Tony have brought sleeping bags; I borrow a blanket from Kevin and lay some cushions down on the floor. It is nine o'clock and Tashigang is still awake: Bhutanese folk music drifts up from the bazaar, a vehicle honks impatiently, trucks lumber up the road, a woman yells repeatedly for Sonam to come home. Eventually, the sounds begin to fade away, Sonam finally comes home and even the thriving metropolis of Tashigang goes to sleep.

The bus to Rangthangwoong turns out to be a truck. We squeeze ourselves into the open back and wait for the driver. People keep climbing in, and soon I must balance awkwardly on one foot until my other foot finds a tentative resting place on a sack of rice. The engine grunts and wheezes to life and the truck lurches off down to the river, over the bridge called Chazam, and onto a rough, dusty road. The landscape is dry and sun-bleached, with chir pine trees dotting the dry, rocky slopes, a complete contrast to the wet, dense green of the enclosed Pema Gatshel valley. I turn my face into the hot wind and the girl next to me smiles and admires my silver earrings. She looks about fifteen, and has a pretty, heart-shaped face. Her earrings are thick, hand-fashioned hoops of gold. "Yours are nicer," I tell her in Sharchhop. She shakes her head shyly. A group of students in their school ghos and kiras begins to sing. A man in a blue-striped gho, smelling strongly of arra, lurches against us when the truck turns a sharp corner and stops. We are at Duksam, two rows of crooked wooden shops along a narrow tar-macked road; several passengers leap out, several more leap on.

When the bus starts up again, I notice the man in blue has pushed himself between me and the girl. He is singing loudly as he clamps his hand over the girl's breast. She looks away but there is no place for her to move. I cannot read her expression. I don't know what to do, if I should do anything. Part of me is thinking, this is not your culture. You've been here for a few short weeks, you don't even speak the language. You don't know what's going on here, who are you to interfere? The other part of me is thinking, it is perfectly clear what is going on here. It is not a matter of cultural differences. But it cannot be *perfectly clear*, except to a Bhutanese, and I am profoundly unsure, paralyzed by this inner argument. Finally, I work my way between the man and the girl. When he tries to reach around me, I elbow away his hand, and he looks into my face, puzzled. I look straight back. The singing around us has stopped. The man grins and shrugs and turns away. I try to look at the girl, but she is looking straight ahead and will not meet my eye. I can only hope I have done the right thing.

Rangthangwoong is halfway up a mountain, a village scattered around three large houses with ground-floor shops. Catherine is dressed in a grey kira, but her bright auburn hair sets her apart in the crowd waiting for the bus. Her quarters, located above one of the shops, consist of a bed-sitting room and, across a communal hallway, a bathroom and kitchen. She has been here for two years already, and she is very excited because the landlord has just installed a tap in her kitchen. We go to admire it, turning it on and off, laughing at ourselves. Someone has brought her a bottle of fresh buttermilk, and she pours us each a cup and then we walk up to the ruins of a ninth-century castle. Sitting below, on a grassy knoll, Catherine points to a mountain at the end of the valley. "That's India," she says. "The town is Tawang, in Arunachal Pradesh. At night, we can see the lights. My headmaster says you could walk there in one day." This, of course, is illegal, she adds. You would run into the army at the border. This is where the Indo-China war spilled over into Bhutan in 1962. After the Chinese invasion of Tibet, India began to station troops along the northern frontier, including along Bhutan's northern borders. The brief war was the result of growing tension along the northeastern Indian border, with both China and India claiming the area as their own. The older people still talk about it, Catherine says, the sudden appearance of helicopters in the sky over a village that had never even seen a vehicle. They thought it was the end of the world.

An old man with a large goiter on his neck stops to offer us betel nut smeared with lime paste and wrapped in a green leaf. Leon accepts, saying he has been meaning to try it. We watch as he stuffs the whole thing into his mouth and chews. "How is it?" we ask.

"God-awful," he says, but keeps chewing. "It's supposed to give you a mild high."

After several minutes, he spits it out. "Are you high?" I ask.

"No, I'm nauseous. Are my teeth red?"

"Yes."

The sunlight has turned a warm, liquid gold. We look up and down the length of the river valley, watching the mountain ranges in the south opening one after the other like gates to a secret kingdom. I love how the landscape gives the impression of vast space and intimacy at the same time: the thin brown line of a path wandering up an immense green mountainside, a plush hanging valley tucked between two steep hillsides, a village of three houses surrounded by dark forest, paddy fields flowing around an outcrop of rock, a white temple gleaming on a shadowy ridge. The human habitations nestle into the landscape; nothing is cut or cleared beyond what is required. Nothing is bigger than necessary. Every sign of human settlement repeats the mantra of contentment: "This is just enough."

We walk back to Catherine's place and cook rice, vegetable curry and dahl, talking about where to go for the first-term break. I had not thought of going anywhere. "Oh, you have to go somewhere," Leon tells me. There are a hundred possible destinations and combinations, other postings to visit, different routes to try out, all the old trading paths that people took before the lateral road was built. There are very old, holy temples to see, Tony wants to go to Dremitse on its own little hilltop, Catherine to Rangchikhar to meet a levitating lama. Two years suddenly seems a very short time. "What about the three-month winter break?" Tony says. "We could all walk from Lhuntse to Bumthang and spend Christmas at the Swiss Guest House."

"What a good idea!" I exclaim, thinking of bukharis and the smell of pine.

"I thought you were going home for Christmas," Leon says to me.

Yes, so I am. I had forgotten.

The lama who lives next door invites us to his room at dusk. The only light comes from the butter lamp on his altar. The lama is absorbed in his evening prayers, and we sit on the floor beside him and drink zim-chang, the good-night arra he has offered us. I am glad there is no need to speak. I want to absorb this moment in this room, the steady flame of the butter lamp, the composed faces of the Buddhas behind the altar, the contented silence of my friends, the great peaceful night settling all around us outside. I feel I could sit here forever. Back in Catherine's room, wrapped in a borrowed blanket, I lay under the window, cold and tired and happy. I study the stars sprayed across the sky and listen to the lama praying softly next door. I remember my arrival in Bhutan and how miserable I was, and all the other teachers who seemed inexplicably content. They were right all along, I think. This is the most remarkable place, after all.

The Vomit Comet

There is no transport from Rangthangwoong to Tashigang; we have to walk back. After a breakfast of fried rice and leftover curry, we set off down the mountainside to the main road which runs along the river valley. Leon and Tony go galloping off, surefooted through fields and rice paddies. I must fly along after them to keep up. As long as I don't think about where to put my foot next, I do not stumble. We are hot and sweaty by the time we reach the row of shops at Duksam, where there is hot tea, warm beer or unfiltered water to drink. We opt for the warm beer, which makes me sleepy, and then continue to trudge along the road. It is sixteen kilometers back to the bridge below Tashigang. There is no shade, and the sun is merciless. Below us, the river is a deliciously cool turquoise surge. Tony says the color indicates its origin: the turquoise comes from suspended particles of stone crushed by the grinding of a glacier. I long to climb down the bank and immerse myself in its blue-green chill.

The flat road is aerobically easy but endlessly tedious. We stop to talk to everyone we pass. *Where are you going, where are you coming from. Gari mala—no truck.* Leon and I become engaged in an inane conversation about soap operas, restaurants, and bad songs from the seventies to help pass the time. We pass the temple of Gomkhora, beside an enormous black rock near the river. "That's the rock Guru Rimpoché used to pin down a demon," Leon says. "He chased the demon all the way from Tibet. There's a really narrow tunnel down there in the rock that people squirm through. If they make it, it means their sins are cleared away." We stand for a moment, looking down toward the river. There is something completely satisfying about the whole spot. The temple is old but well-kept, surrounded by neatly parceled rice paddies and shaded by large, fragrant eucalyptus trees. In the noontime light, everything shimmers but nothing moves except the river. There is no sign of any human activity and that feeling comes over me again, the feeling of being too recent and flimsy for the landscape I am in. I try to imagine who I would be if I had lived all my life here at this temple by the river. I wonder what I would want if I had grown up without ads telling me my heart's desires: to be thinner, richer, sexier, look better, smell better, be all that I can be, have a faster car, a brighter smile, lighter hair, whiter whites, hurry now, don't miss out, take advantage of this special offer. If instead I had spent twenty-four years absorbing the silent weight of the mountains, the constant pull of the river, the sound of hot white light burning into black rocks.

A bird sings out, a two-note song, and I come back to myself. "Let's just stay here," I say, because the road ahead bends and quivers in the heat, and we still have twelve kilometers to go, and standing here is like drinking spring water. Even the river hesitates at this spot, curling around the large rocks and murmuring against the banks before the current tugs it away.

The last two hours of the journey take forever. We turn a corner and see Tashigang dzong, perched on a cliff in the distance, but that's where it remains, in the distance, a mirage, and I limp along, feet burning, stomach empty, with the refrain of "Run Joey Run" on permanent playback in my head. "I wish the Vomit Comet would come along," I say.

"No you don't," Leon and Tony say in unison.

"Which would you rather have right now," Leon says suddenly, "a sandwich with Black Forest ham on thinly sliced rye bread with Dijon mustard and a cold beer or—"

"Oh no," Tony groans. "Not the Food Game."

"OR, a pizza with extra thin crust, sun-dried tomatoes, onions, black olives, cheese and —"

"It's his favorite game on long walks and bus rides," Tony explains. "It's torture."

"AND a bottle of your favorite red wine," Leon finishes.

"The sandwich," I say. "You?"

"The pizza. Okay, now, which would you rather have for dessert, Haagen Dazs chocolate chocolate-chip ice cream or . . ."

Time speeds up. We cross Chazam discussing the merits of seafood over falafel above the loud flap and flutter of tattered prayer flags tied to the bridge railings, and take a short cut to Tashigang dzong, a forty-five-minute ascent up the steepest slope ever to bear a path. I am dizzy and painfully out of breath when we reach the cluster of prayer flags at the top, but now I understand why the dzong was built here, on this unassailable spur overlooking the river.

At the Norkhil bar, we are joined by a class VIII student Tony knows. He begins to tell us about Tashigang, how a local deity had to be subdued before Buddhism could flourish there; a small dwelling halfway down the mountain is said to hold the deity now, The dzong was built in 1688, continuing the Shabdrung's campaign to bring the whole country under one rule. "Hey," I interrupt, "what happened to the Shabdrung anyway?"

"What do you mean, miss?"

"In the class VIII history book, the Shabdrung's reincarnations suddenly disappear."

The student glances over one shoulder, then another, and begins to tell us a story. Sometime in the 1920s or 1930s, he is not sure when, the then-Shabdrung began to cause trouble with the monarchy and soon after died mysteriously "in his sleep," but everyone knows he was assassinated, suffocated with a white silk scarf, and everyone knows the family of the man who killed him was cursed with illness, madness, loss and ruin. The next reincarnation was found somewhere in the eastern districts, but this Shabdrung also disappeared. Some people say he was pushed out of a window in Tashigang dzong.

The student pauses and looks around again. "As he was falling, a bird tried to save him, and caught him with its wings, but the men in the dzong threw stones and he fell again. The river itself didn't want to take him, and sent him back to shore, but the men came again and pushed him back in and so finally he had to die."

He tells us that the next reincarnation was taken out of Bhutan by the Indian army during the Indo-China war, and now lives in New Delhi.

We sit quietly, digesting this, and I remember the Pema Gatshel history teacher's reluctance to talk about the current Shabdrung. After the student leaves, we look at each other. "How much of that do you think is grounded in fact?" I ask.

"Who knows?" Leon says, shrugging.

I think about all the half-complete stories I have heard since I got here, how their incompleteness makes them resonant and powerful. History here seems a combination of official, unofficial, and forbidden stories. This tale of the Shabdrung, for instance: I don't know where to look it up or who to ask for more information. There's no way to know for sure. It could have happened, it might have happened, I heard it happened . . . It is the impossibility of knowing for sure that makes everything possible. I am dying to know (no, I don't want to know) the rest of the story, the whole story, the real story.

We drink several cold beers in silence. "Now where's my ham sandwich with Dijon mustard, that's what I want to know," I say. But what I really want is rice and dahl and potato curry at the Puen Soom, which is fortunate, because that's all there is.

On Tuesday morning, we search the bazaar in vain for a private vehicle going south. "It's the Vomit Comet for sure," Tony says.

"It's full. We'll never get on," I say, watching as a woman with a jerry can of kerosene, a baby, and a bundle of frayed, faded cloth tries to press her way up the bus steps.

Leon walks around the bus, peering into the windows. "That's not full," he reports back scornfully. "Full means the ticket collector has to walk on the backs of the seats. Let's go."

We squeeze ourselves onto the bus, which reeks of mildew, vomit, kerosene, and betel nut, struggling over legs, bags, boxes, sacks, jerry cans, children and bedrolls. It is like being pushed through a sieve. Still more people pile on, until we are jammed in too tightly to move, and the ticket collector has to walk on the backs of the seats. The engine rumbles to life and Hindi film music comes screeching out of a speaker. "Oh misery," Leon groans, "we've got the one with the sound system."

After thirty minutes on the winding road, a few people begin to vomit, out windows if they are near them, onto the floor if not. People cover their noses and mouths with their sleeves against the smell. A chicken escapes from somewhere and a child kicks my shins trying to catch it. Someone spits betel nut juice on my shoes. The ticket collector sways precariously from his perch and clutches at a woman's head to prevent himself from falling into her lap when the bus brakes suddenly. People who want to get off at an unscheduled stop gesture to him, and he pounds loudly on the ceiling or the back wall: bangBANG, bangBANG, bangBANG. Disembarkation requires a contortionist's skill and a great deal of determined uncivility. The open windy ride to Rangthangwoong seems like a luxury now. "Which would you rather have," I ask Leon, "eggs Benedict with freshly squeezed orange juice or . . ." I cannot finish.

"Valium and a Scotch," he answers flatly.

We say goodbye to Tony in Khaling, and Leon gets off in Wamrong, wishing me luck getting a gypsum truck from Tshelingkhor. "If there's no truck, and it's getting dark," he says, "stay in Tshelingkhor. Don't walk in the dark. A kid fell off a cliff last year trying to take a shortcut somewhere along that road."

"Yeah, okay, I'll just book into the Holiday Inn for the night," I say grumpily, thinking of the two miserable, bamboo shacks by the roadside.

"The Hilton has better room service," he says. "Bye!"

There is already a large group of people waiting at Tshelingkhor when I scramble off the bus. It is dusk, and a heavy mist is creeping over the tree tops. Inside one of the huts, Tshering's shop-cum-bar, I study the shelves behind the counter. I have a choice of Orange Cream Biscuits and tea, or Orange Cream Biscuits and several brands of Bhutanese whiskey: Dragon Rum, Triple XXX Rum, Black Mountain

Whiskey, Bhutan Mist. I drink three cups of lukewarm tea and then switch to Bhutan Mist. Tiny knives scrape my throat on the way down but the final product settles warmly in my stomach. "*Gari mala*," the old man beside me says glumly. He is drinking Triple XXX Rum. I ask him where the toilet is and he gestures to the door. Outside. I stand up but he waves me back down. "*Ma di, ma di*," he says, making a strange wriggling gesture with his fingers. "*Pat-ba!*" Finally, a young boy steps forward and translates shyly for me. "He is telling don't go, miss. He is telling leeches." If leeches can get up your nose, they can also get into other orifices. I sit back down. Just then, everyone in the room jumps up. I can hear it too, the distant rumble of a truck. Outside the mist has turned into a fine, cold rain. The truck stops, a flatbed already overloaded with sacks of rice, but the driver waits while we clamber on before turning onto the Pema Gatshel road.

I know we are driving along the edge of a very steep gully, but in the darkness I can see nothing except the occasional glimmer of the truck's headlights on the clouds in the ravine beneath us. In my gut, though, I can feel the immense emptiness between the soft, deeply rutted road we are on and the bottom of the gulch somewhere down below. Beyond, across, I know there are mountains but I cannot see them. It is like driving on the edge of the world.

The truck turns a corner and we are splashed with mist from a waterfall. At the next corner, the truck flounders in mud, rocking back and forth. The Bhutanese begin to pray. I don't know what I am more afraid of: the road giving way, the truck tottering and the whole lot of us tumbling over the edge, or my bladder full of tea bursting. The truck lurches forward, engine straining, then slides back. Everyone is scrambling to stay perched on top of the hard rounded sacks of rice, and I look desperately for something to hang on to. The old man from Tshelingkhor offers me a length of rope which is not secured to anything, a shovel handle, and his own cloth bag full of empty bottles. I shake my head to each. Finally, he grins lewdly and motions at his crotch. "Apa! Yallama!" I say, exasperated. Our fellow passengers, who have been watching this attempt to find me a handhold, burst into laughter. They laugh for the rest of the ride. Just when they begin to quiet down, someone shouts, "Apa! Yallama!" and they explode again. I laugh, too, looking up at the sky of shifting clouds illuminated by the moon buried somewhere deep inside them.

Do Not Eat Your Spelling Tests

In the staff room during morning break, Maya is opening a stack of mail and skimming the letters. I pick up an envelope addressed to "Miss Dorji Wangmo, class VIII B, Pema Gatshel Junior High School" and ask Maya what she is doing. "Girls' mail," she says. "First the matron has to read."

"But why?" I ask.

"Love letters," she says, not looking up. I don't know what to say to this. An inquiry into the privacy of mail is obviously pointless.

"See this one. The boy is writing 'from your dear brother Tandin Wangchuk' on the envelope, but look here, inside. 'My dearest sweet Dechen, I am missing you a hell lot,'" she reads triumphantly, then crumples up the letter. She looks up and sees my expression. "We have to," she says. "Otherwise these girls will spoil their studies."

"But you don't read the boys' mail," I say.

"No," she says. "I am the girls' matron."

"But does anyone read the boys' mail? The boys' warden?"

"No," she says.

I stand there, chewing on the end of my pen, remembering Mr. Om Nath's strange tone when he talked about looking after the girls, thinking of how often the boys are singled out for responsibilities and recognition by the staff while the girls are pointedly ignored, how the number of female students decreases sharply in the upper classes. During the orientation, we were told that women in Bhutan enjoy much more freedom than women in other Asian countries. Women in Bhutan own shops and hotels and small businesses, they travel when and where they want, and schooling is free and open for both sexes. Unlike India, there is no dowry system and very few arranged marriages; daughters are as valued as sons, divorce is acceptable, widows remarry, and family property is usually passed down matrilineally. And yet, in the school, another set of values seems to be at work. In the lower classes, the girls are still bold and confident, but they become increasingly shyer as they move into the upper grades. They put their hands over their mouths and giggle when addressed; they defer to the male students and seem to shrink a little more each year. I wonder if sexism is somehow a by-product of Western-style development, or the number of Indian teachers in the school system, or if chauvinism is just as deeply embedded here as anywhere else. When I ask the older girls why so many of their friends have dropped out, they tell me they were needed at home, or they had gotten married, or their parents thought that education was irrelevant since their daughters were going to inherit the family house and land.

"One letter is there for you, in the headmaster's room," Maya says, and I slip across the hall. It is a letter from Robert. I have this idea that I will put it, unopened, into the top fold of my kira until lunch, that I will take it home and savor it slowly. I do not. I rip open the letter and read it right there, standing in the headmaster's office. Robert writes that he misses me. He has received my postcard from Thimphu and my first long, long letter. He wishes he could call me. He writes about school, what's gone wrong with his car this time, the weekend with his parents, the skiing is finished, it has been a mild spring. The letter is full of details of daily life, and I feel reconnected and homesick, close and far, at the same time. And then I get to the end, just before the love and Xs and Os. He says he has read my letter over and over again, but he just can't get a handle on where I am and what I am experiencing. "Where *are* you?" he writes.

The bell rings for the next period but I stand in the office, the letter dangling from my hand. I don't know how he can ask where I am, how he cannot understand. I wrote everything.

The monsoon has begun in earnest. The rain in March was just a little prelude. The mornings are often clear, and I get up early just to watch the sun float up over the dark hills behind the school. By early afternoon, the clouds have rolled in again, blocking up all views. It rains most heavily at night, and I like the sound of the falling water on the corrugated iron roof now, the steady reassuring pressure of it. I no longer worry about the road and what it might or might not bring—mail, visitors, supplies. I will not starve. I will be taken care of, I know that now.

If I get up early enough, I have an hour or two to myself before someone knocks at the door. I boil water for coffee on the new gas stove Trevor has brought me from Samdrup Jongkhar. It cost one month's salary (which I had to borrow from the headmaster) but it is worth it. Back in bed with my coffee, I read, write in my journal, listen to the now-familiar sounds of chickens and roosters and cows and children. Once or twice, I have gone out for a walk at dawn, and have been surprised at the number of people already at work: tending cows, carrying water, collecting firewood. I think of the students who have already begun their three-hour walk to school, having risen and dressed and eaten a breakfast of cold rice in the dark.

The first knock at the door is usually one or two kids, bringing me vegetables. I pay for these things, even though the headmaster told me not to. "It is because you are the teacher," he said. "They want to give something." He said that respect for the teacher is a Bhutanese tradition, and the parents do not expect to be paid for vegetables. But I don't know how I can suddenly stop paying them now that I have started, and it is such an inconsequential amount (for me)—not even a dollar for a week of fresh tomatoes or spinach. The news of this payment has spread, though, and now kids from other classes are bringing me vegetables as well. Dozens of kids, armfuls of spinach, baskets of onions and radish and beans. I cannot possibly eat all they bring, and yet, I do not know how to refuse it. I cannot take from some and not from others, cannot pay some and not others. I regret my misplaced generosity and then wonder if it is even generosity at all, or just guilt at having so much, and a desire to be liked, to be accepted by the village, to be thought well of. I have upset something, changed expectations, brought something foreign into the picture. I have created a transaction.

I wonder what other things I have unthinkingly done, if I will do more harm than good here. I do things without thinking, I forget where I am. This is harder than living without a refrigerator and hot running water, harder than being cut off from family and friends. This is, in fact, the hardest part: the same imperfect self immersed in a completely new and incompletely understood setting, the same desires and longings clouding judgment, the same old heedless mind, leaping from impulse to action.

No mindfulness, I think. Every Buddhist treatise I read stresses the importance of bringing the mind to focus on itself, developing the awareness necessary for right thought and speech and action. Mindfulness is both a means and an end, the way to enlightenment and the product of it. It has allowed me several times to pull myself out of a quagmire of homesickness and futile longing for material comforts, and bring myself back to the moment or task at hand, but I wish I had a stronger, less random sense of it. Perhaps I expected that I would automatically become wiser in a Buddhist culture, maybe through osmosis. But mindfulness will only come through effort. Meditation is one way to acquire it, but I am also beginning to wonder if all the Buddhist rituals I have witnessed so far—the turning of prayer wheels, recitation of mantras, circumambulation of prayer walls—are practiced in order to develop mental discipline.

I think about this through morning assembly, watching my kids' heads bent in prayer. I love them, each and every one of them. They have already taught me far more than I can ever teach them. Jane was right: they make everything worthwhile. I bow my head and pray that I do not do more harm than good. I pray to remember where I am.

I push open the classroom door and they leap up. "Good morning, class II C," I say. They are class II C, and I am Miss: Miss Jamie, also Miss Jigme, sometimes Miss Jammy, nurse and babysitter, cheerleader and referee, general assistant and, occasionally, teacher.

"Good morn-ing, miss!" they shout back, beaming. And we begin.

Most days are still a travesty of pedagogy. Today, I hand back spelling tests and Sonam Tshering promptly stuffs his in his mouth and swallows it. For a moment, I am too surprised to speak. Karma Dorji says, "That boy is very hungry," and everyone laughs, but I am not amused. Frowning, I fold my arms and say crossly, "Class II! Listen to me!" They sit up straight, serious, expectant. "Class II," I say sternly, "do not eat your spelling tests." And then I burst into laughter. My announcements and queries are growing more absurd daily. Tshewang Tshering, you cannot write your test with a cat in your gho. Sangay, put away those chilies. Well, eat them if you're going to eat them, but don't play with them during math. Class II C, who is bleeding all over the floor? Class II C, who is gassing? Class II C, why is there a bottle of pee in our room?

Moments of work and understanding and order arise briefly out of the uproar. In between accidents, emergencies, spontaneous expressions of affection, and moments of brilliant mischief, they learn the five senses, the months of the year, the rain cycle. Miss, they tell me, you is very good. Miss, you is coming my house, my mother is very happy to you. Miss, you is always teaching us English, today we is teaching you our language; you say *long-sharang*. I repeat it—long-sharang—and they fall over laughing. I have just learned the Sharchhop for dick-head.

After school, they come to take me roaming. There is so much to show me: a crumbling chorten, a flowering orange tree near a stream, a grove where ghosts are seen at night. They have so much to tell: the woman in their village who can talk to the dead, the time someone saw a demon and fell ill, the great hairy ferocious beast that lives in the mist on the tops of mountains and feeds on human flesh (one kid demonstrates by trying to bite another kid's head). They tell me what they will be when they grow up: a dasho, a driver, a farmer. They tell me about their parents, who drinks arra and who does not, whose house has glass windows and whose does not, who died and when and why. They talk about God. God is Sangay, the Buddha, and God is also Guru Rimpoché. And Chenresig and Jambayang, they say, naming the

Bodhisattvas of Compassion and Wisdom. *Lha shama.* Many gods. I ask if they believe in heaven. Yes, yes, they say. "Being very good, then going up to Guru Rimpoché's place. Being bad, then going down." I ask them what it means to be good. They say "good" means being kind, giving, not killing, not even a bird, not even a bug.

"But you eat meat, yes?" I ask. They nod. "So isn't that also bad?" No, they say, they themselves do not kill the animal. "Only eating, not killing." This reminds me of stories I have heard about pigs being tied near cliffs. The pig eventually falls off and then it can be said that the animal killed itself. I don't really understand how this solves the prohibition on harming any sentient being, but they obviously do.

We walk back up the mountain in the cool evening shadows. At home, I write Robert another letter, reiterating, describing things again, in more and better detail. I am so lucky to be here, I write. Even when it is difficult and confusing. Maybe especially then. I am so glad I came. But I wonder if Robert will take this as a sign that I do not miss him, that I like Bhutan more than him. I rewrite the last page, saying I can't wait to see him at Christmas. *Christmas.* The word looks foreign and unreliable on the page.

Beating Nicely

It is the language that confuses me at first. "Our sir is beating nicely," a class IV student informs me. Beating means hitting, with a strip of willow or a thin stick, across the palm or the backs of the legs. But beating nicely? Perhaps it means a beating without force, a mild or apologetic beating: this hurts me more than it hurts you. But nicely is used in Bhutan to mean well-done. So this is a thorough beating, a terrible beating. The sir in question is Mr. Iyya, but almost every teacher in the school has a stick and they are all beating nicely. An ugly narrow piece of bamboo, brought whistling down onto a trembling hand, a vicious crack, an indrawn breath, silent tears. I do not often understand what the beating is being given for. One morning during assembly, several of the smallest students receive a stick across the back of the legs. Mrs. Joy tells me it is for coming to school without shoes. "But what if their parents can't afford to give them shoes?" I ask, horrified. She shrugs. "They have to wear shoes. Headmaster has been telling and telling," she says.

In the classroom, students are hit when they come late, when they talk out of turn, when they have forgotten their books, when they don't understand, when they can't remember, when they dare ask a question, when they give the wrong answer and, occasionally, especially in Mr. Iyya's class, when they give the right answer. Teachers come to school with a notebook, a pen, and a stick. When the stick gets lost or broken, they send a student outside to find another. I should have expected this the first time I heard the Alphabet Song sung with a sinister twist: "Oh my madam don't beat me, now I know my ABCs."

I remind myself that this is not my country, not my education system. I remember fragments from our orientation session, a lecture about the monastic system, harsh punishments meted out by the guru to the student as a way to achieve total submission. The goal in the monastery is not submission for its own sake but the breaking of the ego, liberation from a false sense of self, leading to enlightenment. But it is very hard to see how this applies to class III students who do not understand multiplication. The final goal in school is knowledge, understanding, and a stick will not help. Another part of me argues: it is part of a bigger cultural system, it involves different values. You can only judge it from your perspective, from your own cultural background and upbringing, and even if you are right, what can you do about it? Back and forth I argue, right-wrong, east-west, judgment is possible-impossible. It reminds me of arguments in a first-year university philosophy class, the impossibility of ever saying anything, one way or another.

One afternoon, from across the playing field, I watch Mr. Rinzin slap Karma Dorji across the face and I go running across the grass, heart swollen with rage, how dare he, how *dare* he? "What seems to be the problem?" I ask Mr. Rinzin. My voice is shaking but he does not seem to notice. "Nothing, nothing. There's no problem," he says, smiling, and walks away.

"What happened, Karma?" I ask.

"He is calling me to come, but I am coming there too slowly." He shrugs and plods off to join his friends, and I burst into tears.

I go to talk to the headmaster. He listens sympathetically as I explain. I say that hitting a child for disobedience is one thing, *maybe,* but children are being hit all the time, for everything, even for things they have no control over. They are hit when they don't understand and become afraid to ask questions. How can they learn if they cannot ask questions? Learning and fear are not compatible, and, as for discipline, there are other methods. The headmaster nods. He has heard this before. He says that he agrees in principle with me, but that students in Bhutan are used to the stick, and perhaps they will not behave without it. He says that if he stopped using the stick, the students might think he had no authority over them. "But all the students are so well-behaved," I say.

"Yes," he agrees, "they are, but why? Because they've been brought up so strictly, isn't it?" I feel my throat tighten, and I command myself not to cry. The headmaster does not speak for a while, and then he says that I can use whatever method I choose in my own classroom, and that maybe I will be an example to the others. I nod because I still cannot speak. He asks me if I have heard of NAPE, the New Approach to Primary Education, which the government is introducing. Under the NAPE system, he says, there will be no hitting. But it will take some time for people to get used to the new ways, he says.

These things take time, it is true, I want to say, but what about Mr. Iyya? Time is not going to help Mr. Iyya. There is a big difference between Mr. Iyya's beatings and everyone else's. A few days ago, I stopped outside class I B, my heart in my throat at the sound of weeping. Inside, the entire class was lined up in front of the Dzongkha lopen who was seated at the front of the room with a bucket of water and a handful of stinging nettles. He dipped the nettles into the water and struck each student across the palm. He did not look angry or happy or not happy to be punishing the students for whatever infraction they had jointly committed or their simple failure to learn. He just looked tired. But Mr. Iyya is different. I have heard him shout himself gleefully into a black twisted rage over a misspelled word. The senior girls tell me that he slaps them in class and says nasty things to them. "What kind of nasty things?" I ask, but they are too shy to tell me. His methodology for teaching English to class IV is to make them copy out and memorize pages from the dictionary.

That afternoon, as we walk out of town, I ask Karma Dorji if his parents hit him. "My mother is not beating," he says.

"But what about when you are very naughty?" I ask.

"Then shouting," he says. "My father is shouting and then sometimes beating. But Phuntsho Wangmo, you know Phuntsho Wangmo, miss? Our class Phuntsho? Her mother is beating. Her mother is very *kakter*." Kakter means hard, difficult, rough.

"And the teachers at school, they are beating, yes?" I ask. They all nod, and Norbu says, "Only miss is not beating. Why not beating, miss?"

"Because class II C is very good," I say, and they laugh. "Not good, miss. We is very naughty."

Then I tell them, slowly so that they will understand, "In my village, in Canada, if I beat my students, their parents would get very angry. They would call the police and I would have to go to jail." But even as I say it, I hear the falseness in it. I try to calculate how many years ago corporal punishment was used in schools. I remember the strap in my elementary school. I cannot explain to them the complexity of the issue, the debate over physical punishment, the legal aspects, parents suing teachers, children suing parents. I cannot explain the state of things in North American schools, where teachers do not hit the students but students sometimes hit the teachers, the slow poisoning of the relationship between teacher and student, breaches of trust and abuse of authority, the hopeless lack of self-control that no one seems to know how to address. Things are different in North America, but in the final analysis, not any easier or any better, and I am sorry now that I have given that impression. Here again is the mind, leaping from emotion to speech without reflection. I have learned nothing.

Three days after this conversation, tea break in the staff room is interrupted by a disturbance outside the headmaster's office. A man with a stick is speaking quietly, angrily in rapid-fire Sharchhop. Maya tells me that Mr. Iyya split open a girl's knuckles in class and her father has come looking for him. The door to the office closes and we can hear nothing more. We sit in the staff room, watching the mist settle over the school yard, listening to the start of the rain on the roof, waiting for the end of the story. The office door opens, and the man leaves the school. The headmaster looks exhausted. The father was furious, he says, and he was hard-pressed to stop him from taking that stick to Mr. Iyya. He has promised to keep Mr. Iyya under control. The father in turn has promised not to beat Mr. Iyya on school property, but warned that Mr. Iyya now comes to the bazaar at his own risk.

I walk slowly across the playing field, letting the cold rain soak me. The hem of my kira is wet and heavy against my ankles, and my flip-flops sink into the mud. I feel like I am struggling through deep water. You do nothing, you keep quiet, and a teacher breaks open a girl's hand. But at least something has been done. Perhaps it was right to stay out of it and let the parents come forth on their own. But if the girl had been a boarder, if she had had a different, less confident father, perhaps no one would have come forth. The girl would have been sent to the hospital for stitches, and Mr. Iyya would continue to hit and degrade the students. I want to know whose responsibility it is to do something. Just because I am a foreigner, an outsider, just because this is not my home, does that mean I should stay silent while children are beaten by a crazed, vicious adult? It's a slippery slope on all sides, and I do not know where to draw the line between cultural sensitivity and plain old cowardice.

The Shrub's Name Is Miss Jammy

I am perched on a counter in the kitchen, waiting for a pot of water to boil, remembering how in the beginning, I hated to come in here. The discolored walls and cracked concrete sink made me think longingly of warm and well-lit kitchens with shelves full of pretty things. Porcelain cups and saucers, ceramic canisters, quilted pot holders and matching oven mitts. Table cloths, place mats. A bread box, a butter dish, salt and pepper shakers. Junk and clutter, I think now. Clutter and junk.

I have one kerosene stove (used only for boiling water), a plastic jerry can, and a shining new gas stove with cylinder. A few tin plates, mugs and tumblers. Three spoons. A flour sifter, a tea strainer. One sharp knife. Two woven bamboo baskets, an assortment of empty cans with plastic lids. A frying pan, a pressure cooker, two pots. A beer bottle with the label washed off (the rolling pin), two shoulder pads (the oven mitts), one plastic bag full of plastic bags and one water filter. Overall it is still the ugliest, coldest, dirtiest, bleakest, barest, least comfortable kitchen I have known, but I have everything I need.

First-term exams have finished, and I have just started marking class II C's science papers. Even the preprimary students wrote exams. All week, students wandered around the school yard memorizing their textbooks. Class II C wanted to join them. "We *have to* by-heart it," they said.

"No, you don't have to by-heart it," I argued. "You have to *understand* it. Do you understand it?"

"Yes, miss."

I pour boiling water into the tin mug, stir in coffee powder and carry it to my desk where the papers are stacked up. *What is a shrub?*

A shrub is a shrub. Shrub is mugspit. I am not a shrub. The shrub's name is Miss Jammy. Shrub is I don't kanow Miss. Most of them fail science. Maybe I should have let them by-heart it. I press my head against the window. *I don't kanow Miss.*

Outside, the wind picks up, sounding strange and ominous, and a flock of crows settles on the edge of the playing field. From a neighbor's house the sounds of a puja, horns and drums and a chanted prayer, rise up over the crying of a baby. The puja is for the baby who is thinner and more yellow each time I see her. I swat at the flies that buzz angrily around my head. I cannot grade any more papers. I have to get out. I open the door to find Lorna climbing the staircase. "Howdy," she says. "Wanna go shopping with me tomorrow in Samdrup Jongkhar?"

Samdrup Jongkhar, on the Indo-Bhutan border, is three hours away from Pema Gatshel by truck. At the orientation in Thimphu, it was referred to as sort of a shopper's paradise for eastern Bhutan, where Indian goods of every kind were readily available. "Are you kidding?" I say. "Let's go right now!"

We get a ride in the back of a gypsum truck, sitting on a pile of stones as the truck roars out of the valley and onto the main road. The sky is clear, a brilliant, heartbreaking blue. "This is so much better than the Vomit Comet," Lorna says. I tell her about a teacher who claimed the woman behind him on the Comet gave birth and no one even knew about it until the ride was over and the happy woman and her husband got off the bus with their new baby. Lorna says a very young monk peed on her foot on her first bus ride and a Bhutanese man proposed to her.

"Really? What did he say exactly?"

"He didn't speak English, so he got his friend to ask," she says. "His friend said, 'Bhutanese man wants marriage you.' "

"And what did you say?"

"I said I'd think about it. There wasn't anything in our contracts about remaining celibate, was there?"

"I don't think so."

"Good," she says, laughing. "The old libido is starting to rage."

"Yeah," I sigh. "I've got the same problem, and Robert is seven thousand miles away."

"How long before you see him again?"

"Seven months."

Lorna whistles. "Good luck to you, girl."

The truck turns a corner and we gasp: the mountains have dwindled into soft emerald hills which in turn subside into the scorched and impossibly flat plains of India. The heat grows as we descend through lusher, more exaggerated tropical vegetation—flowering bushes with star-like leaves, groves of banana trees, umbrella trees with flame-colored blossoms. We see grey langurs, scarlet birds, black butterflies the size of my hand with electric blue markings, a large hornbill, waterfalls. Then we pull into Samdrup Jongkhar, and the wet heat rushes over and wraps itself around us. We thank the truck driver and leap down onto the tarmac—I can feel the heat burning through the soles of my shoes—and stagger down the road to the Shambhala Hotel.

Inside, under a whirring fan, we gorge on french fries and chicken and chocolate and wait for the sun to drop. It is a little cooler without the unrelenting sun beating down on our heads but still very humid, and my lungs feel full of slush. We walk to the Indo-Bhutan border, which is half a brick wall painted with slogans: ULFA! ANTI-ULFA BE CAREFUL! BODOLAND! I know from the Indian newspapers the school receives that ULFA is the United Liberation Front of Assam, fighting for separation from India, and that the Bodos are a tribal people who want a separate state carved out of Assam. On the other side of the wall, the roads and shops and teastalls continue, but the buildings look more run-down, and there are piles of bricks and sand and garbage in the streets. We walk back along the main road past shops selling everything. Jeans, umbrellas, pineapples, refrigerators, cassette players, canned vegetables, spices, hand cream, flashlights, car parts, bolts of cloth in hundreds of patterns and colors. I buy a new and hopefully chicken-proof flashlight (50 ngultrum, about $4), and we decide to get new kiras with matching blouses and jackets. Lorna studies the shelves of cloth for about thirty seconds before choosing a stripy green print, but I spend ages comparing swatches of cloth, much to her annoyance.

"What do you think of this?" I ask, holding up a plain dark-gray fabric.

"Yeah, it's nice."

"Or this one? I like the checks better than the plain."

"After a month of washing it in Surf, you're not going to be able to tell the difference." This is true: the washing powder we use sucks the color out of our clothes and gnaws little holes in everything.

"Oh, here's a nice one. What do you think of this maroon?"

"It's FINE. Come on, Cinderella, you'll be late for the ball."

I buy the maroon. Back in our room at the Shambhala, we sit under the fan and talk about our kids. Lorna tells me how she tried to describe a vacuum cleaner and washing machine to them. "God knows what they've constructed in their minds," she says. "Just imagine how it must sound to them: a big pipe that sucks up dirt and a box that washes your clothes."

I tell Lorna about class II C's dismal science exam answers. "I'm really feeling my lack of teacher training," I say. "I don't know if I'm doing much more than babysitting."

We talk about beating. Lorna says that she is a strict teacher and hopes to show that you can be strict without hitting. "But shouldn't we try to do something about it?" I ask.

Lorna shrugs. "It's not our place to do anything," she says. "And anyway, what would we do?"

The electricity suddenly fails, and we lie on the beds in the damp heat, listening to the crickets and one hysterical dog. I am almost asleep when Lorna's voice comes out of the darkness. "I just remembered something. You can't wear that new kira."

"Why not?"

"Only monks and nuns can wear that color."

I had completely forgotten. "Well, I can always make curtains out of it."

"Or become a nun," Lorna snickers.

In the morning, we decide to flee the heat and go to Bidung. The owner of a white hi-lux parked outside the hotel, a tall, boyish-looking Australian man, agrees to give us a ride to Tashigang. His name is Will, and he is a consultant, he tells us, making Seventy-Five Thousand American Dollars a Year, *Plus* Living Allowance and All Travel Expenses, and he cannot understand why we have come here for anything less. "You teachers make what, a hundred and fifty dollars a month?" he snorts.

"It's enough to live on," I say.

"It's what all the other teachers live on here," Lorna adds.

Will just shakes his head. "One hundred and fifty dollars a month. You couldn't get me to do it, no way."

"No one asked you to do it," Lorna mutters.

Will talks all the way to Tashigang. This place, these people, can't get a damn thing done, no work ethic, no idea of how to build a proper bridge, equipment thrown here and there, two new drills broken to pieces in a week.

"So why do you stay?" Lorna asks. "If it's that bad."

"I told you," he says. "Seventy-Five Thousand Dollars a Year."

In Tashigang, we scramble out of the vehicle and don't even thank him for the ride. It is late afternoon; we will have just enough time to get to Bidung before dark. We walk up through cool pine forests in the falling evening, to the ridges where the winds stay, stopping to rest under trees, at the base of a chorten, beside a cluster of prayer flags. We arrive in Bidung at nightfall. Lorna's quarters, at the end of a dilapidated row, consist of a bed-sitting room and a dank, spidery kitchen with a mudstove. I rummage in my bag for my new flashlight to take to the latrine. "It's true to its name, *pit latrine,*" Lorna warns me. "They're building a new one. This one is so disgusting, I don't use it."

"What do you use then?"

"The maize fields," she says. "The maize is just high enough."

"Oh, Lorna!"

But she is right, the latrine is exceedingly disgusting. Where the floorboards have not rotted away, they are covered in excrement, and

I hope for Lorna's sake they finish the new latrine before all the maize is harvested in the fall. When I come back, Lorna says we have just been invited to dinner by her "headless master." "A nice man," she says as we walk to his quarters, "but a hopeless headmaster. And he drinks too much, but then, there's not a lot else to do out here, is there?"

Sitting on straight-backed chairs in a room identical to Lorna's, we sip large cups of arra. "Dinner will take some time," the head-master tells us, pouring more arra. "Please have." Two bottles of arra later, I am sitting with an empty plate in my lap, although I cannot remember having eaten. We stand up to go, and Lorna has to hold onto my arm.

On the way back, she says, "How did you eat that awful meat?"

"There was meat?"

"Yes, you idiot. It was putrid. I don't know how you ate so much of it."

I don't know either. I awake hung-over. Lorna is getting ready for class. She has no classroom and teaches on the school verandah. Five small faces appear at her window. "Miss *niktsing*," they whisper excitedly. *Two* misses. On her way out, Lorna throws a packet of chicken noodle soup at me, part of a recent package from Canada, and asks me to make lunch. "Use wood instead of the kerosene stove, okay?" she says. "I have to haul the kerosene up from Tashigang. There's plenty of kindling in the bucket in the kitchen." I nod and go straight back to sleep.

Hours later, I carefully layer pieces of kindling and scrap paper in the bottom of the stove, sprinkle everything with kerosene and throw a lit match. The fire blazes up and I am pleased. Ten minutes later, the soup is still cold: the fire has gone out. I use more kindling, more paper, more kerosene. I poke, I blow, I curse. How is it that whole houses have been known to burn to the ground with one electrical spark, and yet I cannot warm a pot of soup with a bucket of highly flammable substances? I hear the door open and Lorna calls out cheerfully, "Hi honey, I'm home." She is decidedly less cheerful when she sees that I've used all her wood and paper, and almost all the kerosene, and the soup is still cold. She fiddles with the charred remains in the stove, and the fire leaps to life.

We sip the hot soup and eat cream crackers, and discuss various romantic developments among the expatriate teachers. Lorna has already ruled out the possibility of romance with any of the Canadians. "They're good buddies," she says. "But nothing more." I ask her if she has seen anything like the night-hunting we heard about during our orientation, where young men court women by climbing through their windows at night.

She says yes, and this is why the girls at school are locked in.

"What do you mean, locked in?"

"Locked in the hostel. At night. From the outside."

My mouth drops open. "They're locked in from the outside? What if there's a fire or something?" I say. "Why can't the girls lock themselves in from the inside?"

"I don't know," Lorna says. "They don't trust them?"

"But who are they locked in against? The boys?"

"I guess so."

"So why don't they lock the boys in, then?"

"I don't know," Lorna says.

"But isn't it weird? Even the word 'night-hunting.' And if everyone is so relaxed about sex, and if women are so free, why are they locking the girls in? It's just not acceptable."

"It's not acceptable in our culture," Lorna says.

Outside, a hard heavy rain begins. There is something ominous in the force of it. I cannot see farther than the edge of the playing field. At 3:30, I begin to worry about the road back to Pema Gatshel. "If this keeps up, I'll be stranded in Tashigang," I say. "I'd better get back." Lorna lends me a rain cape, and I set off. The path is now a mudslide, and at several places I have to sit and slither down. My pants are slick with clay, and rain runs down my neck.

The road south is already closed by the time I reach Tashigang, and I have to stay for several days, waiting for the landslides to be cleared and then for some form of transport. Each morning I sit at the Puen Soom, praying for a landcruiser, a hi-lux, a truck, a scooter, a donkey. One morning on the way down to the bazaar I even pray for the dreaded Vomit Comet and my prayers are instantly answered. There it is, revving up in a swirl of blue fumes.

The Question Why

The rains have turned Pema Gatshel a thousand shades of green: lime, olive, pea, apple, grass, pine, moss, malachite, emerald. The trees are full of singing insects, flowers, birds, hard green oranges, children. I walk along a stone wall, feeling my foot connect with every step to the earth, listening to the whirring humming world around. I stop to watch a woman weeding her garden. Her children are playing a game with stones in the shade of a flowering shrub, while three plump chickens scratch in the dirt. A little further on, I rest on a mossy boulder beside a waterfall, cooling my face and hands in the mist. A class II student and his father stop to offer me a handful of plums, and I refuse politely. Offer-decline, offer-decline, offer-accept. The plums are firm and faintly sweet. Above, the cleanest whitest clouds I have ever seen are banked up against the sky. It's hard to believe now that I once thought this a landscape of lack, that I was afraid I wouldn't have enough, wouldn't fare well, wouldn't be happy.

Yesterday, the kids brought me seven tiny, withered apples, obviously the last of last year's harvest. Under the darkened, spotted skin, the yellow heart was almost unbearably sweet. In Canada, I would have thrown them out and gone to the grocery store to choose new, perfectly shaped, unblemished apples, the taste genetically engineered out of them.

Everything is more meaningful here because there is less of everything. Every brown farm egg is precious. I make yogurt out of sour milk, and turn overripe fruit into jammy desserts. A plastic bag is a rare and immensely useful thing. The first few did not last long, but now I am careful. I wash and dry and fold them away. I clean out jars and tins and plastic containers and save the tinfoil liners from cartons of milk powder. I stand in my kitchen, satisfied with the meaning of every item, thinking that my grandfather would be pleased. I am beginning to think that his cautious saving and counting and putting away have more to do with this measure of meaning than fear of future lack.

I like knowing where things come from. The cheese in my curry comes from the cow belonging to the family in the first house behind the hospital with the banana trees out front. I buy the cheese, fresh, still warm, wrapped in a banana leaf and tied with a piece of dried vine. The new flip-flops I am wearing are a present from Sangay Chhoden's mother for the antibiotic ear drops I gave her for Sangay Chhoden's baby brother's infected ear. The cloth bag of peas in the kitchen came from Sonam Tshering, whose family lives in a bamboo hut at the end of the road and who cannot afford to be giving away peas or anything else. I forget the peas until they begin to rot, and am about to throw the whole lot out when I think of the hut and the meager vegetable garden behind it. I force myself to pick through pods, separating the edible peas from the slime, keeping in mind a Tantric Buddhist teaching about overcoming squeamishness, facing the inevitability of death and decay by immersing oneself in all forms of unpleasantness.

Everything is more meaningful because it is connected to the earth. There are no signs to read, no billboards or neon messages; instead I read the hills and the fields and the farmhouses and the sky. The houses, made of mud and stone and wood, are not hermetically sealed. The wind blows in through the cracks, the night seeps in through the rough wooden window slats. The line between inside and outside is not so clear.

Everything is more meaningful because understanding requires struggle. I have to hold on to all the half-explained, half-translated, half-imaginable things, hoping that I will meet someone someday who will be able to explain. One evening I am called to the boys' hostel to see a sick class VIII boy. He is sitting slumped in his bunk, eyes unseeing. When I touch his arm lightly, he shudders. The other boys explain: he has these fits, no not epilepsy, they know epilepsy, it is not that. It is like possession, they say. Last year a lama gave him a protective amulet and he was fine until he lost the amulet washing in the river last week and now, just see, miss, he is sick again. I don't know what to say. They didn't cover possession in the health course. Keep him warm, I say, but not too warm. Let him be but stay close by. Later, when I tell the other teachers, they nod. Yes, this happens. They don't know how to say it in English. There are things here too old to be translated into this new language.

The headmaster asks me to teach class VIII English in the afternoons while class II C is learning Dzongkha. I stay up late the night before my first class, reviewing the lesson, hoping that I will be able to handle the senior students, many of whom are at least eighteen. I do not have to worry: they are well-behaved and meticulously polite. They are eager to answer questions with definite answers: What is the past participle of eat? What happens to the main character of the story? Other questions, though, produce a strained, confused silence. Perhaps they are shy, I think, perhaps they will express themselves more freely in their written assignments. But I am disappointed and puzzled by the sameness of their writing. Every piece begins with a cliché or a mangled proverb. *As they say, student life is golden life, and it is true also. As saying goes, the cleanliness is next to the godliness and I agree to it.* Every piece concludes with some hackneyed piece of advice or fawning praise (*so let us ever thank our kind teachers who make so many sacrifices for the poor and undeserving students*). I cannot get them to write in their own voices, and wonder if it is because individual expression is not valued here as it would be in the West. Originality seems to count for very little; the community is more important, conformity and accordance and compliance.

But there must be some dissent, I think. I listen more carefully outside the classroom, and begin to hear different stories. Some senior girls tell me they were forced to cut their hair at school. They are ethnically Nepali, from the southern districts of Bhutan. (According to government policy, students above class VI are sent to schools outside their home districts. Southern students are sent north, eastern students west, western students south, to promote greater integration.) The Nepali girls tell me that it is their custom to keep their hair long. "We wept like anything," they say, "but what to do? Short hair is driglam namzha."

I casually ask the headmaster why the female students must all have short hair. "Lice," he says matter-of-factly. The hostels are alive with fleas, lice and bedbugs, this is true, and given the school's erratic water supply, short hair makes sense. But this driglam namzha is appearing more and more. There is the new dress law: all Bhutanese citizens have to wear national dress in public or face fines and possible imprisonment. In the staff room, I leaf through back issues of the *Kuensel*, Bhutan's weekly newspaper, which I rarely bother to read when it arrives, a week or two late. An article explains that the national dress rule is part of efforts to preserve and promote Bhutan's national identity. A larger country can afford a diversity of customs and traditions which enrich and add color to the national image, but "for a small country like Bhutan, maintaining and strengthening a distinct national identity will always be a most important and vital factor for its continued well-being and security." These messages seem particularly aimed at the southern Bhutanese of Nepali origin. According to the *Kuensel*, the southern people have expressed full support for strengthening Bhutan's unique cultural identity by wearing national dress, speaking the national language, and following the ethics and practice of driglam namzha. The government announces that it will import machine-woven cloth to make ghos and kiras that can be sold at cost price to the people of southern Bhutan. The people of southern Bhutan express their gratitude.

This is the reason I have not read much of the *Kuensel*. Everyone is always expressing support and gratitude, no one ever seems to have a contradictory point of view. It seems strange, for instance, that the people of southern Bhutan would be so keen to wear the northern dress in the hot tropical plains, and that not a single person of Nepali origin expressed concern for preserving their own culture and language. Perhaps with time, an identity can be replaced, but it is hard to overwrite the names people call themselves. Either dissenting views were felt but not expressed, or expressed but not reported, but there must have been *some* people who were not happy with this idea.

I ask a class VIII student to explain the dress law to me. He says, "Our national dress is part of our culture." I ask why it must be legislated then. He isn't sure, but says that the Dzongda recently told his class the question why should not be allowed in Bhutan.

"Why ever not?" I ask, incredulous.

"Asking why is not driglam namzha," he says. I stare, openmouthed, but in the end I say nothing. I am afraid to contradict the district administrator. Maybe it is not even true. Maybe it is a misinterpretation. Maybe I do not understand. Most definitely I do not understand. *The question why should not be allowed?* A completely different system of values is at work here, based on another history. Obedience to authority, respect for elders and preservation of the status quo form the bedrock of Bhutanese values. I tell myself to see the Dzongda's statement objectively, as a part of a cultural context . . . but I wonder if this is ever truly possible: what does "objectively" mean anyway?

Movement Order

"Miss, your friend is here!" Sangay Chhoden comes to the library after school to tell me. I lock up and follow Sangay down the stairs to see who has come to visit. "Well, hello Medusa," Leon says, looking at my hair which has been made particularly unruly by the July humidity. "I'm starving. What do you have to eat? Let's make pizza." We set off, skirting the playing field, but the soccer game comes to a complete stop anyway so that everyone can watch us walk away. "Does this happen to you in Wamrong?" I ask Leon.

"Oh, all the time. I can't buy tomatoes in the market without the entire town talking about it. What's the phillingpa doing, he's buying tomatoes, how much is he paying, where did he buy them last time, how much did he pay then. It's part of being here, I know, but it still gets on my nerves sometimes. We have such a strong concept of privacy and it just doesn't exist here."

I know exactly what he means. I sometimes long for anonymity, to walk down a crowded city street unnoticed, unremarked upon, to be surrounded by strangers who couldn't care less where I am going when I step out of my door on a Saturday morning. Everyone in the village will know by this evening that my friend has come to visit. It doesn't really matter, but still, I wish my private life could be . . . well, private.

We stop between my building and the bank and furtively cut a few stalks of "pig food." I have noticed that many of the foreign teachers, even those that would not normally smoke it, take advantage of the wild marijuana that grows so luxuriantly everywhere. I dry the leaves in a frying pan while Leon churns together onions and Druk tomato sauce for the pizza. We stay up late drinking warm Golden Eagle beer and smoking the marijuana. Leon is certain that he will extend his contract and is already thinking of where he would like to be posted next. "Somewhere off the road," he says. "I know it's too early, but do you think you might extend?"

"I can't," I say. "There's Robert, for one thing . . ."

I am worried about my relationship with Robert. I miss him, but our letters only seem to emphasize the distance between us. They have become monologues, except for a few lines tacked on at the beginning or the end: I hope you got over your stomach trouble, I hope you did well on that last essay, be careful with the water there, your new car sounds lovely. I do not write that a car now sounds like a terrible indulgence in a city with buses, trains, trams and a subway system, or that the condominium Robert raved about sounds like an expensive prison. And I have a feeling he does not write how inexplicable he finds the stories in my letters. "It's like we're on two different planets," I say.

"Well, in a way, you are," Leon says.

I stare glumly at my bottle of beer. "I'm supposed to go home at Christmas," I say. "Maybe he can come back with me for a visit after." There's that odd word again, Christmas. *Home* has a strange ring to it now, too.

Too many bottles of beer later, I sweep the rest of the "pig food" into a Ziploc bag. "Leave the mess," I tell Leon, who is stacking up plates and pineapple rinds, and go crashing off to bed.

Someone knocks loudly at the door a few hours later. I lie in bed in the grey morning light, fully resolved to ignore the knocking. Go away, go away, I think, it's too early to be bringing me vegetables or a bleeding limb. I'm not getting up, go away. The knocking grows thunderous. I march to the door in my nightshirt and yank furiously at the bolts. "What?" I say. "What!"

The headmaster steps back, looking disconcerted. "Uh, Miss Jamie, this is the new principal of Sherubtse College," he says, gesturing to the heavyset man beside him. He has a broad, genial face, and is wearing a richly embroidered orange-and-yellow gho. "He would like to talk to you. . . ."

I apologize profusely for keeping them waiting, for my rudeness, for my nightshirt, for everything in general, and lead them into the sitting room, where Leon is sitting up in his sleeping bag, blinking. He leaps to his feet as I dash off to put on a kira. When I come back, the headmaster and the Sherubtse principal are sitting at the table while Leon clears away the empty beer bottles and dirty plates. He goes off to the kitchen to make tea, and the college principal explains that he has just been appointed to replace Father Larue. One of the English lecturers is leaving this month, he says, and he has heard from someone that I have a master's degree in English. Would I be interested in the job?

"Father Larue thought that I was too young," I say lamely.

"I know," he says, shaking his head. "I say, if someone has the right qualifications, what does age matter? It's like saying that someone is too short for the job. No, no, we aren't worried about your age."

Leon brings in the tea, and we notice at the same time the Ziploc bag in the middle of the table. He has thoughtfully cleared away the pizza remains and pineapple rinds for this impromptu job interview, but has forgotten the bag of pot. Our eyes meet and I can see that he is on the verge of an explosion. He bites his lip and looks away, his shoulders shaking with laughter.

We drink our tea while the principal tells me more about the college. A forty-minute drive south of Tashigang, surrounded by the village of Kanglung, the college is Bhutan's highest institute of education. About five hundred students are enrolled in undergraduate degrees in arts, commerce and science. The English curriculum is set by Delhi University, there's some poetry, some Shakespeare, a few novels. The library has thirteen thousand books. The other lecturers are mostly from Delhi, they all live on campus, the staff quarters are very nice, and he is sure I will be very happy there. . . .

I don't know what to say. The college sounds like a dream (thirteen thousand books!) but it is all so sudden, and it's unclear whether or not I have a choice in this matter. The principal stands. "So, I'll send a message to the Education Department for your movement order," he says. "And we'll send the hi-lux for you next week."

When they are gone, Leon dangles the plastic bag of pot in front of me. "I can't wait to see that movement order," he says. "It's going to say TRANSFERRED BACK TO TORONTO."

"Do you think I can refuse to go, Leon?" I ask.

He says I could probably ask to stay in Pema Gatshel, but thinks I should accept the transfer. "I think you'll get a whole different perspective on Bhutan at the college," he says. "The students are from all over the country, and from every type of background. It's a great opportunity."

When Leon leaves for Wamrong, I drag my empty hockey bags and suitcases out from under the bed and stare at them, as if this will make the idea of Kanglung more real, and help me decide what to do. I can hear kids pounding up the stairs. I am not ready to see them, but they persist, rattling the door handle and barking, "May! I! Come! In! Miss!" I get up wearily and let them in. They stop in the middle of the room and stare at the bags.

"Miss, where you is going?" Tshewang Tshering asks.

"I've just been transferred to Kanglung," I say. They look at me to see if I am joking, and then they look at each other. There is a long, terrible silence and we all look at the floor. Karma Dorji wipes his runny nose on his sleeve and looks up. "Oh, miss," he says sadly. "Please don't go."

"Just a minute," I say, and go into the bathroom. I latch the door and turn on the tap full force. When the water is running noisily, I lean my hot forehead against the damp, flaking concrete, and cry.

By Monday, the news has spread. When I open the door to class II C, I am besieged by questions. Miss, you is going? Kanglung collitch going? Miss, you is transfer? When going? Is true, miss?

I tell them yes, it is true. I am transferred, I am going. In maybe a week. I will go to teach at Kanglung College, but I will write to them, I say. I will miss them but I will come back to visit them. And a new teacher will come for class II C. And now we will have spelling dictation because if we do not, I will cry again.

In the staff room, I am congratulated and felicitated. I am so lucky, they tell me. I will have electricity, better quarters, bus service to Tashigang. Kanglung is a much better place; I will be working alongside tiptop lecturers, I will be teaching the cream of the crop. Mr. Iyya tells me I will be at the zenith of my glory. Yes, who wants to teach class II in such a remote and backward place? they ask each other. My throat hurts and I cannot speak.

At lunch time, I sit on the front steps of the school, watching some of my kids playing soccer. I think about that library, reference books open on a long polished table in front of me, I think about preparing lecture notes instead of spelling tests, teaching *Macbeth* instead of *Herbert the Mouse.*

I think about my kids, my dear, sweet, smiling, smelly, runny-nosed, barefoot kids. The school is already suffering from a terrible teacher shortage, and it will take weeks and weeks for a replacement to arrive. My kids will fall behind. But since their first-term exam results, I've been wondering what good I am doing them anyway. I love them, but I don't seem to be teaching them anything. Surely they would be better off with a trained primary-school teacher, someone who could explain the concept of division without using the word "divide."

On the other hand, my replacement could turn out to be another Mr. Iyya. I cannot bear the thought of someone beating them. And perhaps it would be foolish to move now anyway, after I have finally become used to Pema Gatshel, the Lotus of Happiness. I have acclimatized, and it was no small feat. No, I should speak to the headmaster and tell him I don't want to go, ask him if I can stay.

A wireless message arrives for me after lunch, from the field director in Thimphu. *Received notice of your transfer,* he writes. *Will process if you want to go. However will support you if you decide to stay in P/G.*

There, I can stay if I want to.

But I want to go. I am pulled away by the idea of new stories, a different view out over other valleys and ridges, another way of understanding Bhutan. A new posting. I send a message back to say that I will go to Kanglung, and ask if a new WUSC teacher can be sent to Pema Gatshel to replace me.

The kids come to visit in the evening. They stay for dinner, five of them, and afterward sing songs in Dzongkha and Sharchhop and Nepali. Karma Dorji translates for me: a mother cries for her child, the teachings of Buddha bring light, oh Lhamo I told you not to go, the song of the river tells the coming of spring. The session ends with their favorite English songs, "Chili Eating," sung to the tune of "Clementine," and the "Momo Song":

Five fat momos
Sitting in the shop
Round and fat with chili on the top
Along comes a boy with a ngultrum in his hand
Gives it to the shopkeeper and eats one momo up!

It is too late for them to go home after, so they spend the night, sleeping on mats and quilts on the floor, covered with blankets and kiras and towels. The next night there are eight, the next, sixteen. After dinner, they act out skits for me in costumes made of kiras, a badminton racquet, sunglasses, plastic bags and my woolen tights. They do homework and flip through magazines and draw pictures for my new house. They write me goodbye letters and leave them in elaborately decorated envelopes on my bed.

They tell me ghost stories while we cook dinner, all of us crammed into the tiny kitchen chopping onions and chilies in the wildly flickering candlelight, and then they are too scared to leave the kitchen and must go to the bathroom in groups of three and four. They wash the dishes, argue over the Walkman and fall asleep on the floor.

I check their homework and admire their pictures, settle disputes and explain magazine pictures as best I can. "*Doen*," I say of an ad featuring Freddie Krueger of *Nightmare on Elm Street*. "A ghost. But not a real one." I go to the market for extra rice and eggs and butter and salt (I have finally been paid and now have a cartoon sack of money containing four months' salary—twelve thousand ngultrum—all in fives and tens). I peel massive quantities of tubers for meals, but make no dent in the pile I have accumulated. I never did resolve the money-for-vegetables dilemma with the students, and when I leave for Kanglung, I will take with me a twenty-five kg jute bag of carrots, radishes and potatoes. I fall into a dead sleep around midnight. I know I have to leave at the end of the week, but for now, I am here with my kids, and I am happy.

Finally, I have to tell them to go home. I have not packed a single thing. They leave, but just before dark, Norbu and Karma Dorji return. A man died suddenly in the house next to Norbu's, they explain, and they are afraid to sleep at home. The people are saying the man was killed by black magic. They sit at the table quietly and refuse all offers of tea, crayons and books. Occasionally, I hear one of them murmuring a mantra. It begins to rain, a sudden, completely familiar rush of sound. "See, miss," Norbu says sleepily. "That man is died and now rain is coming."

I go into the bedroom to pack, but I get nothing done. I sit at the window instead, thinking about doen, all the possible meanings, all the possible ghosts, from demons and the spirits of the dead to gods of rocks, trees and earth. I think about the magicians who still know the old religion, the rituals from before the arrival of Buddhism over twelve hundred years ago. They are said to be able to summon the spirits and send them off to do their bidding—bring hailstones to flatten crops, dry up rivers and wombs, suck out someone's life force, cause madness, disease and death. I can no longer say, "I don't believe in ghosts and black magic." Everyone around me believes. Even the other foreigners are unsure. A Canadian teacher in Dremitse awoke to see green lights dancing at the foot of her bed, a British teacher saw a child temporarily possessed by the distraught spirit of a dead uncle, the teachers who lived in this flat before me reported voices coming from empty rooms, too close and distinct to be from outside or downstairs. I heard these stories in Thimphu, ages ago, when I could still say, "Nonsense." If, as Buddhism teaches, separateness is an illusion, if we all partake in and help create a much vaster reality than we can know, then everything is interdependent, and anything is possible. The rain grows heavier, a thunderous roar, the hair on the back of my neck stands up, and I am cold. I light every candle and lamp I have, and sit with Norbu and Karma Dorji until they fall asleep at the table.

The rain stops, and I wake Norbu and Karma and put a mattress on the floor for them. They curl up under a blanket, and I stand in the doorway, watching their small faces relax into sleep. I must squeeze my eyes tightly to stop the tears. If I feel this sad leaving Pema Gatshel after five months, I cannot imagine how I will feel leaving Bhutan after two years.

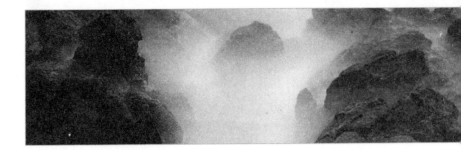

Peak of Higher Learning

If there is a
paradise on the
face of the earth,
It is this, oh!
it is this, oh!
it is this.

Sliced Bread

The college truck swings off the main road through a gate, stopping outside a row of white two-story houses separated by well-tended gardens. Four young men step out of the shadows of a cypress tree. "Good evening, ma'am," they say, bowing gracefully before heaving my hockey bags out of the truck and carting them off. I am struck by how neatly they are dressed: the folds of their ghos are perfectly straight, their white collars and cuffs are immaculate, and they are all wearing dark knee-highs and polished shoes. The vice-principal, a soft-spoken man in a plain navy-blue gho, appears with a ring of keys. "Welcome to Sherubtse College," he says. "We're very glad to have you here. Shall I show you to your quarters?"

I follow him over a wooden footbridge. "Here we are," he says, stopping outside the last house. "Each house has four flats. The upstairs flats have balconies, which are quite nice, but the downstairs ones have gardens. I prefer a garden." He opens the door to the downstairs apartment, and we file into a sitting room. I stand gawking at the peach-colored walls, the fireplace, the bookshelves, the divans with rose-colored cushions. There is another fireplace in the bedroom, a white-tiled toilet, shower room, dining room, and a kitchen with cupboards.

"I hope these quarters will be adequate," the vice-principal says. "They're very simple, of course, but if there's anything you would like us to do to make them more comfortable, please let us know."

Is he kidding? After my place in Pema Gatshel, this looks like a spread from *Better Homes and Gardens*.

In the sitting room, the four students who carried my luggage are examining my keyboard with interest. I smile, remembering how class II C had subsided into an awed silence the first time they saw it. Karma

Dorji had pressed a key gingerly, and they had all backed up, startled at the sound. *Zai, yallama! What is inside, miss?*

"That's an electronic piano," I inform the four college students.

"Casio or Yamaha?" one asks. "What's the voltage?"

"Uh, Yamaha."

The vice-principal clears his throat and the students bow again. "Thank you," I say.

"Thank you, ma'am. Good night, ma'am," they answer, and disappear into the growing darkness outside.

The vice-principal invites me to dinner and leaves me to unpack. I wander through the rooms again, running my hand along the fireplace mantels, turning the lights on and off. I arrange my books on the shelves, and then sit on one of the divans, overwhelmed. It is all so neat and orderly, I don't know how I will ever adjust. Even my thoughts seem sloppy and unruly, and I struggle to impose some order on my perceptions. I've only been here for an hour and already I want to go back. I want my rough unpainted flat in Pema Gatshel and my barefoot, grimy students. From the open window, the smell of flowers drifts in.

At dawn the next morning, I sit on the front steps, watching the sun set fire to the clouds above a dark ridge. The staff quarters are set on an incline, over the campus which looks like a cross between a community college and a summer camp. From my steps, I can look across the valley to the temple of Dremitse on a hilltop, or north to the sharp toothy peaks along the border. The strip of garden all around my house is ablaze with crimson poppies, orange gladioli, yellow dahlias, and several varieties of roses. A flowering shrub climbs up the door frame and drops tiny pink petals on my lap. Huge crows swoop and circle overhead, and a bird I cannot see sings sweetly from the gracious arms of a cherry tree. I sip milky coffee, missing the sound of one of my kids climbing up the stairs to present me with an armful of potatoes or infected flea bites.

Later, I put on a kira and walk across campus to the main academic buildings. "Good morning, ma'am," students say, bowing politely as I pass. I wonder why I have gone from "miss" to "ma'am," and notice again how neatly everyone here is dressed. I am conscious of my bare feet in rubber flip-flops and my wild hair. My kira is faded, and I am wearing it too short, hoisted up over my ankles (for walking through mud, of course, but there is no mud here, only smooth rolling lawns and neat paved pathways). I may have to buy a new kira, and I will definitely have to find my shoes. I haven't worn them since March, when the first rains rolled into Pema Gatshel.

I study the framed pictures of English poets on the walls of the vice-principal's office as he explains the history and functioning of the college. He is extremely precise and formal, but his smile is warm and his whole face lights up when he talks about teaching. Over dinner last night, he spoke primarily of the students, and the difficulties and unexpected insights he had gained teaching another culture's literature in Bhutan. "But, of course, there are universal stories," he said. "How else would we ever be able to connect?"

Sherubtse, which means "peak of higher learning," started out as a public school, the vice-principal says, and is now affiliated with the University of New Delhi, which fixes the curriculum, sets and marks the final exams, and issues the degrees. Most of the lecturers are from Delhi, although the number of Bhutanese lecturers is slowly growing. Canadians have been involved at Sherubtse since Father Mackey founded it in the late '60s, the vice-principal explains. Mr. Rob, the WUSC lecturer who I am replacing, taught here for five years. The students are divided into two groups: the pre-university students (called, most unpoetically, PU) who are completing classes XI and XII, and the college students who are majoring in arts, commerce or science. "You'll be teaching all levels," the vice-principal says as a typist enters with my timetable. "Do you have any questions at all?"

What I really want to know is how old the students are, and are they all as sophisticated as the ones I met last night, and is it too late to change my mind.

"I couldn't help noticing the phone on your desk," I say instead. "Is the college connected by phone to —?"

"To Tashigang and Samdrup Jongkhar," he says. "Do you want to make a call?"

"No, no." I smile down my disappointment. For a brief moment, I had imagined calling Robert.

I walk up the road into the village of Kanglung, which seems no bigger than Pema Gatshel, but much more prosperous. Past a row of large shops with verandahs, at a deep bend in the road marked by a dozen white prayer flags, I sit and look out over the land below. Pema Gatshel, two thousand feet lower, was wild boisterous green, overgrown, uncontained. Here, the forests are less dense, growing in small groves, and the fields are larger and flatter. Wide footpaths wind around rice paddies, past chortens and clusters of prayer flags, to solid farmhouses. I watch the sun sink into a bed of cloud, staining it pink, and wonder what class II C is doing right now.

Back at home, I rummage through my luggage in search of my shoes in between myriad visitors. The man from upstairs, Mr. Chatterji, economics lecturer, comes to say hello and welcome. Next is Miss Dorling, who teaches history, an exceedingly thin lady of indeterminate age and nationality, in a long pink skirt and jacket, leading two white yapping Apsoo dogs on a leash, welcome, welcome, she says, if there's anything I need. . . . Mr. and Mrs. Matthew from southern India are next. Mrs. Matthew has warm, smiling eyes, but Mr. Matthew reminds me of a loud, disagreeable uncle. He gives me a short history of the college's past principals, all Jesuits. "Now that Father Larue is gone, there is no one to say mass," he tells me grimly. "You are Catholic, yes?"

"No," I say firmly. I have learned my lesson from Mrs. Joy. "I'm not Christian at all." Two students arrive, bearing a stack of books for my courses: *Macbeth, Pygmalion,* collections of poems and essays, a syllabus. Two more lecturers come to fill me in on the advantages and disadvantages of college life: the store, which stocks dry goods, vegetables and sometimes meat, the electrician who runs the generator and changes lightbulbs if he's not drunk, the *dhobi* who washes clothes for the staff, the infirmary. And did I know that the college has its own VCR? And a grand piano? And a bakery? Yes, bread is available from the bakery on Wednesdays and Saturdays but I should be knowing this, since the bread slicer was just purchased with funding from WUSC. Bread slicer! Wait till the others hear this, I think. Lorna doesn't have a classroom to teach in, and I can get sliced bread.

When I finally return to my luggage, it is dark outside. Pressure cookers sound in the flats around mine, students' voices float up, doors bang, vintage John Lennon competes with Duran Duran in the hostels. By this time in Pema Gatshel, an exquisite silence would have settled over the valley and I would have been reading in bed by candlelight, not looking for a pair of proper shoes. I find the nun's kira I bought in Samdrup Jongkhar, which I cut into curtains and staple over the wooden curtain rod in the sitting room. I set my blue teacup on the mantel. I find the pictures drawn by class II C, smiling suns, golden dogs, dancing girls, a bounteous blue moon, and tape them up all over the house. And finally, I find my shoes, wrapped in plastic at the bottom of a cardboard box. They are completely covered with the thickest green fungus I have ever seen.

Oh Dear

The college has everything that was promised: a library with racks of newspapers and stacks of books, an auditorium with a red-curtained stage and a public address system. The science labs have microscopes, Bunsen burners, test tubes, snakes and mice pickled in formaldehyde. There is a photocopier, and a computer room for the new computer-science course. The buildings themselves seem remarkably well-kept after the corroded cement corridors of Pema Gatshel Junior High School. There are blacktopped basketball courts, volleyball and badminton courts, a soccer field with bleachers. I walk around and around the campus, trying to adjust to the sudden and staggering luxury of it.

I meet Shakuntala, the librarian, a tall Indian woman about my age, dressed in gray corduroy trousers and a dark-red blouse, her expressive face framed by wavy, shoulder-length dark hair. Her direct, unconstrained manner puts me at ease, and I know instantly that I have a friend. "Let's go to Pala's for lunch," she says, and we walk across campus to a canteen overgrown with bougainvillea just outside the college gate. Inside the low-ceilinged room, Pala, a silver-haired man in his fifties, gives us a brief smile, and his wife, Amala, clears a space for us at a table under the window. Beneath her short, feathery black hair, she has lively eyes in a sharp, thin face. "Come in, come in," she tells me briskly. "You from Canada, I think, yes?"

Students swarm in and out, asking for lemon tea, fried rice, Pala where's my thukpa, Pala can I put this on my tab, two coffee one cigarette how much? Pala remains unruffled, counting out change from a drawer, calling out orders to the kitchen, knocking a persistent gray kitten off the counter. In spite of the faded gho tied sloppily around his waist and his rubber flip-flops, he has a stately, dignified bearing; Shakuntala says that he was born a Tibetan prince and came to Bhutan when he married Amala.

We order *baleys,* wheels of soft Tibetan bread, and the national dish of chilies and cheese. It is so hot that my eyes run and I choke. "Today ema datsi very hot," Amala advises me, clucking sympathetically. "Better you eat more baley."

On the wall across from me is a collage of pictures cut out from fashion magazines, lollipop models in severe makeup and frizzy pink hair. Someone turns on a cassette player and pop music bubbles out around us. Two young men enter, exhaling ribbons of cigarette smoke. They are wearing jeans and tee shirts emblazoned with "Guitar Heroes" and "Metallica." I am surprised to see them out of national dress. I feel very far away from Pema Gatshel, from class II C who had never seen a keyboard before and thought Johann Sebastian Bach was my mother. I have a strange feeling that I have left Bhutan.

But when the students see Shakuntala and me, they put their cigarettes behind their backs and bow gracefully. "Good afternoon, ma'am."

I look up at the same time and notice the picture above the window. Instead of the usual formal portrait of the King of Bhutan, there is a black-and-white photo of His Majesty as a teenager, dressed in a gho, accompanied by a young woman, perhaps his sister, in a white miniskirt and high white boots. A fitting photo for this place, I think, a mix of tradition and fashion, Guitar Heroes and driglam namzha. I am still, most definitely, in Bhutan.

Back at the library, I begin to prepare notes for my first lecture. The information seems to be coming from a small dark room far back in my head, and my notes are sparse. The literature section of the library has two ancient critical texts on Shakespeare, neither of which helps much. The next morning, I sit in the empty staff room, practicing my lecture in my head. My hands are damp, my stomach queasy. I have managed to clean most of the fungus off my shoes but cannot get my kira down past my ankles. Lecturers drift in and out, greeting each other with an exaggerated formality. Good morning, my dear sir, and a very good day to you, and I thank you most kindly, sir. Mr. Bose, the other English lecturer, a small, dapper, grey-haired man from Delhi, is explaining the intricacies of attendance to me, pointing out the registers on their shelf by the door. "You have to be careful," he says. "The boys bunk from class but get their friends to answer for them during roll call."

"The boys? But not the girls?" I am confused. Out of the five hundred students, only eighty are female.

He waves a hand impatiently. "No, no. When I say the boys, I mean the girls, too. And you mustn't forget attendance. It must be taken in every class."

"Even for the degree students?" I ask.

"But of course!" he answers cheerfully. "Especially for them! They're the worst rascals."

The bell rings, and I pick up my chalk and notes. "You forgot the attendance register," Mr. Bose calls out. "Good luck!"

I open the door of the classroom and walk into a heavy silence. "Good morning," I say. The class slowly rises, and there is a weak chorus of half-hearted "good-mornings." I introduce myself, write my name on the board, smile brightly until my face hurts. Class XII stares back coolly. According to my attendance list, there are six *girls* and forty-nine *boys*. No one in the room looks younger than twenty.

"I, uh, I've been told that I have to take, uh, attendance," I say, wondering why my voice sounds so thin and apologetic, how I can stop my hands from shaking. The attendance list contains several Nepali names which I have not seen before. How do you say Bahadur? Bah-hay-der? Bay-hah-der? I settle on Badder, which elicits a few snickers and an outright snort.

Enough of this. I launch into my lecture. Who was Shakespeare, what is tragedy, why do we study it. I ramble on and on. After several long minutes, someone calls out from the back, "We finished *Macbeth* last term."

They have finished *Macbeth* and I still have forty minutes left before the end of class. "Oh dear," I say, chewing on a thumbnail, and someone repeats mockingly, "Oh dear." I scan the rows: one student meets my gaze. He has longish hair and a proud handsome face, and he is leaning back in his seat, legs stretched out in the aisle. For a brief moment, I think he is going to smile but it turns into a smirk.

Now what? I think. We cannot very well draw pictures or sing the "Momo Song." "All right," I say, "then . . . write me a composition."

There is much scuffling and rummaging for paper and pens.

"On what topic?" someone asks.

"On anything," I say.

"*Anything?*" someone echoes. It is Smirk.

I am suddenly very tired. This is not class II C. This is not fun. I should have stayed where I was. I sit at the front of the class, watching the students write and waiting for the bell to release me.

My next period is a batch of new admissions. At least they cannot have finished *Macbeth* last term, I console myself, but when I push open the door, I am unnerved. The long, narrow classroom is packed. As far back as I can observe, students are squashed together on the wooden benches. I cannot even see the back rows. I pull out the attendance list: nine *girls*, seventy *boys*.

"Good morning," I say, and the response is deafening. Benches are pushed back as the class rises and the room echoes with "good mornings." Someone misses the seat on the way back down, a desk is overturned, and laughter rises up in a wave. "We'll take attendance first," I say, but they cannot hear me. I can barely hear me. "Class Eleven," I say. "Class Eleven!" Finally I shout, "Class Eleven!!"

The noise subsides, but there is still some kind of disturbance going on in a back corner. Two students have straitjacketed another with the sleeves of his gho. "Class Eleven! Untie him! Don't tie each other up with the sleeves of your ghos." And then I am laughing because it's just like class II C, only there are more of them and some of them have mustaches. I stand at the front of the room, staring at the class. Seventy-nine students! "It's a zoo," I marvel aloud. They seem pleased with this description.

After class, I find Catherine from Rangthangwoong and Pat, a

Dutch nurse posted in Tashigang, sitting on my doorstep. "We've come for afternoon tea," Catherine says, "and then we're going back to Tashigang on the four o'clock bus."

"But how did you find out so fast that I was here?" I am pleased to have company already.

"There are no secrets in eastern Bhutan," Catherine says. "Come on, let's go visit the Fantomes."

"Who?"

"You'll see."

Behind the infirmary is a cottage hidden by cypress trees. On the wooden verandah, dozens of orchids grow out of clay pots and mossy logs, the names of the flowers inscribed neatly in English and Latin on wooden plaques. I stop to examine a spray of delicate white blossoms with scarlet tongues. Lady's Slipper. "People eat this one," Pat says. "Orchid curry. It's a great delicacy."

In a book-lined sitting room, Mrs. Fantome, a plump woman in a crisp, apple-green sari, pours tea into porcelain cups. "Cream or lemon, dear?" she asks. Cucumber sandwiches cut into dainty triangles and slices of vanilla pound cake are passed around. Mr. Fantome wears white trousers and a worn brown sweater and speaks with a faintly British accent. He studied at Oxford, Mrs. Fantome tells us. They have been at Sherubtse for the last twelve years, she teaches chemistry, he is a retired English lecturer. They used to teach in Sikkim but had to leave after the tragedy. I have no idea what this tragedy might be and am too embarrassed by my ignorance to ask. Mrs. Fantome gives Pat her recipe for pound cake, and Mr. Fantome and I discuss Milton, or, rather, Mr. Fantome discusses Milton and I try to look like I remember what Milton wrote.

On the way back to the college gate, where the bus to Tashigang will stop, Catherine explains the Fantomes' unusual name. "Mr. Fantome's grandfather or great-grandfather was a French convict who apparently jumped ship in India and then changed his name to Fantome," she says.

"And what was the tragedy in Sikkim?" I ask.

"It was annexed by India in the seventies. Sikkim used to be a separate country, like Bhutan. Remember there was that American woman who married the King of Sikkim?"

"Sort of. But why did India annex it?"

"I'm not sure. Something about a power struggle between the Sikkimese and Nepali immigrants."

Over the next week, I am invited to almost every lecturer's house for sweet tea spiced with cardamom or ginger and plates of samosas, pakoras, fried peanuts. During these visits, I begin to piece together the network of alliances and shifting hostilities that exists beneath the daily my-good-sir routine. At Mr. Gupta's house, I am warned to keep away from Mr. Matthew, at Mr. Matthew's house, I am warned to stay clear of Mr. Bose. Mr. Bose advises me to have nothing to do with Mr. Chatterji, Mr. Chatterji claims that the Mr. Bose is not trustworthy. Mr. Ratna says Mr. Nair is a drinker, Mr. Nair says Mr. Harilal is a troublemaker. Mr. Krishna allegedly carries tales to the principal, and I would do well to be careful of what I say, to whom, and where. "I wouldn't pay the slightest attention," Shakuntala says when I see her again in the library and recount the various warnings and dark allusions. "Some of them are well-meaning and genuinely interested in their work, but a lot of the others are only here to make money. These little plots and subplots keep them amused. I stay clear of all of them. The students are much better company, anyway."

I am not sure about the students yet. The Zoo is my favorite class because they are loud and enthusiastic, but last week, one young man informed me that I looked "damn fat" in my kira. (He himself looked as if he was put together out of wire coat hangers.) I had barely recomposed myself when another chimed in, "But ma'am is very simple." Fat—*damn* fat—and stupid! Thank you, I thought to myself, you've both just failed English. And Smirk's class continues to be difficult. Difficult in comparison to class II C. By Canadian standards, their manners are exquisite. They still stand up when I enter the room. They hand me their homework with both hands and bow when I pass them in the hall. But they are also testing me. They mimic the way I say their names but when I ask for the correct pronunciation, they remain silent.

They ask me how old I am, and if I am married, and how long I have been teaching. I refer to the poetry of Wordsworth and Coleridge, and Smirk smirks and calls out, "What do you mean by *Romantic?*"

I fold my arms and try to look bored, but I am thinking that maybe Father Larue was right after all. "What do *you* mean by 'Romantic'?" I ask.

There is an uncomfortable silence that stretches out and out.

"I don't know, ma'am," he finally says, embarrassed.

The small class of third-year degree students is easier because they are mostly silent. They are extremely attentive, sitting quietly with pens poised above thick notebooks, but they will not speak. I spend a week on a Shakespearean sonnet, talking about structure and imagery and language, and I have no idea at the end of the week what the poem means to them, if it means anything at all. I have no idea why I am teaching it beyond the fact that it is in the syllabus, and the fact that it is in the syllabus *here,* of all places—well, this is what we should be discussing, instead of laboring over the intricacies of every metaphor. I ask the students if they have any questions, comments, *anything*. No ma'am, they say, no questions. I pick up a piece of chalk and fill the blackboard with big white letters: TALK. They laugh at this, but they do not talk.

In my other degree class, I am to teach "language," but the only set topic in the syllabus is précis writing. "What am I supposed to teach them for the rest of the year?" I ask Mr. Bose. He advises me to take attendance and then release them. "No, seriously," I laugh, "what should I do with them?"

"I have told you seriously," he replies.

In the evening, I sit at my desk under the glare of a bare bulb and write letters. I write to class II C, telling them that I have put up their pictures and that I think about them every day.

I write to Lorna: *We have a VCR and a grand piano and a bread slicer. The students are all very cool and sophisticated. Some of them have informed me that I am damn fat and simple. I think I hate it here.*

I try to write to Robert. I want to tell him how everything has changed for me, how I marvel at the distance I have come. I want to tell him how difficult it is to imagine going home at Christmas, but I cannot. My mind seizes up. I reread the letters I have received from him, but I cannot reconnect myself. I can still close my eyes and see him in the armchair in his apartment, but the picture gets smaller each time I call it up.

Class II C writes back. The letters are addressed to "The Miss Jeymey," and the envelopes bear instructions: "Fly my letter very quick" and "Open with smile face." Sangay Chhoden writes: *Dear Miss, I am very happy to write without no reason. How are you that side. Here I am fine with my kind teachers and friends.*

Karma Dorji writes: *Dear Miss, I am very unhappy at pema gatshel, why means you is went.*

Norbu writes that they have a new sir and he is beating them nicely. I put my head down and cry.

Lorna writes: *Cheer up, simple is a compliment here. It means good-natured. My kids told me I was damn fat and homely and later I found out that homely means easygoing. Homely people make you feel at home. Get it? There's absolutely no consolation I can offer on damn fat, though, and you'll just have to put up with the sliced bread.*

Cultural Competition

I walk to the bend in the road before breakfast, the wind soft and warm against my face and bare arms, carrying the smells of green things and earth. Kanglung is drier than Pema Gatshel: apart from a few afternoon showers, the days are mostly warm and bright. In the new light I see a peak in the north that I have not noticed before, a black stone spire much higher than the ridges and crests around it. Yesterday, some students told me that gods and other spirits reside in naturally sacred sites called *nheys*. Peaks, rocky outcrops, a circle of cypress trees, a waterfall, all can be nheys, and if you disturb one, you will fall sick, or some other misfortune will overtake you. Everyone knows this, they said. If you damage the natural world, you must suffer the consequences.

All around me are constant reminders of Buddhism: rough prayer walls along the path, a prayer wheel turned by a stream, prayer flags soaring above the ridge. If I close my eyes, I can conjure the Toronto skyline, giant hypodermic needle jabbing the sky, glass facades of office towers, all cold perfection. Here, things grow and fade and die, and no one pretends otherwise. The older walls of a house remain mudbrown and rutted beside the smooth white walls of the newly built addition. The old and the new grow out of each other and there is no attempt to make everything perfect and perpetually modern. There would be no point, when everything is changing, is fading away.

In class, I battle against clichés, cant and bad grammar. "I want to hear what you have to say," I tell the students. "Write me something different, something you haven't already written a hundred times before." I spend hours marking their homework, drawing arrows from subjects to verbs, restructuring convoluted sentences, and writing notes of encouragement beside any signs of original expression. Mr. Bose tells me I am wasting my time.

In a shop outside the college gate, I stop to buy laundry soap. The shopkeeper hands me my package and I recognize my own handwriting. ". . . careful with subject-verb agreement," I read. "Don't use clichés." The soap is wrapped in one of the compositions I corrected this morning. "Where did you get this?" I ask.

The shopkeeper shows me a stack of papers. "The students are giving," he says. "I tell them not to throw, I will use in my shop. Instead of plastic. Plastic is too expensive."

Shakuntala shows me past exams set by the University of New Delhi. *Write a composition on one of the following: Time and tide wait for no man. A book is the best of friends.*

It occurs to me that Mr. Bose may be right.

But there are also signs of hope. A student named Tobgay writes about how education has changed his family life. When he was first admitted to Sherubtse, his parents were thrilled, especially his father who was illiterate. During his first-term break, at a family gathering, his father proudly asked him what he was learning at the college, and Tobgay told him. *I told that we saw the picture of the first man walking on the moon and everyone laughed at that. I told it was true, the people had gone up to the moon even and then my father became angry with red face and bulging eyes. Don't tell lies, he told. It is not a lie, I told. After my cousins went, he told that he felt shame by me telling such things and, now that I am in college I think I am a high shot to tell such things like this or what. How people can go to the moon, he told. So now when I go home for holidays I am never telling what I learned at college and when I am at home all the things we learn at college seem impossible, like people walking on the moon.*

And in the Zoo, I can actually hear the students listening as we read *Macbeth*. There is a palpable tension in the room, and when the bell rings in the middle of Macbeth's dagger soliloquy, Singye in the front row gasps. "He will not do it," he says, aghast at the thought. There is no need to explain the significance of the crime Macbeth is about to commit, or the evil omens, the unruly night and strange wind, the wild behavior of Duncan's horses, the appearance of Banquo's ghost. These are not literary symbols to the students but the real and obvious results of a monstrous deed. It is impossible to gauge the distance between what I am supposed to be teaching them about the play and how they read it in the light of their own culture, but their insights are bringing the play to life for me, and it has never seemed more horrifying.

One Saturday morning, two students bring a note to my door: there will be an evening cultural competition featuring song and dance in Dzongkha, Nepali and English. Mr. Bose and I are to judge the English items. "Will you be in the competition?" I ask the students, and they say yes, they have been released from SUPW in order to practice their song.

"What's SUPW?"

"Socially Useful Productive Work," one says.

"Some Useful Period Wasted," the other adds.

I laugh, delighted, and from the garden next door, Mr. Matthew clears his throat loudly. I am not sure who this warning is meant for.

Shakuntala and I go to the college store, a windowless room behind the student mess, to collect our weekly supply of vegetables. Baskets of chilies, tomatoes and beans are emptied out onto shelves, where they are pawed through and pinched. Everything is weighed on a rusty scale suspended from the ceiling. The man in charge, Mr. Dorji, shakes his head when I show him my handful of chilies. "Not even half kg," he says. "Take for free." My chili intake has increased steadily but I am still no match for the Bhutanese teachers who are loading up large jute sacks. My students tell me they cannot eat without chilies. When I prepare Western food for them, pasta or pizza, they tell me it is too sweet and go into the kitchen to make *ézé*, a condiment of chopped-up chilies, onions, tomatoes and cheese.

168

Outside the store, we step over a butchered pig and collect bread from the bakery window. At home, I eat several pieces with Bumthang honey, then fall asleep on the divan.

Canadian voices wake me up. "Hey, Medusa, open the door. We hear you have freshly sliced bread in there." It is almost the entire Canadian contingent from eastern Bhutan, plus Mary, an Irish teacher posted in Samdrup Jongkhar.

"It's not sliced," I say, throwing open the door, "and I've eaten half of it."

They traipse in, laying down jholas, bottles of Dragon Rum and lemon squash and Golden Eagle beer, a cassette player and tapes. "We were all in Tashigang and decided you needed a proper house-warming party," Margaret from Radi says.

"Look at this bathroom!" Lorna shrieks from the hall. "It's TILED."

"Oh my god, two fireplaces!"

I tell them they are in time for the cultural competition in the evening, but they are disappointed.

"Cultural competition! I could have that in Radi. I was promised sliced bread and a video," Margaret complains.

"Closets!" Lorna says. She looks well, her long golden-brown hair full of sunny highlights and her face tanned the color of honey. "She has two *closets*. I have to keep all my clothes in the food safe."

Leon and Tony look even thinner and blonder than the last time I saw them in Tashigang. Leon is handing out drinks made of Dragon Rum and lemon squash. Someone has plugged the cassette player in and the Traveling Wilburys are singing about last night. Margaret is in the kitchen making something out of sweetened condensed milk, cocoa, peanuts and dried "pig food." Kevin and Tony are reading magazines, Lorna is dancing a jig with Leon, and Mary is knocking back Bhutan Mist and *knitting*. We are a motley crew, I think. What brings us together, aside from skin color and language? We would not all be such good buddies if we had met outside of eastern Bhutan. But I like being with them because I can slip back into my old Canadian self, I can speak a faster, sharper, more direct English. It is like going home to your family. Everyone understands the basic framework, you don't have to explain yourself at every turn. It's the same with these friends; no one asks me why I am not married yet or why my mother let me come all the way across the world to teach, was it because I couldn't find a job in Canada? I don't have to explain who Ed Grimly is, or why I am talking like him.

But there is a negative side, too. The stress of being fully immersed in our villages, of trying to live mindfully in another culture, makes us overanxious to be purely ourselves when we are together. We drink too much and talk too loudly, we shriek with laughter and fall over in little bars in Tashigang, not caring what impression we are making. We want to forget where we are, and yet we keep calling ourselves phillingpa and making comparisons to Canada; we keep reminding ourselves that we are here, and isn't it amazing.

If many of these friendships are destined to fade after we leave Bhutan, we are bound now by the knowledge that we need each other here. Any mention in a letter of an ailment beyond the usual giardia will bring packets of instant soup in the mail or a visit, and in emergencies our nearest Canadian neighbor will become our next-of-kin.

We walk to Pala's for a dinner of *shabalay*, deep-fried turnovers stuffed with minced meat. Students drift in and out, glance over at us but pretend not to, and I am relieved that we are not quite the spectacle we would be in Pema Gatshel. A well-built young man in a long black trench coat and a beautiful woman in a denim skirt and cashmere sweater float past. Leon shakes his head. "I don't know how you teach here," he says. "The students are all absolutely gorgeous."

"It is a little unnerving," I say.

"What would happen if you had an affair with one of your students, though?" Margaret asks.

"I don't know, I haven't really thought about it," I lie. I find myself noticing over and over again how attractive this or that student is. The older male students have a very fine, courtly charm, and some of them are quite flirtatious.

"Well, we'll think about it on your behalf," Lorna says, and the others agree enthusiastically.

The cultural competition begins with a traditional Bhutanese dance. The men and women move slowly in a circle, raising and lowering their hands in front of them in simple, lulling gestures as they sing. The beauty is in the measured, synchronized movements; this is not a dance about performance but participation. There is no instrumental accompaniment, only the voices rising and falling in the melancholic, pentatonic scale, and lingering over microtones that no tempered instrument could ever match. The style is called *zhungdra,* the oldest form of music in Bhutan, and the melody climbs and climbs and then falls suddenly, rhythm changing unpredictably, evoking perhaps the soaring sinking Bhutanese landscape itself, mountaintops plunging into deep valleys and rising steeply again.

A Nepali dance follows. Two women in gorgeous red-and-gold silk saris twirl and kick and throw up their arms to loud taped music over-full with instruments and competing melodies and rhythms. I am sitting between Leon and Margaret, a pen and clipboard on my lap, preparing to judge the English selections, the first of which is a "Break-Dance," according to the MC. The lights go off, pulsating disco music starts and stops and starts again, and two lithe young men appear on stage in tight pants and tee shirts. The dance is a combination of some genuine break-dancing and a lot of straightforward calisthenics.

"Where *am* I?" Leon mutters. I know exactly what he means. In spite of its closed-door policy and ban on TV, Bhutan is not hermetically sealed. Fashion trends and music cassettes find their way in, but it still seems utterly bizarre that I should be sitting in a concrete auditorium in the Himalayas watching Bhutanese students break-dance to American disco. The music ends and I have no idea how to judge the first English item. On what basis? In comparison to *what?* In the end, I give it a very mediocre mark. The other English selections include CCR's "Proud Mary" accompanied by an electric guitar and an amplifier that thinks it's an instrument in its own right, and a remarkably good version of Elvis's "Love Me Tender" by the well-built young man in the black trench coat. Elvis wins the English competition.

There are more songs in Dzongkha, Nepali and Sharchhop, and dances from Tibet, Assam and the nomadic yak-herding communities along Bhutan's northern border. The instruments are remarkable: the six-stringed, dragon-headed mandolin called a *drumnyen*; the many-stringed *yangchen* laid flat on a table and played with thin bamboo sticks; a gleaming new harmonium; a tabla played with deft fingers. Although the official government line might speak of one identity, there are many voices here, many dances and many songs, and perhaps it is my Canadian upbringing, being raised on the strengths of the multicultural mosaic over the American melting pot, but I am glad of the plenitude.

Back at my house, we lay mattresses, mats, kiras and quilts in a row on the bedroom floor. There is much wriggling and giggling and negotiation for space, and when I finally fall asleep, I dream that I am dreaming of break-dancers. You're just dreaming, I tell myself in the dream. There is no break-dancing in Bhutan.

So Lucky to Be Here

My dreams change and change again. Gone are the airport dreams and drugstore dreams and the dreams of in-between places, not really Canada, not really Bhutan, all dreams of longing for home. Now my dreams of Canada are grievous. I dream that I get on the Comet and it turns a corner and turns into a Greyhound bus with plush seats and a sign ordering passengers to not stand forward of the white line, and we are driving over a bridge, passing out of Bhutan onto a Canadian highway. It is the beginning or the end of winter, dirty crusts of snow, dull sky, a flat paved road leading into a sad, colorless city. I have made a terrible mistake; I do not want to go home at all. I get off the bus, but Bhutan is gone, and I do not know how to get back.

I dream more often of Bhutan itself. I am walking through narrow green valleys with rivers rushing through them. The mountains rise up so steeply on all sides, I have to look up and up to find the sky above. I walk through forests at night to a ring of dark-fringed fir trees, to a rocky pool beneath a waterfall, to open spaces where I can see the stars thrown across the deep blue-black sky. In my dreams, clouds climb down from the sky, fill up ravines, melt into fields, darkening the green of the rice and the maize. I watch the mist and tell myself I am dreaming, the world cannot possibly be so beautiful, but I wake up and it is.

We walk through the forests and fields around Kanglung, Shakuntala carrying a sketch pad or camera, I my journal. I am enraptured by the space, the size of the mountains, the stretch of the sky. I am always wondering what is beyond the next ridge. It is only about 150 kilometers as the crow flies from the Indian border in the south to the snow-peaks in the north, and yet it would take years to get to know the lay of the land by foot, to learn what is hidden in the folds of these mountains. I want to see what the crow sees.

We turn off main trails, following narrower tracks into forests, through fields. I am no longer dismayed at the way a wide, worn trail can splinter into a dozen smaller paths, one of which winds down a slope and disappears at a log. We climb over the log, slosh across a stream and another path picks us up, carries us through rice paddies, to someone's backdoor. A dog chases us around the kitchen garden into a forest, where a path brings us to the road. There are always large stones to sit and rest on, trees to sit and rest under, there is no restricted place, no lines and bars separating what clearly belongs to someone from what belongs to everyone.

We pass through villages where the entire community is at work in one family's fields, or where everyone has gathered to help build a house, plastering the woven bamboo walls with mud. Each village seems a world unto itself, a tightly knit, closely related, interdependent community, with an elected *gup* who as acts the headman, settling minor disputes and keeping whatever community records exist. A wealthier family may have paid for the grinding stones to extract oil from mustard seeds, or a manual threshing machine, but these are often used by everyone. Everyone knows what everyone else has— their belongings, their business, their plans, their problems. It is not possible here to close your doors to your neighbors, to live in tiny isolated units, nodding impersonally as you pass each other. In fact, the privacy that we so zealously guard in the West would be fatal here, where a mountain stands between one village and the next, between one village and the nearest hospital, wireless office, shop.

We emerge from an oak forest one afternoon into the courtyard of a very old temple. The paintings in the vestibule have darkened with age, the reds and blues becoming deeper and richer instead of lighter. The door is padlocked, we cannot go inside, but we circumambulate the temple clockwise, turning the worn prayer wheels built into a bracket along the outer walls. The prayer wheels are inscribed with *Om Mani Padme Hum,* Hail Jewel in the Lotus, the mantra for the benefit of all sentient beings. You accumulate merit by turning the prayer wheels—if you do it mindfully. I spin the wheels but my mind usually spins off elsewhere.

Scattered readings and occasional attempts to meditate will not make me mindful. I read the theory and I think yes, this makes sense, but my life—my mind—goes on as usual. While I am actually reading the texts, I think I understand. Nothing in the world is permanent, everything changes, breaks down, dies, and this is why attachment to things in this world causes suffering. The Eightfold Path is the way to nonattachment. Then I pick up an anthology of Romantic poetry, and I wonder what is wrong with attachment anyway, and what poetry could be born out of nonattachment. Why shouldn't we throw ourselves into our lives and love the world deeply and break our hearts when it changes, fades and dies? I paddle back and forth between the Four Noble Truths and Wordsworth, Coleridge, Shelley and Keats. Contemplating the paintings of Buddha sitting in calm abiding, I have a thousand questions and no one to answer them, and wonder if this is a sign that I am on the wrong path. But then I remember Buddha's last words to his disciples—work out your own salvation with diligence—and I am encouraged in my questioning.

A packet of mail. My grandfather writes that I must really appreciate life in Canada now. *You see now how lucky we are here.* My mother writes about how proud she is of me, enduring all this hardship. They have it all wrong. There is no hardship any more, I write back. I love my life in Bhutan. I do see how lucky I am—to be here. A letter from the field office in Thimphu reminds me of the upcoming conference for Canadian teachers in Tashigang. No letter again, still, from Robert.

Lorna appears at the door two days before the conference. "I just came to use your bathroom," she says, bolting through the sitting room.

"Haven't they finished that new latrine yet?" I call out.

"Yes," she yells back, "but it doesn't have *tiles.*"

Over coffee on the front steps, Lorna tells me she is having an affair with a man in her village.

"How did it begin?" I ask, thrilled.

"In a maize field," she confesses, and I have to spit out a mouthful of coffee so that I won't choke. "Don't laugh. We were coming back from a village party and he grabbed my arm and said, 'Miss, I lob you.' I couldn't resist that."

"So he speaks English?"

"No, I wouldn't say that. He speaks a few words." She is suddenly convulsed with laughter. "The first night, after we made love, we were lying there in my bed, trying to think of what to *say* to each other, and finally he turns to me and says sadly, 'My little brother is dead.' And I'm like, 'Aww, that's so sad, I'm so sorry.' I thought that he was confiding some tragic childhood memory. Then I realized he was saying he couldn't get it up again."

I laugh until my stomach hurts.

"It's true," Lorna says. "I swear. But listen, don't tell anyone. Not that I think anyone would care, really."

"Well, it's all very romantic," I say, surprised at the wistfulness in my voice.

Lorna looks at me quickly. "How's Robert?"

"Who knows. I haven't heard from him." I am making it sound like Robert is the problem, but I know in my heart it is me. He hasn't written very often, but when they do arrive, his letters sound just like him, affectionate and loyal and full of practical advice. It is me who is changing. My letters to him sound false and forced to me.

The conference passes in a sleepy blur, under the swish of the ceiling fans in the Royal Guest House resplendent with blue-cloud painted walls and brocade hangings. In the afternoons, we trudge up a path behind the bazaar, following the river to where it widens into a pool. It is too shallow to swim, but we sit in the water and talk quietly. Children stare at us curiously, ten grown-up foreigners sitting in the river, doing nothing. They strip off their school uniforms and wash them in the river, passing around a sliver of soap as they scrub and pound their clothes on the rocks, and then hang them in the trees to dry.

In the evenings, we eat at the Puen Soom. The three new teachers, fresh from Canada, pick at their food and send their plates back, asking for smaller portions of rice, half of this, no, a quarter. "How do you eat so much rice?" Marnie asks me. She is wearing a white blouse and peach-colored jeans, one of several perfectly coordinated outfits with matching accessories that she puts on each day; each morning in the guest house she curls her bangs with a propane-powered curling iron.

I look down at my hill of rice and shrug. "You get used to it."

"I don't know if I'll get used to anything here," she says doubtfully, looking around. "I hope my quarters are not like this."

I remember this feeling. You really will get used to it, I want to tell her again; your clothes will fade and fray, and you won't have time between study duty and morning clinic to curl your hair, and the walls in your house will look exactly like this plus your roof will leak and you'll have rats, but you won't care because you'll be in love with the place you have suddenly woken up in. You will feel so lucky to be here. But I know she won't believe it until it happens.

Blessed Rainy Days

Blessed Rainy Day, September 22, is supposed to be the official end of the monsoon. I sit under a blue-and-white canopy with the other lecturers, balancing a cup of oily suja and saffron-colored desi on my lap, watching an archery match. Only half the players are using traditional bamboo bows to hit the targets, short wooden planks set in the ground about 150 meters apart, and they are no match for the new compound fiberglass bows imported from abroad. I quickly grow tired of watching the actual game. Far more interesting are the players, the graceful dances they do when they hit the target, and the lewd gestures and songs they use to distract their opponents. The sky overhead is a fresh expanse of blue with a border of clean white cloud, except for a grey swelling in the south, which looks suspiciously like more rain.

It is more rain. It begins just before dawn the next morning and continues for two weeks, days and nights of falling rain and drifting mist and water trickling in drains, until I am sick of the sound of it, and the tiresome wet and chill of it. The damp insinuates itself into my sheets and blankets, and none of my clothes will dry. A cold turns into an ear infection and I cannot hear, it is like walking underwater. The sky sinks lower and lower under its own weight until the clouds are among us, breaking apart and hurrying past us like distracted ghosts.

After two weeks, I awake at dawn to the remarkable sound of nothing. Even without looking outside, I know: *now* the monsoon is over. The sky is clear every morning, and in the north one peak is bright with snow. The clarity is stunning. I feel dizzy, almost drunk on the amount of light. The hills all around are plush and green, and the trees are full of cicadas and flocks of birds that have migrated down from higher altitudes. The days are soft and warm and buttery; the sharpness in the early morning air melts away in the full sunlight. In my garden, the summer flowers are crowded out by rusty marigolds and orange and yellow nasturtiums. In the villages all around, sliced pumpkin and apples are set out to dry in flat baskets, and on farmhouse roofs green chilies turn a rich dark crimson in the sun. Long strips of bloody beef and chunks of pork fat are hung over clotheslines. When dry, they will be chopped into flaky pieces and served with chili sauce, or cooked for hours into a stew. The rice paddies turn gold around the edges, and the rice stalks droop under their own weight.

I cannot write to Robert anymore. The writing comes out slowly, stiffly, it sounds like another language in my ears. When I try to write about my love for Bhutan, it feels like a betrayal of him, and I am not sure why. Perhaps because I feel I have fallen in love with the place, the way you fall in love with a person. I write letters addressed to no one and stick them in my journal.

What I love most is how seamless everything is. You walk through a forest and come out in a village, and there's no difference, no division. You aren't in nature one minute and in civilization the next. The houses are made out of mud and stone and wood, drawn from the land around. Nothing stands out, nothing jars.

Time has become a melding of minutes and months and the feeling of seasons. The colors are changing, the light that comes slanting over the rim of the mountain grows cooler. I have trouble remembering the date. I ask my students what day it is, but by the time I get to the next class, I have forgotten and must ask again. Yesterday, I started a letter home and wrote July and realized only when I looked outside and noticed the gold and brown creeping into the hills all around. Leon says it is the Bhutan Time Warp and I know what he means. Time does not hurl itself forward at breakneck speed here. Change happens very slowly. A grandmother and her granddaughter wear the same kind of clothes, they do the same work, they know the same songs. The granddaughter does not find her grandmother an embarrassing, boring relic. Her grandmother's stories do not annoy her, and what she wants is no different from what her grandmother wanted at her age. In the village, there is little to keep up with. When change does come, everyone has time to get used to it. Glass windows, a corrugated iron roof, electric lights, immunization, a school. Everything that happens in the village will be remembered, because what happens affects everyone, it is everyone's story. It is not something happening to strangers on the other side of a city, on the other side of the ocean, announced today, displaced tomorrow by newer news, the latest development, this just in. Just how fast development will change this is impossible to know. In school, the kids are taught a new order of things. There must be many students like Tobgay, no longer able to tell their parents what they are learning. When the outside world catches up, everything will accelerate, and grandparents will shake their heads and sigh over their grandchildren. The wholeness that I love will be lost, and yet I cannot say that development is bad and that people should go on living the way they have always lived, losing four out of eight children and dying at fifty. Development brings a whole new set of problems as it solves the old set. I must be careful not to fall into the good-old-days trap.

For now, though, I am glad to be a part of the Time Warp. I feel exhausted when I remember my last year in Toronto, rushing to class, the grocery store, the bank, a movie, a meeting, always feeling that I had not caught up, fearing that I never would, because there was so much to do and see and buy and say you've done and seen and bought to be on the cutting edge, to be where it's happening, not to be left behind. Now I have time in abundance. There is no one to catch up to, and I don't have to be anywhere but here. I have no idea what is happening in the outside world, what wars or famines are being turned into ten-second news clips, what incredible new technologies are revolutionizing the way people die or dream or do their banking. I lost my watch in Tashigang and the digital face on my alarm clock faded out in the monsoon damp, but I am learning to tell time by the sun and the sounds outside, and I am hardly ever late.

I have fallen into this world the way you fall into sleep, tumbling through layers of darkness into full dream. The way you fall in love. I am in love with the landscape, the way the green mountains turn into blue shadows in the *late afternoon light, the quality of the light as the sun rises above the silver valley each morning, the unbearable clarity of everything after rain, the drop to the valley floor far below and the feeling of the great dark night all around, and knowing where I am, and being here. I am in love with the simplicity of my life, the plain rooms, the shelves empty of ornaments, the unadorned walls. I don't want to go home at Christmas (I don't want to go home, ever). They never warned us about this at the orientation.*

The field director in Thimphu sends a wireless message saying the flight to Toronto that I asked him to book several months ago has been confirmed.

Durga Puja

Shakuntala and I spend most of our time together. We are united against the knot of bickering staff members by our love for the place and our easy relationship with the students. Some of the lecturers begin to treat us with cool disdain; Shakuntala thinks they disapprove of two unmarried females being let loose upon the world. We make up bogus Latin names for the worst of them and cackle loudly in the library; we excuse ourselves from the dreary staff parties where the chairs are pushed back against the walls, funeral-parlor style, with the women demurely sipping orange squash on one side of the room and the men belting back Bhutan Mist on the other, while students scurry back and forth with platters of food. Instead, we invite the students to dinner and eat in a circle on the floor; afterward the students bring out guitars and sing, we play charades and word games and talk.

The students visit frequently. They come to borrow books and tapes, they come to get their homework checked, they come to sit and drink coffee and talk. I have broken through some barrier, have even made peace with Smirk. He still makes wisecracks in class, but I have grown to like him. With his longish hair and his smart-ass comments he is asking questions about the accepted order of things. His full name is Dil Bahadur, which means Courageous Heart.

Shakuntala was right: the students are very good company. The ones from wealthy families in Thimphu and Paro are more Westernized, at least on the surface. Their fathers are in key positions in the civil service and their families often have extensive land holdings. They are found most often in jeans and leather jackets under a haze of cigarette smoke at Pala's. Their conversation is laced with a mix of slang from across decades and continents: chaps and chicks, cat and cool. Ten ngultrum is ten bucks, money is dough, drunk is boozed or boozed out. "But" is stuck on the end of a sentence (*I don't know but*), and "damn" is merely a synonym for very. Every phrase is punctuated by the ubiquitous "ya." *I told her, ya, last time, ya, but she never listens, ya. No, ya.* Shakuntala says that "ya" is not "yeah" but a corruption of "yaar," Hindi for mate or man or friend. Many of these students have been educated in private boarding schools in Darjeeling and Kalimpong, and they refer to their less worldly classmates as "simple." Simple in this instance means unacquainted with the world outside. Simple means the village, definitely not a cool place to be from. In less tactful moments, they use the word "rustic."

My favorite students are the "simple" ones. They are shyer and more difficult to draw out, but utterly sincere. The wealthier students seem more like teenagers, preoccupied with their clothes and hair and who has a date with who at Pala's (ignoring the ridiculous new rule, set down by the principal, that bans "couples" in order to put an end to the "gossip and scandal"—i.e., pregnancy—that allegedly flourished under the Jesuits' noses). The so-called simple ones have not had the opportunity of adolescence. They became adults at puberty. A surprising number of the men have wives and children back in their villages. (Female students who get married or pregnant, though, must drop out of school.) Unlike their private-school classmates, they have had limited exposure to Western culture. Their ideas of universal wealth and privilege are drawn directly from the few videotaped movies they have seen at the college, and they refuse to believe that there are people living on the streets, begging for coins in the cities of North America. They flip through my old magazines with the same absorption as class II C, looking up occasionally with the same puzzled expressions. "Ma'am, what is a UFO?" or "Miss, why it says here about a psychologist for cats?"

The students learn that excessive formality makes me uncomfortable. They do not behave as casually as if I were a fellow student, but neither do they treat me with the same rigid protocol as the other lecturers. I am still "ma'am" and "madam" and sometimes "miss," but they are warm and friendly and at ease, and I like them more each day, and I learn and learn and learn, far more than I teach.

Because of their fluency, I can ask them things I could not ask class II C, and they answer many but not all of my questions about Buddhism. It is okay to appreciate the world and all that is beautiful in it, they tell me, only we must not become attached to it. "We have to remember that it is not permanent, and anyway, ma'am, isn't that why it is so beautiful in the first place? If everything was the same forever, well, we can't even imagine that," one student says. I think of Keat's Grecian Urn, frozen perfection, and agree. He is a slight young man, with a quiet, reflective face and a brush cut. His name is Nima, which means "sun," and he has a smile that lights up a room. I ask him about the practices of tantric Buddhism, how they seem to contradict the Buddha's teachings against superstition and empty ritual. He says that the lamas know the real meaning behind the rituals. "We know only the simple meaning. Like when we are filling the water cups on the altar, we must not spill one drop because we say it will draw the demons. But actually, miss, we aren't supposed to spill one drop because we are supposed to be doing it carefully, and if we aren't concentrating, then we aren't doing it right. So maybe the people couldn't understand this, and the lamas tried to think of a way they would remember, so they made up the story about the demons coming."

"So you don't believe in demons," I say.

"No, miss, I am believing. We just can't say about them, so it is better to believe, isn't it?"

There is a lot of this in the students, this preference for both/and over my insistence on either/or. Either the Buddha said there is no God and therefore Buddhism is not theistic, and therefore tantric Buddhism with its pantheon of deities is a contradiction of the original school of thought, or there are gods and therefore there is no contradiction. It is not so for the students. Yes, they say, the Buddha said he was not a god, and at the same time we worship him as a god, and there are many other gods as well, and there is no contradiction.

"Anyway," Nima says, "my father says it's not what you believe or say you believe that matters, it's what you do." Nima's father is a gomchen in a village three hours walk from Tashigang. He brings my questions to his father when he goes home and carries the answers carefully back to me. "Like for example, you must be knowing that in Buddhism we say all beings were our mothers in our past lives."

This is the rationale behind treating all beings with loving-kindness. It is why you should not kill any sentient being, even an insect. In our millions and billions of past lives, every being was at one time our mother. "Yes, I've read this," I tell Nima. "But I don't know if I believe it literally."

Nima says, "You see, miss, what matters is not what you believe but what you do. The important thing is whether you treat all beings the way you treat your mother. With that much love and respect. Of course, for we Bhutanese, it is best to believe and do. But if you believe and don't do, then the belief is nothing."

Nima visits regularly, along with his roommates, Arun, a tall, emaciated southern Bhutanese who wants to be a doctor, and Wangdi, short and sturdy and almost irritatingly cheerful. I try to learn the subtle tonal differences between a "no-thank-you" that really means "no" and one that means "yes but I'm being polite." Often I resort to asking, "Is that a Bhutanese no?" They are so tactful that I have to learn to read the most minute indicators. Nima winces slightly when I flip a spoonful of sugar into his cup backhandedly but says nothing. "What is it, Nima?" I ask.

"Nothing, miss."

"Did I do something wrong?"

"No, miss . . ." He clears his throat and runs his hand across his shorn head. "Actually, miss, in Bhutan, we never pour anything in that backward way unless someone in the house has died. That is how we serve the dead."

During these visits, I learn not to whistle inside someone's house (it may call in spirits) or step over religious books. I learn to flick a drop of tea from a full cup before I drink as an offering to hungry ghosts, whose excessive desire in previous lives has left them wandering in a realm of perpetual lack and longing; their stomachs are grotesquely swollen with hunger and thirst but their throats are knotted up. I learn to eat rice like the Bhutanese do, with my right hand, using my thumb to sweep the food neatly into my mouth. I learn to make butter tea, and eat chilies for breakfast.

The students balance my view of rural Bhutan. Yes, they say, things in the village are peaceful . . . on one level. "People are very jealous," one young woman named Chhoden tells me. Her hair is cut in an asymmetrical bob, and her kiras are bright silky prints imported from Bangkok. Her immediate family lives in Thimphu, where her father is employed in the civil service, but she says they still visit their ancestral village in Mongar once a year. "You don't see it, ma'am, because you are just seeing from the outside. There's a lot of jealousy and backbiting. And people have very strict ideas about what is proper. When I go home to the village, I have to become a different person. Boys can roam about and do as they please but if girls do that, everyone will say oh that girl, she's a bad character, always roaming here and there. If I try to argue, my parents say that I have been spoiled by school."

I talk a lot about language with the students, about English and Sharchhop and Dzongkha and Nepali. The Nepali-speaking students advise me to learn their native tongue; Nepali is more useful, they say, more people speak it and anyway it is easier to learn. The Dzongkha-speaking students frown at this. Madam, why you are learning Nepali? You should learn our national language.

I want to learn both, I say. Isn't that okay? Thinking to myself, it must be okay, you can all speak each other's languages plus English and Hindi with a smattering of Bengali or Tibetan. But we are talking about something more than language here, I only wish I knew what. I want to learn both, I repeat, and neither group looks very pleased. As if, in choosing both, I had chosen neither.

I learn that thank you very much in Dzongkha is *namé samé kadin chhé*. *Namé* means no sky, *samé* no earth. *Namé samé kadin chhé* means thanks beyond the sky and earth. I learn that the script was developed in Tibet in order to translate the teachings of the Buddha, and it is therefore called *Chhoeki*, the language of religion. I learn to write the alphabet, which hangs from an invisible upper line, with the tails and heads of letters stacked together to create combined sounds. The spelling is murderous. "Why does *joba* have to start with an 'm', of all things?" I complain, exasperated, to Nima. "Why not a 'q' or a 'p' or heaven forbid a 'j'?" He explains that because the language is mono-syllabic, extra silent letters are used to distinguish one homonym from another. I almost give up, but the language looks so beautiful on the page, with birds flying above the words and lines ending in swords. The birds are Os, the swords full stops.

Another student gives me a list of "everyday phrases" in Nepali:

> *what is your name, why are you laughing, wooden leg, heart's disease,*
> *warm bed, mother's blessing, permission, advice, dark night, song of the river*
> *truth, love story, remember, again, voice, enemy, friend, forget*
> *setback, lack, lake, fire, water, mountain, sun, rain*
> *king, minister, rich, poor, apple, pear*
> *good morning, good evening, good bye*

A very small announcement on the notice board invites all staff and students to attend the Hindu celebration of Durga Puja in the auditorium. Shakuntala tells me the story behind it, from the Hindu epic *Ramayana*: Ravanna, the demon king of Lanka, abducts Sita, the wife of the god Ramchandra. Ramchandra worships the goddess Durga for nine days, and on the tenth day is empowered to defeat Ravanna and bring his wife home. Durga is also Kali, the goddess of destruction, smashing the old to make way for the new in an endless cycle of change.

On the auditorium stage, an altar has been set up with a fierce statue of Durga garlanded with marigolds and silver tinsel. Incense hangs in delicate streamers in the air. There is an offering of milk and honey to the goddess, and then we are given *tikka*, a smear of red pow-der on our foreheads. Dil Bahadur is looking unusually somber as he assists with the ceremony on stage. His longish hair has been cut, and he is wearing loose white pants and a white shirt. He ties a piece of colored thread to my wrist, and another student gives me a handful of sweets: these are *prasad,* the offerings made to the goddess and given back to the worshipers. Tomorrow they will go to the river to immerse the statue, a female student named Gayatri says, and invites me to come along and see. I sit for a while in the auditorium after the other lecturers have left, listening to the songs flowing one into the next without pause, with a tabla and bells as accompaniment.

Scholars claim that Buddhism developed as a reaction to negative elements of Hinduism, in particular the rigid caste system and the excessive, empty ritualism that had built up over the centuries in India. Hinduism and Buddhism are not wholly separable, however. Most of the Hindu deities turn up in the Buddhist pantheon, and the two systems share many concepts, including reincarnation and the idea of karma. Moreover, by the time Buddhism came to the Himalayas, it had picked up many of the practices of Indian Tantrism. Although Durga Puja is more flamboyant than the Buddhist rituals I have seen, its colors more gaudy and its music less somber, the two do not seem fundamentally different.

Offstage, something is wrong. There is much running off and returning and urgent whispering. Beside me, Gayatri is twisting her handkerchief into knots. "Is something going on?" I ask her. "No, ma'am," she says, but her face is strained and unhappy.

The next morning, she appears at my door dressed in a cream-colored salwar kameez, a knee-length dress over loose pyjama pants, her hair freshly washed. At the auditorium, a large group of students is waiting, holding flowers, incense, jugs of milk, a tabla, the statue of Durga, and *khukuris,* fierce knives, long and cruelly curved. At the college gate, the crowd stops unexpectedly. I am lost in the middle and must stand on tiptoe to see what is happening. What is happening is the older students are having an argument with the principal. It is the first time I have seen authority openly challenged in Bhutan.

"Principal wants them to put on national dress and they are telling they have to wear their Nepali dress because they are the pundits doing the puja," Gayatri whispers.

This is serious—I can see it in the principal's anger-blotched face and the physical stance of the students, in the number of khukuris catching and throwing the sharp October light. And then there is this: balanced precariously on the wooden fence is the newly appointed administrator of the eastern zone, whose office is ten kilometers away. He is grinning around the cigarette jammed into the corner of his mouth, and he is recording the scene with a sleek new video camera. It seems highly unlikely that he was just driving by with a camcorder in the backseat and decided to stop at the college in the hopes of catching a bit of defiance on tape. A cloud of nebulous fear begins to form in my gut. Don't be silly, I tell myself, a bit of resistance to authority is to be expected. This is a college, after all. In Canada this would be nothing. But this is not Canada, and the video camera makes me very uneasy.

The crowd breaks up, and the students return to their hostels to change their clothes. Since the dress law does not apply to foreigners, I go back to the auditorium and wait. It occurs to me that I could slink off, go back home, stay out of it. But no, I will not. These are my students, and they invited me to go with them. Besides, I am too curious to stay at home. They return wearing ghos and kiras that have been put on in haste, bunched up and tied loosely. When I see Dil's dragging on the ground behind him, I realize it is not haste but defiance.

The group moves silently forward, out of the gate, down the road past Pala's, and as soon as we have turned the corner, the students begin to sing. Gayatri says the song is devotional, but the voices are too loud and khukuris are flashing everywhere. At the river, the statue is immersed in the rushing white water, and milk and flowers are poured over it. Dil and his friends clamber up and pose for photos on boulders above the river, shouting and raising their fists in the air. Beneath the singing, the ringing bells, and the wild, joyous rhythm of the tabla, the whole celebration has this antagonistic undertone. When it is over, the men and women separate into two circles and sit at the side of the road. The men talk urgently in Nepali, the women wait for them to be finished. Annoyed with the segregation, I get up to return to campus. Down the road, I am joined by a senior student named Rajan.

"Rajan, can I ask you what's going on?"

"Oh, now the puja is over," he says, "and we will all eat—"

"No, no," I interrupt. "I mean: What. Is. Going. On."

He is silent for so long that I think he will not tell me. Then he says, "You know, ma'am, they did not want us to have our puja."

"Who didn't? The principal?"

"Not only the principal. They—the northern Bhutanese." And he tells me that there is trouble in Bhutan, between south and north, Nepali and Drukpa. "They don't want us to be Nepali anymore," he says. "We have to wear their dress and speak their language. We can no more be who we are."

The others catch up with us, and we walk in silence.

The campus is oddly still. The students return to their hostels, and I go home, wondering about Rajan's comments, and how long the alleged trouble has been bubbling beneath the appearance of calm, wondering about that videotape and who arranged for it and how they knew there would be a confrontation at the gate, and what will happen. It strikes me that I may be on that videotape, and I wonder if I will be implicated in what is happening, whatever it is.

The Situation

And now there is a Situation. This is how the students speak of it. This situation, they say. *The situation is serious.* Sometimes they speak of the Problem, which calls to mind the Irish Troubles, but I can't believe that things will go that far in tiny, peaceful, quiet Bhutan. Aside from a few oblique comments in the staff room, none of the lecturers speaks of the incident at the college gate. But overnight, there is a physical division between the students. They change places in the classroom: north sits with north, south with south. I talk to Shakuntala about it. We are in her dining room, drinking lemon tea. We often sit here until late at night, talking and working and laughing. On her walls are portraits of students she has drawn, pencil studies of leaves and flowers and ferns, photographs of chortens and prayer flags. I feel nostalgic, looking at her work, as if that Bhutan is already over. I cannot shake this feeling of dread. I tell her about the video camera at the gate and the flashing khukuris, and the separation in class of northern and southern. "The thing is," I say, "why do they have to make dress into such a big deal? If the Nepali students want to wear Nepali dress for a Hindu puja, let them."

But Shakuntala doesn't agree. "It's not such a big thing to ask," she says. "To wear your national dress when you leave the campus."

"But it's a religious custom," I say.

"Still, it's not much to ask," she says. "No one is saying they couldn't have their puja. No one is saying they couldn't be Hindu anymore, that they all had to become Buddhist. They were just being asked to obey the dress law."

Not a dress code but a dress *law.* "I understand that it's to preserve Bhutan's culture, but shouldn't it be voluntary? How will it ever work, otherwise?" I say. I don't say, "What about the other cultures and traditions that exist in Bhutan? What about preserving them?" I am caught between two ways of seeing, two possible interpretations, unable here to have faith in either one.

I study the next issue of *Kuensel,* looking for some mention of a Situation, but there is nothing. I want to hear more directly from the students, but the atmosphere on campus has grown increasingly oppressive. Fear and anger pinch their faces, and they answer my questions elliptically. No one will give me a full explanation. I want someone to start at the beginning, I want someone who can complete a sentence, who can say it straight out: here is what's been happening, here are the two sides, now make of it what you will. I feel that I have come into the theater during the second act. I don't want to get on stage with the actors, I only want a summary of what has happened so far, but everyone seems afraid of saying too much. The only agreed-upon facts I have on the Situation so far are these: the Nepali students resent having Drukpa dress and etiquette imposed on them. The government feels that this imposition is necessary for Bhutan's survival. But there must be more to it than this.

There must be more to it than this because there are night patrols on campus, room checks each evening. When the students come to visit, they speak so softly I often can't hear half of what they say. Sometimes, one stands at the window, watching, while the others talk. There are spies now, they say. They have to be very careful. Some southern students have received pamphlets, they tell me, calling for the southern Bhutanese to rise up and demand their rights, demand democracy.

"But do you think Bhutan is really ready for democracy?" I ask. "What do you think is necessary for a country to be a democracy?"

They do not know, they whisper. They haven't thought about it.

"But how can you support something you haven't thought about?" I demand.

They look alarmed at my rising voice and shake their heads frantically. They cannot talk about these things here.

They do not come to visit me in mixed groups anymore. Even Nima and Arun come separately. "Where's Nima these days?" I ask Arun. Studying. Busy. Don't know, miss. I feel I can ask Nima anything, but he is a terrible source of information. He spends most of his time in the library reading religious books. When I ask what's happening, he says, "The Nepali students don't want to wear national dress."

"Oh, Nima, even I know that! What is really going on?"

"I don't know, miss, and I don't want to know. Buddhism teaches us not to get involved in politics. It distracts us from the real things." He has more important things to think about: he has been helping one of the Dzongkha lopens translate a Buddhist book into English, and he is trying to decide if he should become a monk after he finishes class XII.

"But Nima, there must be values in Buddhism that people could apply to politics. Like tolerance and seeking the truth. Didn't the Buddha say to question everything? Wouldn't that help get to the bottom of things?"

"Yes, miss, but I don't think we can apply Buddhism to politics. Look what happened to Tibet. And Sikkim also."

I am chilled by this. I know full well what happened to Tibet but nothing about Sikkim beyond the Fantomes' mention of tragedy. I make a mental note to find out.

The whispered drifts and snatches grow more distressing. I hear that some students at the National Institute of Education in southern Bhutan have been arrested for writing pamphlets. I hear they have been tortured in prison. Tortured? I ask the students who bring this news. Surely not tortured? This is a Buddhist country. They look at each other and shake their heads at my naïveté. I will remember their looks later when I find in my Sharchhop grammar book a section entitled "Punishment," which contains translations of "to torture, torture instruments, to slap, whip, fetters/chains."

I hear that one of those involved has committed suicide in detention. I hear that two British teachers at the institute have fled the country. I hear they were also involved. I hear they helped write a pamphlet. I hear they were not really involved, they only edited the grammar. I hear that all foreigners will have to leave the country because of them. I hear this is just a rumor. I hear a hundred different fleeting whispered stories but I do not hear anyone talking openly. Without talk, nothing will be explained or understood, solved or learned. I want to write it on the sides of mountains, across the autumn sky. TALK TALK TALK.

Each week in the library I search the newspaper for some mention of the Problem, but each week there are only the usual development reports and farming news: irrigation workshop held, World Food Day celebrated, Australian wool for Bumthang weavers, two-headed calf born in Paro.

Dil and his friend are arrested and taken to the Tashigang for not wearing national dress outside the campus. They were on their way back from Pala's when the police picked them up. Many students, both northern and southern, wear jeans to Pala's. The arrest seems malicious and provocative. Dil and his friend return to school but a few days later, they disappear again. We are in the middle of a final review before exams. "Are they coming back?" I ask. The students study their notebooks, look out the window, do not answer.

I hear they have run away. They have gone to join unnamed others across the border after they were beaten up by northern students for wearing Nepali dress under their ghos. And then, five more southern students disappear. They are taken at night. Arrested, gone, delivered to Thimphu for questioning, I hear from the other lecturers. The students will not talk about it; they look terrified at the mere mention of the five who are gone. This is the most frightening thing.

The Situation finally merits a mention in the *Kuensel.* During the 68th session of the National Assembly, the Ministry of Home Affairs announces that several anti-national and seditious letters and booklets were mailed into Bhutan. The allegations made in these publications were found to be baseless, malicious, and against the fundamental principles of the *Tsawa Sum,* the Three Jewels of the King, the Country and the People. As such, they constituted an act of treason. The culprits and miscreants responsible could not be traced, the Ministry adds. There is no mention of a movement or any arrests.

The View from Here

We are going to visit a holy lake above Khaling, Tony and two Dutch aid workers from an agricultural project near Kanglung, and me. Tony is two months away from the end of his contract in Khaling, and will not extend. He is still quite thin, the result of a bout of typhoid and a stomach parasite. His nickname among the other Canadians is Bean, short for Bean Pole. His weight loss has no impact on his walking speed, however, and thirty minutes into the walk, I am winded. But I plod on, determined to keep up. I want to see the lake. I also want to be away from the Situation for a few hours.

We walk through an oak forest cool with early morning shadows, and I am thinking about Robert and Christmas and home. Nothing in me wants to go to Canada this winter. I finger memories, hold up images, run a scan through muscle blood bone, trying to find some tiny fiber that still wants to go. There is not one. Not even for Robert.

The forest opens into a meadow and the meadow rises into an immense hill, smooth and rounded and extremely steep, covered with golden grass and yellow flowers. The path zigzags up for almost four hours. We pass Brokpa, the nomadic yak herders from the easternmost settlement in Bhutan, with their herds of shaggy, lumbering yaks coming down from the mountain tops where it is already winter. My legs are screaming at me to stop!stop!stop! and I do for a moment, huffing and puffing, sweat running into my eyes. A tiny Brokpa child in cracked blue rubber boots motors past me, sturdy legs churning effortlessly. "Are we almost there yet?" I call out. "A few more minutes," Tony calls back. "A few" turns out to be forty-five, but then we arrive and stand gazing at the small lake set in a shelter of ancient pines and mossy boulders. Stone cairns have been built along the shores, and we can see the blue of one-ngultrum notes in the clear cold water, offerings made to the lake spirit. Tony says that all lakes in Bhutan are considered holy. His students warned him not to pollute the lake, or bring meat anywhere near it, or leave any garbage nearby. They were full of stories of what would happen otherwise: you would get sick, or the lake would send mist and clouds to make you lose your way in the forest, or the spirit might even rise out of the water right then and there and that would be the end of you.

We eat our lunch of bread and cheese and hard-boiled eggs and as I am packing up, I am tempted to leave something behind, to test the stories, just to see what will happen. I tear off a minute piece of chocolate-bar wrapper, but at the last minute put it in my pocket. Tony proposes that we walk to a peak called Brangzung-La, not far from the lake. It is only an hour or so from here, he says, and the view is fantastic. We are exhausted from the long climb up in the broiling sun, but the promise of a view lures us onward. An hour or so turns out to be "or two and a half," and I trudge along behind the others, muttering and panting and cursing Tony who must have been a mountain goat in his last life. As we ascend, the tall fir trees shrink into weeping blue juniper bushes and dwarf bamboo, knotted tightly against the cold, and I begin to feel pale and stretched and thin. Tony says it is the altitude. I cannot walk another step but I do and I do and I do. I hate walking, I tell myself, and I don't care if we can see the entire world from up there, it's not worth it.

But it is. The treeless peak is marked by a white chorten and ragged white prayer flags, the printed prayers blown completely off by the constant wind. The view lasts forever: snow peaks along the northern border, frozen white fortresses against the blue sky, and far away in the south, the plains of India, shimmering in the last of the afternoon light, and in between the north and the south, the valleys and ridges of eastern Bhutan spread out in waves. The others are taking pictures, but I want to memorize the view. I want to be able to close my eyes anywhere in the world and see this. We are not even very high up, and yet it is the best thing I've seen in my life.

"I don't want to go home at Christmas," I say suddenly.

"So don't go," Tony shrugs, adjusting his lens. He is trying to get a shot of Gangkhar Puensoom, the highest mountain in Bhutan.

Don't go. But if I don't go home at Christmas, that will be the end of my relationship with Robert. There will be no way to reconnect after two years.

Exactly, says another voice. It's not that you don't want to go home at Christmas . . .

Everything about my relationship with Robert, in fact everything about the life I left behind, seems small and narrow in comparison with where I am now. Everything I imagine in that life is repulsive to me: a house in an affordable suburb, a car that I will hate because it is too big, sprinklers keeping the lawn green in the summer while we sit in air-conditioned rooms inside, sealed off from the elements, safe and smug. Part of me knows this is unfair to Robert but the rest of me doesn't want to hear it. I can see only what I have now, this view, and the dark, bright world below, with its stories of kings and curses and guardian deities, flying tigers and thunder dragons, religious scrolls hidden in rocks and valleys hidden in mountains by magic or Buddhism or both, and yetis and ghosts and the levitating lama in the temple on the ridge the sun rises over each morning, and all the places I haven't been to, and the stories I haven't yet heard, all the things I haven't figured out, like the Situation. Even with the Situation, and the frustration of being in it but apart from it, and the whispers and fear, I want to stay. I can't go home yet.

The sun begins to set, and a few stars chisel their way out of the pale sky. "It's only an hour down," Tony says, but by now we know what this means. We finish the last of our water and chocolate and follow Tony along a tenuous muddy track through dense bamboo. The shadows around us thicken, and Tony urges us to hurry. "This trail breaks off at some point, and if we take the wrong path, we'll end up in a nightmare of a bamboo forest above Khaling with no way down."

We hurry but the bamboo does not thin out, and the trail grows steadily worse. I am so tired I want to cry. We have been walking since seven this morning. The track is now the merest memory of a path. I know we are lost, and I know it is superstitious and silly but it is all because of that piece of paper I was tempted to leave at the lake. Tony stops abruptly. "I think we're lost," he says. "We should be able to see the lights of Khaling by now." It is completely dark, and we have one slim flashlight between the four of us.

I explain about the piece of paper. The others listen without comment, but Tony says, "That is just about the stupidest thing I have ever heard."

Then we notice a lustrous sheen low in the sky, the rising moon. The light grows brighter and the moon appears, rising quickly, a full pretty silver face, rising higher and higher, throwing down armfuls of light. We walk single file along the path, which climbs out of the mire and joins another wider trail. When we come to the long edge of a dry grassy slope, I sit and slide down the hill, toward the steady yellow lights of Khaling.

Back in Kanglung, I sit on my doorstep, looking at Brangzung-La. A chill lays over the campus now until the sun is quite high above the ridge. More green has seeped out of the fields and hills, and outside my door, one cold white lily opens amidst the burnished marigolds.

I have just written two letters. One is a message for the field office in Thimphu, canceling my flight reservations. The other is a long, winding letter to Robert, full of my love for Bhutan, if he could only understand, I just cannot come home, and I cannot marry him because Bhutan has changed me, and I don't want the same things anymore. I add apologies and excuses, secondary reasons and supporting material, sign it and seal the envelope. I take it straight to the post office before I can change my mind.

Winter Break

The days in December are thin, empty, short. The students have left for the winter vacation, returning to their homes across the country, and the college bus took the Indian staff, including Shakuntala, to the nearest Indian town several days ago. The college will not reopen until February. After one year of service, the WUSC field office in Thimphu gives us a travel grant for a holiday in the region; I will go to Thimphu with the other Canadian teachers when their teaching terms finish next week, and decide where to spend the winter.

I sweep the floors, sort through clothes, preparing to go, and in the evenings, huddle in front of an electric heater that throws as much warmth as a Bic lighter. The staff houses were designed for India, with concrete ledges fixed above the windows to keep out the scorching sun, and a breezeway in the back hall to let in monsoon-cooled wind. I wish for a traditional Bhutanese house, with thick mud and stone walls against the cold.

When the power goes out, as it frequently does, I go to bed. Sometimes, I am in bed for the night at six p.m., under two woolen blankets, a sleeping bag and quilt, and all of my kiras. I cannot move, but finally I am warm.

I pack a rucksack for the winter holiday, and then repack, getting rid of all the extras in case of this, in case of that. I think of all those things I brought with me from Canada, my bags stuffed with things I didn't actually need. I could not have learned this freedom in Canada. But the feeling of lightness is counterbalanced by the worry that sits in my stomach. Several southern students swore they would not come back to the college in the spring because of the Problem, and some northerners went around boasting about what they would do if "these people" try anything. People do not become "we" and "they" overnight. This is a problem with a history behind it, and I feel desperate to understand it.

In my last days, I flip through old *Kuensels* and history books, hoping to find the missing pieces. Nepali immigration into Bhutan began as early as the end of the last century when laborers from the lowlands were recruited for timber and stone extraction; the laborers eventually cleared plots of land in the malaria-infested jungles of the south and settled there. Similar patterns of migration were occurring throughout northeast India, especially in Sikkim, where the British tea plantations and roads offered plenty of jobs. According to Nari Rustomji's *Sikkim: A Himalayan Tragedy*, the immigrants were an energetic group, hungry for land and extremely mobile. Because there was plenty of land, however, the indigenous tribal Lepchas, and the Bhutias of Tibetan origin, did not feel threatened, even when the immigrant population began to grow. "The Nepalese made no attempt to assimilate themselves with the inhabitants of their host country. Due to the rigidities of the Hindu caste system, they could not inter-marry freely with the Lepchas and Bhutias. . . . Few Nepalese cared to learn the languages of the land. . . ." Under the Buddhist monarchy, which had been established in 1641, the Nepalese felt they were being treated as second-class citizens; though they were now a majority, they were not in a position to aspire to the true political power under the existing system. Their calls for democracy in the 1960s and 1970s were an attempt to establish a government that would reflect the demographic balance and promote their own interests. Relations between India and China were still tense, and increasing political unrest gave India the opportunity to absorb the kingdom under the "sensitive border area" excuse. In 1975, the 334-year rule of the Sikkimese Buddhist kings came to an end.

In Bhutan, the 1958 Citizenship Act gave citizenship to anyone who had lived in Bhutan for at least ten years and owned land. With the implementation of the country's first economic development plan in 1962, there was plenty of work to be found building roads, schools and hospitals, and Nepali immigrants continued to move into the country. Integration did not seem to be a concern; apparently, travel to northern Bhutan was restricted for the southern Bhutanese until sometime in the 1970s. South was south, north was north.

The south became an issue in 1988, when census records indicated a disproportionate increase in the population in the southern districts. In the neighboring Indian states of Meghalaya and Assam, Nepali immigrants were being evicted. No room, no room, the state governments insisted. Go back home. We can't help it if there is no room for you there either. You are not our problem. At the same time, the Gorkha National Liberation Front in Darjeeling began calling for the establishment of Gorkhaland, which would spread across northeastern India, including parts of southern Bhutan.

A new exhaustive census was ordered, and local officials in the south were accused of allowing large numbers of illegal immigrants to enter Bhutan and register themselves as Bhutanese citizens. There was mention of unhappiness and dissatisfaction felt in the south over the harshness with which the census was being conducted, but these feelings were put down to rumors.

I don't know if I am any closer to understanding the Situation. I can see why Bhutan, living in the dark shadow of an annexed Sikkim and Tibet, must be concerned about demographics and sovereignty. But I can also see why the southern Bhutanese feel harassed and afraid. I close up the history books. The historical backdrop does nothing to alleviate the anxiety I feel for my individual students. If anything, it makes it worse.

On my last day, I lock up my house and take my rucksack to the college gate to wait for the vehicle. At Pala's, Amala calls me over. Her short straight hair is wrapped around pink sponge curlers, and she is carrying a trowel and a bucket of wet cement to repair a wall at the back of the restaurant. I have just eaten lunch, but she insists on feeding me again, and we drink tea out of shot glasses and talk about Amala's plans for the winter. She will go to her ancestral home, in Sakteng, on the eastern border of Bhutan, where her late father was once a high lama. His reincarnation has not been found, and his temple and house in Sakteng stand empty, except for a caretaker.

"Listen," Amala says. "Vehicle." It is my ride, a hi-lux packed full of Tony and Leon and several of their students. I thank Amala and climb in. Amala waves her trowel at me, and I begin the reverse journey, back across the country to Thimphu.

We arrive three days later, turning a corner in the dark to see the net of lights spread out in the valley below. "But it's enormous," Sasha says, and Lorna breaks into a chorus of "New York, New York."

We spend several bewildering days in the capital sorting out travel plans and visas, stumbling along the main road alarmed at the traffic and the number of streets, surprised by our sudden anonymity in shops and restaurants, feeling shabby in our monsoon-streaked, sun-bleached clothes. Our field director takes us for lunch at the elegant Druk Hotel, and we giggle and fiddle with the silverware and knock over the salt and pepper shakers. Hefty expatriate consultants in dark suits and polished shoes raise their eyebrows at us. The shops are full of so many *things*: paper clips, wall clocks, air freshener, plastic coasters shaped like fish. There are three video shops on the main road now, and "Fancy Shop" sells greeting cards and black high-top trainers.

A poster in a travel agency announces that Bhutan is the Last Shangri-La. There seem to be more tourists in Thimphu this winter, and we scoff at their heavy camcorders and expensive travel clothes. Thinking about it later, I hear the ugly, arrogant tone in our voices. Ugh—foreigners! As if we were not. Bhutan is so difficult to get into, such an unusual and desirable location, that I have become swollen with pride, as if my being in Bhutan were a great personal achievement and not simply a matter of luck. It is one of the dangers of being associated with Bhutan. At first you cannot believe your good fortune, and then you begin to think it has something to do with you. Look at me, look where I am! Bhutan is special, and I am in Bhutan, therefore I must be special too. Travel should make us more humble, not more proud. We are all tourists, I think. Whether we stay for two weeks or two years, we are still outsiders, passing through.

We hear the story behind the British teachers who fled. They not only fled, they contacted Amnesty International, and their involvement, we are told, was viewed "most seriously" by the government. Aid agencies were reminded that it is strictly forbidden for foreigners to become involved in Bhutanese politics. I tell the field director about the videotape at the college gate. He makes notes grimly and says he will have to make inquiries. He reminds us to do nothing and say nothing and stay out of it. "We all came within centimeters of getting turfed out," he says. Even he seems infected with the Fear of Talk. "Don't ask questions and don't discuss it with the Bhutanese," he tells us, lowering his voice and glancing over his shoulder. In another context, it would seem laughable, a spy-novel spoof. No one is laughing, though, as we whisper nervously about upheaval and ethnic conflict in the Last Shangri-La.

Leon, Tony, Lorna and several others go to Thailand for the winter, and they urge me to come along. I want to see Nepal, though, and fly to Kathmandu with Jane from Tsebar. From there, we travel overland to Delhi. Northern India is exhausting. Along the way we are stared at, glared at, honked at, swerved around, groped, grabbed, pinched, poked, fondled, bullied, propositioned, lied to, proposed to, and sang to. It is a relief when we finally reach Shakuntala's book-lined flat in Delhi. Jane returns to England, and I continue on alone to Kovalum Beach in Kerala, where I spend my days swimming and reading and walking from one end of the beach to the other, eating yogurt, fish, pineapples and coconut. The three-day train journey back to northern India is warm and intimate. We pass through cool morning forests, hot midday plains and hills turning purple in evening shadows, and the Indian families in the compartment share their food with me, aloo dum and paratha and an assortment of homemade pickles, sweet basmati rice and chickpeas in tangy sauce. I have nothing to offer in return, but buy fruit drinks and ice cream for the kids, and we make stars and boats and flowers out of the back pages of my journal.

By the time I reach Calcutta, I am longing to see the mountains again. All winter, my thoughts have never been far from Bhutan. The bus from Calcutta to Phuntsholing barrels over a deeply gouged and rutted highway. The air becomes suddenly cooler, and I look up: ahead, without a prologue of knolls or hills, the mountains rise straight up. I feel a familiar surge of happiness. I am back home.

Involvement

*And if you hit upon the idea that this or
that country is safe, prosperous, or
fortunate, give it up, my friend . . . for you
ought to know that the world is ablaze with
the fires of some faults or others. There is
certain to be some suffering . . . and a
wholly fortunate country does not exist
anywhere. Whether it be excessive cold or
heat, sickness or danger, something always
afflicts people everywhere; no safe refuge
can thus be found in the world.*

—Buddhist Scriptures

We the Lecturers

The college is awash in mid-morning sunlight when I step off the Comet from Tashigang. I unlock my house and fling open all the windows. Mrs. Chatterji calls down to me, asking about my trip to India. She is very beautiful, with large brown eyes and pale skin and a fall of straight dark hair. Over her flowery sari, she wears two thick handknit sweaters against the cold, but when I suggest that she comes out into the sun, she shakes her head. "Bad for the complexion," she says, and points to the broom in my hand. "So today you are doing spring cleaning?" Actually, I was only going to sweep off the front step so that I could sit on it, but I nod. After living below her for six months, I know that housework is her entire day. She begins as soon as her husband leaves for class in the morning—sweep the floors, beat the rugs, tend the garden, do the laundry, cook the meals, wash the dishes. "She needs a child," Mrs. Matthew once whispered to me.

"Or a job," I whispered back. Mrs. Chatterji has a master's degree, but when I asked Mr. Chatterji why she didn't teach, he laughed. "My wife does not have to work. She is happy at home." But I do not believe it. In the late afternoon, waiting for her husband to return, she descends the stairs and paces back and forth along one wall of the house. I have never seen her go farther than this by herself, and I cannot imagine how long that stretch of time is between the last thing cleaned and folded and put away and the sound of her husband's footsteps on the stairs.

On the other side, Mr. Matthew is working in his garden. He offers to lend me his gardening tools. "Your garden has become like jungle," he says in his musical Keralan lilt. I tell him that I like the undomesticated look, but he frowns.

I change the subject. "It's so quiet without the students, isn't it?"

"Quiet is good," Mr. Matthew says. "You know, we were talking about you just before our winter holidays."

"Who was?"

"We, the lecturers. You are becoming too familiar with the students. This is not good. They will be taking advantage."

"I haven't had any—"

"You must not lower yourself to their level. You are a lecturer, not one of them, isn't it. Lecturers cannot be friendly with the students."

"It's all right, really—"

"No," he says. "It is not all right. I hope you will improve yourself this year."

I sit in the sun on my front step all afternoon, reading and drinking in the view, and in the evening go out to the tap in the backyard to wash my journey-stained clothes. Mrs. Matthew stops on her way upstairs. "Washing your clothes at night?" She is aghast.

"It was too nice a day to spend inside," I say.

"In the *dark?*" She goes clucking loudly up the stairs to her apartment, where she and Mr. Matthew will discuss the errors of my ways, and they will be legion.

This is the other side of small, which Chhoden had warned me about last year when she spoke of the constricting uniformity of village life. After six weeks in total anonymity, I had forgotten this, the smallness and narrowness of the community here. I had forgotten all the implied criticisms of my teaching methods and general behavior, the falsely cheerful questions in the staff room. *What for you are bringing this tape player to class? Playing music—in* class? *What were your students doing sitting outside today? Writing poems is in the syllabus? Why you are having so many students visiting you, Miss Jamie? Are you giving extra tuition in English?* Not really asking. Really telling. Telling me this is not the way we do things here. Real lecturers do not behave like this. Real lecturers call the students boys and girls; they take attendance religiously and do not play Dire Straits songs in class to illustrate satire. Real lecturers do not sit on their steps drinking coffee with the students, and they do not hang out their clothes to dry at night. If it weren't for Shakuntala, I would be very alone here.

At the post office, there is a parcel from Canada that has taken nine months to reach me, a few Christmas cards, and a letter from Robert. I carry it to the bend in the road and read it hastily under the prayer flags. Robert is hurt and angry and bewildered. He doesn't understand how I could have turned away from so much in such a short time. I am unable to look fully at the pain that I have caused, and I fold the letter away into my pocket, wishing I could fold away my remorse and guilt as easily.

We have been back only for a few days when Shakuntala receives a message from home. Her father is seriously ill, and she may have to return to Delhi. She waits for news, hardly daring to leave her house. "Maybe he'll be okay," I say, and she nods but her eyes tell of an immense grief to come.

That same weekend, a student shows up at my window late at night, and we have a whispered conversation through the shutter—you can't come in, but why not, you *know* why not. He begs, pleads, promises to tell no one, he swears to Buddha he would never tell, and what harm can come of it, just this once, if you only knew how much courage it took for me to come here, you would not send me away. I do not recognize him—he is not in any of my classes, and in my mind, this somehow justifies letting him in. I am hungry for physical contact, and in a quick, unthinking moment have convinced myself that this is night-hunting, part of the experience of Bhutan. I open the door.

Almost immediately, though, I regret it. Physically, it is a rushed, blurry, wholly dissatisfying encounter, but the real problem is how his demeanor changes. The sweet, pleading routine is replaced by a smugness that turns my stomach. I hurry him out of the house after, cursing myself for not having had more sense. I doubt that he will keep his word about telling no one, and I dread the thought of seeing him in daylight. My only consolation is that he mentioned his final-year exams. This means that in a few weeks, he will be gone.

By the next morning, I have worked myself into a blind panic over the encounter, and the possibility of it becoming public. I am not sure if I could be fired in Bhutan for this, but certainly my reputation among the students would be irreparably damaged, perhaps to the point of making teaching impossible. I don't know how I could have been so reckless. Next door, Shakuntala is packing to return to Delhi, but I am so caught up in my own predicament that I barely notice her distress. I pace her bedroom while she folds clothes into a suitcase, half-listening to her describe her father's latest symptoms. He is going to tell someone, is all I can think, and what then. Shakuntala stops talking, and after a long strained moment, I realize she has asked me a question, the only word of which I heard was "remission." I rush into the silence, telling her what I have done, appalled at the way I turn it into a lighthearted, light-headed encounter. "I don't know," I conclude. "Do you think he'll tell?"

"I—I don't know," she says blankly.

"Maybe no one would believe him," I say. "Do you think?"

"Jamie," she says. "My father is *dying*." She is weeping.

For the next few days, I live in a state of pure neurosis. I see him on campus, and we look carefully past each other, and slowly the worry about what *might* happen *if* he tells begins to dissipate. The worry, but not the regret.

Then I realize that Shakuntala is gone. She writes briefly to say that her father has died, and that she must stay in Delhi with her mother. The thought of my callous behavior on the day of her departure shakes me out of sleep at night, thrusts itself into everything I do, look here, it clamors, look at this. I try meditating to empty my mind of all cognitive thought, but I am unable to get away from myself. After a few minutes, I leap up, looking for some book or task to throw myself into. There is no quick confess-and-forgive formula in Buddhist practice. Buddhism requires a constant, relentless internal honesty, and I know I will be unable to proceed until I face my own behavior, my utter thoughtlessness in sleeping with the student, and my failure to be a true friend to Shakuntala. The only way out of this is straight through it.

And while you are there, a voice adds, you might take a real look at the grief you have caused Robert.

Without Shakuntala, I am alone, neither part of the staff nor of the student body. I resolve to try to make amends with the staff members, but the thought of becoming one of "we the lecturers" makes me feel cold and cross, a hundred years old. It rains for several days, and I stay in bed, preparing lessons, eating peanuts, wrapped in sweaters and a heavy woolen kira against the cold damp. When the rain subsides, I put on my shoes and walk to the shops to get something more substantial than peanuts. The tops of the mountains are all engrossed in cloud, and the wind comes down from the dark peaks in the north, sharpened by its passage through brambles and thorns, carrying icy droplets of rain. While the shopkeeper packs my groceries in newspaper, I read the astrologers' calendar on the wall, printed in Chhoeki and English. It is the Year of the Iron Horse, and the predictions are ominous, full of conflict and rain and the movement of peoples.

Four of the five who were arrested last year are back. They are subdued, associating with neither north nor south, nor with each other; they are years older, eyes shadowed and faces haggard. As for the one who is still missing, all I can find out is that he was "involved" and is now in jail. Dil has not returned. The southern students say the Situation deteriorated over the winter: there were curfews and travel restrictions, the government is canceling Nepali instruction in the southern schools, and families have to produce a land-tax receipt from 1958 in order to be counted as Bhutanese citizens. The northern students say that thousands of illegal immigrants have been found in the southern belt, and what country in the world wouldn't take action against this.

In the newspaper, treason is still the key word, along with *ngolops,* traitors. The government was "deeply saddened to learn that some southern Bhutanese teachers, trainees, students and civil servants had taken part in activities aimed at harming the Tsawa Sum." It is a matter of "great regret and disappointment that these people had become involved in anti-national activities against the government that had fed, clothed and educated them since their childhood." The government says that clemency has been shown to all except the ring-leaders, and the people's representatives express disappointment at the government's lenient stand. I have serious doubts about this expressed disappointment; the entire discussion sounds stilted, as if it had been scripted.

I begin asking direct questions. I get two sides of a story, two halves that do not make a whole.

See ma'am, it's about democracy and human rights, the southern students tell me. We have a right to wear our own dress and speak our own language.

But the northern students say it is about their survival as a nation. Bhutan is a small country stuck between two giant neighbors, threatened by demographic pressures. We have to protect and preserve our traditions and culture.

What about our traditions and culture, the southern students ask. What about our rights? They are imposing their culture, their driglam namzha, on us.

It's our country, after all. We've been here since time immemorial. They came here from Nepal only when Bhutan started to develop. They came here because they had nothing in Nepal, a northern student tells me.

My family has been here for a hundred years. I have just as much right to be here as they do.

If they don't want to abide by the law of the land, they should leave. If they want to be Nepali, they should go back to Nepal. They've never been loyal to Bhutan. In their houses, they put up pictures of the king of Nepal instead of our His Majesty.

They never wanted us here. When our people first came, it was because they needed us to work. They gave us land in the south where the jungles were full of malaria. And our ancestors cleared the land and planted oranges and cardamom and we became prosperous. That's what they don't like.

They've been bringing their people in illegally, the border with India is open. If we don't take care of this problem, we'll be swamped. We'll be a minority in our own country.

We've never been treated equally. Just look at all the ministers—there's only one southern Bhutanese. Our people can only go so far. There's always been discrimination.

There has never been any discrimination against them. They get free schooling and health care just like the rest of us.

You can't trust them. They appear very simple on the outside, but inside you don't know what they are thinking.

You can't trust them. They want a "greater Nepal" and that would include part of Bhutan. They want to take over, like they did in Sikkim.

The voices grow shriller. I try to present each side with the other side's arguments. There are angry denials. Don't listen to them, that's all propaganda. You can't trust them it's all their fault they want to destroy us our culture our rights those people this is what they're like.

Ordinary words swell with heat into rhetoric, and no real discussion is possible, only the same script, recited again and again. *Il n'y a rien dehors de text*—this comes back to me from a poststructuralist seminar, with a distressingly different meaning, and I wish I were back in a Canadian university, engaged in discussions about language that would make no difference to the world outside; how easy it was to talk about hegemony and discourse from the margins in a well-lit classroom where no one had to whisper and keep watch out the window and students did not disappear at night.

This is not about democracy or rights, I think. At the most basic level, it is about tribes. Loyalty to one's race, and fear of the other. Each half thinks it makes a whole story on its own, and neither side will acknowledge that there is another side. I have not heard one person speak of mediation or negotiation or even the listening that is necessary for understanding. There is no recognition of any overlap, any common ground. Already it is a case of two solitudes.

One morning, I fall asleep during a meeting, and wake up to find I have been appointed to the "exam committee" which will meet "today itself only" after lunch. I arrive ten minutes early to find my colleagues already engaged in a blistering debate over a title for the head of the committee. Convenor? Controller? Supervisor? Excuse me, my dear sir! I beg your pardon! If you will kindly listen! They go on and on until I think I am going to scream.

"But let us ask our Canadian colleague," Mr. Ahmed says, and five heads swivel toward me.

"Convenor, controller, head honcho," I answer. "This is a complete waste of time."

There is a slight pause and the discussion resumes. Mr. Gupta is finally elected controller, Mr. Ahmed coordinator, and they decide that they will decide between them who will go to Delhi to pick up the exams. They exchange smug smiles, and I realize the whole debate has been about this, an all-expenses-paid trip to Delhi. Shakuntala and I used to laugh at the wheeling-dealing schemes of the more mercenary lecturers; today I am infuriated. I walk out. Silence follows me to the door and down the hall.

I flee to Pala's where I sit at a table outside, churning with anger. I don't care if I make outright enemies among the rest of the staff now. There are too many façades to maintain. Nothing is going on, nothing is wrong, no students were arrested, no students were beaten up, no students ran away. No students are talking about joining a movement, no students are talking about joining the militia to fix up the students who join the movement. No students are talking because there is nothing to talk about. I am a foreigner, I do not know what is going on (nothing is going on), I am not involved. I have no opinion on anything. I am here to teach Shakespeare and the present perfect continuous and if the country falls apart around me, it's none of my business. My business is with the staff members, all competent, dedicated professionals who get along famously.

Inside the restaurant someone is tuning a drumnyen, and voices try out a melody, stop and start and dissolve in laughter. At the next table, a student is poring over a tattered copy of *Rolling Stone,* another is engrossed in a biography of Bob Dylan. They are eating *zow,* rice crisps, which they throw by the handful into their mouths. I have seen the Bob Dylan fan in the library and on stage a number of times. He has a handsome face: high cheekbones, a luscious mouth, and a long fringe of jet black hair falling into his eyes. He looks over and smiles, and the result is dazzling. "Good meeting, miss?"

"How do you know I was in a meeting?"

"I was in the classroom next door." His eyes are bright with laughter.

"You weren't eavesdropping on your lecturers, were you?"

His answer is long and ridiculous, full of words like "sanctimonious," "plethora," "scalar," ending with "sound and fury, signifying nothing."

I burst into amazed laughter. "So you *were* eavesdropping!"

His friend gets up to go, but he stays and talks. He speaks English faster and more fluently than any Bhutanese person I have met, darting from topic to topic, the British in India, Indian immigrants in Britain, Sufi mystics, Bhutanese methods of dream interpretation, international intelligence agencies, the Booker Prize. I can barely keep up. I cannot figure him out. He is worldly and obviously extremely well-read, but instead of the cool, breezy nonchalance that I have come to associate with the private-school set, there is an intensity about him that I find very attractive. Or maybe it's just that he is unsettlingly good-looking. At any rate, I am sorry when he says he has to get to class. "Economics," he says, "which I detest and despise."

"Abhor."

"Revile. Loathe."

"Your nickname should be Roget," I say. I wish he was in my class. I wish I could talk to him every day. He shoves his book into the front flap of his gho, and makes a funny little bow. "Good afternoon, miss." He has a quicksilver smile and very mischievous eyes. His name is Tshewang, I remember. I find myself smiling long after he has gone.

A Silly Passing Infatuation

All around us spring unfurls. Peach and plum trees explode into blossom, the sky loses its hard winter glare, and the days begin to stretch out, afternoon light lingering on the mountaintops. A new English teacher arrives, a brilliant young woman from southern India with a sharp tongue and a head full of Marxist feminist literary theory. Her name is Dini, and she deconstructs the English syllabus one morning over coffee on my front step. "I'm not teaching that," she says, stroking off a selection of essays, "or this poetry, and oh god, Shakespeare is so overrated."

"You have to teach it," I say, laughing. "It's in the syllabus."

"Syllabus shyllabus, I am not teaching it."

We spend hours playing Scrabble and cooking vindaloo dishes that smoke with twenty-five different spices. She is a Christian, and her boyfriend is from a strict Brahmin family. They want to get married but his family will not allow it. She tells me stories of life in an Indian village, untouchables beaten for allowing their shadow to fall on an upper-caste man, or killed for drinking from the upper-caste well. She explains the four major castes and the thousands of subcastes, the concept of untouchability. She talks about recent Indian history, the situation in Jammu-Kashmir, the problems in the northeast, the Naxalite movement. For Dini, the recent political developments in Bhutan are similar to a dozen other demographic conflicts in the subcontinent. "This is nothing new," she says. "It may be new to Bhutan, of course, but not to the rest of the region." I listen carefully as I slice tomatoes and long red chilies, peel garlic, learn to use a pestle and mortar to grind seeds and spices into a paste.

Dini thinks I should deconstruct my love for the landscapes of

Bhutan. "You're projecting things onto the place," she says, "all the things you feel your own culture is missing. The pre-industrialized world, communion with nature, all that Shangri-La-Di-Da business."

"But the people are safe and content here, Dini."

"And poor."

"Well, yes, there is material poverty," I agree, "but not misery."

"What's the difference?" she asks.

I say that lives in the villages might be hard and short, but the people seem genuinely content with what they have, and this is a function of their faith, which recognizes that desire for material wealth and personal gain leads to suffering. Dini says they are content with what they have because what they have is all they know. How deep do you think those values go? she asks. Their lifestyle is not a matter of choice but a function of the environment. If they could have cars and refrigerators and VCRs, they would. Let the global market in here with all its shiny offerings, she says, and see how fast everything changes.

I remember the video shops, the air freshener and plastic coasters shaped like fish for sale in Thimphu.

Dini doesn't see why the Bhutanese should not choose for themselves. "If they want fish-shaped coasters, why shouldn't they have them? You want Bhutan to ban consumer goods just because they ruin your quaint notion of an untouched magical little world. It reminds me of all those environmentalists coming to India and telling us we have to cut down on CO_2 emissions, what do we think, every Indian can have a car or what? Every American has a car, but oh, that's different."

I can say nothing to this.

"Look," she says. "In your mind, Bhutan can be whatever you want it to be. But only the Bhutanese know what it really is."

The next time I stop to watch a family transplanting rice into flooded paddies, I feel how Dini's adamantine edge has cut away some of my sentimental attachment. The family stands in muddy water, backs bent as they stab the rice shoots into the wet earth, their hands fast and unerring. At the edge of the field, a girl of about three carries a baby wrapped on her back with a broad handwoven cloth. The baby gnaws a fist and frets as the terraces fill slowly up with green. Standing there with an armful of rhododendrons I have picked in the forest, I am aware of two possible versions: I can see either the postcard (Lost World Series, Rural Landscape No. 5), or I can see a family bent over the earth in aching, backbreaking labor, the ghosts of two children dead of some easily preventable disease, and not enough money for all of the surviving children to buy the shoes and uniforms required for school. It is too easy to romanticize Bhutan. The landscape cannot answer back, cannot say, no you are wrong, life here is different but if you add everything up, it is not any better. You can love this landscape because your life does not depend on it. It is a merely a scenic backdrop for the other life you will always be able to return to, a life in which you will not be a farmer scraping a living out of difficult terrain.

I love the view, but I would not want the life.

In the twilight, the percussion of frogs and crickets and cicadas rises up from the marsh below the staff quarters, and I meditate, legs folded under me, eyes closed. At first, I itch and squirm and shift, but gradually a stillness settles over me. My goal is mindfulness: I want to be able to hold the stillness inside, to move through the day aware of my thoughts and words and actions. The full concentration I achieve when I am sitting begins to dissolve minutes after I stand up, but a trace of it remains, a small piece of quiet in my head that I carry with me throughout the next day.

I run into Tshewang again and again, and we fall into conversation easily. His parents are from Tashigang, he tells me, but he grew up in southern Bhutan, the middle son of seven children. Like most Bhutanese, he is multilingual, speaking Sharchhop, Nepali, Dzongkha, English and Hindi fluently. His father is a gomchen and his mother a weaver who used to supplement the family income by brewing arra. As a child, he says, he walked five kilometers to school every day, returning home to toss his bag of schoolbooks into the trees before heading into the forest to look after the cows. In the evenings, he played by the riverside, listening for elephants, afraid of snakes. Every morning he would have to search for his school bag in the bushes while his parents scolded him for his carelessness. He did well in school, though, and qualified easily for college. What do you read, I ask, and he says everything. I believe him. He has an incredible store of knowledge, an excellent memory for details, names and dates and cultural trivia. "I was so desperate for books when I was a kid," he says. "I remember picking up empty boxes and wrappers and things, just to read what was written on them. What did you like to read when you were a child, miss?"

I remember the day I got my own library card and checked out ten fat children's classics. I tell him, discomfited at the gap between our worlds. He is not disconcerted at all, and plunges into the gap, and we end up debating the most fitting symbol of decadence. A TV in every room in the house, I say. Imelda Marcos's shoe collection.

"Chocolate milk," he says.

"Chocolate *milk*? How do you even know about chocolate milk?"

"From an ad in a magazine. When I saw that, I thought, it's not enough to have milk? A whole bottle of milk is not enough? People have to add chocolate to it?"

This happens in many of our conversations: we start off in one direction and skid on a cultural difference, ending up in a new place altogether.

He loves to argue by illustration, piling metaphor onto metaphor until I cannot remember what we were talking about. "Okay, it's like this: imagine a blind weaver," he begins, and I cannot keep a straight face. I tell him that his arguments are elliptical and full of annoying contradictions; he accuses me of manufacturing evidence. "Wait, let me guess—" he says whenever I start to prove a point, "they've *done a study.*"

Harmless conversations, I tell myself. I look forward to them because he's so intelligent and funny. I look forward to seeing lots of students, Nima, Arun, Chhoden . . . no, I cannot convince myself that this is the same. Beneath our conversations, running through them, is an energy. I think he feels it as well. He stands or sits very close when we talk, looking directly into my eyes, and I sense that he is reading me as closely as I am reading him. While our behavior is not overtly inappropriate, I would not want Mr. Matthew's disapproving eye observing us in conversation.

He is a show-off, I tell myself, a loud, attention-hogging, limelight-seeking blusterer, a trumpeter of synonyms. He's actually very irritating. But this doesn't work, either. Underneath the persona of the charming chatterbox, I sense a broad-minded, sympathetic person. Intellectually, he is a seeker, unafraid to cross over into another point of view, "to see how it looks from that side," he says. Although he seems to be popular, he doesn't really belong to any particular group or circle. He doesn't quite fit in, and I wonder if he ever feels like an outsider among his classmates.

I ask him one afternoon. We are leaning against the balcony outside a classroom; classes have finished for the day, and below us on the grass, students are gathering for a volleyball game.

"Yes. No. Sometimes." He chews the inside of his lip and touches the back of my hand lightly. "But it's lonely, isn't it, miss, not to think the way everyone else thinks." He smiles that peculiar smile that always makes me want to move closer, stay longer, know more.

I find myself wanting to talk with him about bigger things, Mr. Iyya and the question of beating, history, politics, religion. He listens, agrees, disagrees, tells me flat-out sometimes, "Miss, you are wrong there," and I realize I can say anything to him because he will argue back. It is an immense relief to talk in my own voice.

He remembers everything I tell him, and I am touched and flattered when he asks how my brother, Jason, is, or collects bits of Canadian news from magazines for me. He materializes in odd places, under the eaves of a shop, on the football ground at twilight. I begin to wonder if it is more than coincidence when I find him sitting at my favorite bend in the road. "What are you doing here, Tshewang?" I ask.

"Waiting for you," he says.

"No, really."

He smiles and I cannot tell one way or the other.

I begin to wonder every morning if today I will see him, and I am disappointed at nightfall if I haven't. I, too, have memorized small details: he likes to read late at night, he hates the cold, he doesn't know his real birth date, he has long, spatulate fingers but short, stubby thumbs.

It's a crush, I tell myself. A silly, passing infatuation. Get over it.

The days pass quickly, the rice growing higher in the paddies, the clouds thickening with the monsoon. I walk at dawn, when Kanglung is sunk in mist, the world softened and still in the slow listless rain. One morning, I meet him running with two of his friends. He is wearing a red bandanna to keep his hair out of his eyes on the ten-kilometer run uphill, and his shorts and tee shirt reveal a compact body with well-defined shoulders and arms, and a lot of smooth copper-colored skin wet with rain. We wave as we pass each other, and when he is out of sight, I stop in the middle of the road, put a cold, wet hand against my flushed cheek. I am shocked at the force, the physical density of my desire.

Mr. Chatterji helps me plant chilies among the roses and gladioli and weeds in my garden. He won't take the seedlings directly from my hand because they are a "hot" food and handing them to someone directly will result in an argument. I lay the plants on the ground, and he picks them up from there, popping them into the soil and sprinkling them with water. I put twelve chilies in my curry now, and eat ema datshi every day. "Just like a Bhutanese," Lopen Norbu says when I go to his house for dinner. "Now you need a Bhutanese husband." I shake my head vehemently, as if the thought had never crossed my mind.

Tshewang visits unexpectedly one Sunday morning. He sits uneasily at the edge of the divan, refusing my offers of coffee and tea.

Everything about him is in motion. He chews his nails, taps his feet, fiddles with his pen, and his eyes fly around the room. Our conversation is full of polite abdications, sorry go ahead, no what were you saying? Outside, in full view of the world, we talk effortlessly and endlessly. Inside, alone, we are unable to finish a single sentence. Well, this is a disaster, I think unhappily. Why is it all wrong? I feel thirteen again. He plucks up a magazine and then he is gone, completely absorbed in what he is reading. I lift a notebook from the pile I've been marking, but I cannot read a word with him sitting there. I consider his face and his hands, remembering his legs and the curve of his shoulders from the morning in the rain, wondering what would he do if I went over there right now and kissed him, wondering what kind of lover he would be.

He puts down the magazine and says, "Miss, can I borrow a book?"

I reach over and pull *One Hundred Years of Solitude* from the bookshelf and hold it out to him. "Okay, great," he says, shoving the book into his gho. "Well, I should get going."

"Okay." I want desperately, dangerously for him to stay, and I cannot wait for him to be gone.

At the door he stops, studying a class II C picture. I want to ask him what he is thinking, does he feel this powerful pull or not. Does he think of me the way I think of him. Say something, I think. Please. "Thanks, miss," he says and closes the door behind him.

Miss. Madam. Ma'am. I burst into tears.

Foreigners Can't Understand

Dini and I are asked to judge a debate about the role of women in Bhutanese society. The debate is not taken seriously, and the conclusion is that there is no gender problem in Bhutan. "What about the fact that there are five hundred male students and eighty female students at the college?" Dini asks. "How many women ministers are there? How many women dashos? How many women are elected to the national assembly?"

"And what about how the women on campus are treated?" I add. They are often hissed at and harassed when they get on stage to make a speech.

"There is no discrimination against women in Bhutan," a male debater reaffirms. "If women want to become ministers, they can. If they want to be elected to the national assembly, they can be. They just don't want to be."

"Why don't they want to be?"

He pauses to think. "Because they're busy with their families. Anyway, if they have any ideas they want raised, their husbands can do it. And when we hiss at the girls, we're only teasing them. They know that."

Dini leaves the auditorium in disgust.

I try to discuss this in one of the senior classes. "Let's define gender problem," I begin one morning.

"Is this in the syllabus?" someone asks from the back of the room.

"No, it's not in the syllabus," I answer, unruffled. "But I'm just curious about what constitutes a gender problem to you."

The answers are similar. The way women are treated in India. Widows made to throw themselves on their husband's funeral pyre.

Girl babies aborted, or left to die. Institutional barriers. Discrimination embedded in law. But none of this happens in Bhutan, they say. Therefore, there is no discrimination.

But there are other forms, more subtle but still very powerful, I begin.

A student interrupts. "The government says there is no discrimination against women in Bhutan. And the government must be knowing whether there is or isn't."

I stand silenced at the front of the class. If I persist, I will be contradicting the government. If I stay silent, I will implode. "Write me an essay on it," I say finally, knowing that I will not be able to read them.

I am just beginning to see how large the gap is between what I try to teach and the Bhutanese way of thinking and learning. I give what I think will be an inspiring lecture on Shelley's "Song to the Men of England" to my senior poetry class and the students object to the poem.

"We are not believing like this," one says. "We believe if you are born poor, that is your karma. It means you must have been very greedy in your last life."

"But the rich people in this poem, what about their karma? Are you saying they have a right to exploit the peasants?"

"No," another explains. "If they do all these things like in this poem, they will be reborn poor next time and will have to suffer. So there is no need for uprisings because karma will take care of everything."

"But what about helping to alleviate the suffering of others? As Mahayana Buddhists, aren't you supposed to be acting compassionately?"

Yes, they say, compassion is important, but they cannot see the link between compassion and working to change institutionalized injustices. Anyway, in Bhutan, the social system is handed down to us from our forefathers, one says finally. It is part of our traditional culture. We must preserve our traditions and culture.

And that is the end of that debate.

Like class II C, they want to memorize everything. They are

uncomfortable with ambiguity and keep asking, "But what's the real answer?"

"Why can't there be more than one answer?" I counter.

They shake their heads. For the exams, they say, there is only one right answer.

"But not for literature," I say. "Everything we read is open to interpretation."

"Please, madam," someone says. "If we don't pass English, we won't be promoted."

Mr. Bose, I have noticed, sits at the front of his class and reads from his yellowed notes while the students write frantically. There is no discussion, no room for other interpretations. I remember the kids in Pema Gatshel being hit for asking questions: questions insulted the teacher, the thinking went, because they implied the teacher had not done his or her job properly.

"I won't be insulted if you ask questions," I tell the students. "In fact, I'm insulted when you don't ask."

In private, they sometimes share their critical observations with me, but in public, they wear the smooth, untroubled face of conformity. I ask why they never express their doubts and criticisms openly, and they tell me this is not how things are done in Bhutan. Questions about how things work might be read as dissent. My own questions about the political situation are drawing more hostile answers from both sides. "I'm only asking," I say uneasily, knowing that I am both asking and telling, that my asking holds value judgments. One student tells me with uncharacteristic bluntness, "Foreigners can't understand. This is not their country. They should not get involved."

I turn it over and over in my mind one evening at Pala's, at the little table in the back corner, underneath bougainvillea and orchids. I am exhausted by the constant debate with myself. It is like walking a tightrope—I climb up and manage to balance for a short time, arms out, feet splayed, muscles tightened against the pull of gravity—yes, from here I can see how all values are culturally constructed. From an intellectual point of view, it's a fascinating place to be: here there are no universal standards or ethics, only endless constructions and points of view. But now that I am up here, I realize, there is no place to go, except back down, to my own side and point of view.

Amala brings out a mug of *changke,* a thick tangy drink made out of fermented rice. "Taste," she says. "Just now I am making."

"Thanks, Amala."

"No problem," she sings out as she goes back inside. It is her favorite phrase, acquired from the students. She complains that her English is "all broken" but I love the way she talks.

Tshewang sticks his head around the corner. "Hello, miss," he says softly.

I wave at him and pick up my pen. Go away, I think. I am too demoralized to talk, and after last Sunday's awkwardness, he is the last person I want to see.

"What's wrong, miss?"

"Nothing. I'm writing some letters."

"Can I sit here?" He pulls out a chair across from me.

"Isn't it time for your night study, Tshewang?"

He sits down anyway and waits, his eyes trained on me. "What is it, miss?"

I cannot resist the kindness in his voice and eyes. I tell him about my frustration in class over the students' reluctance to debate issues. "I just want them to talk," I say. "What's wrong with really debating the issue of gender in Bhutan?"

He considers this. "There's a time and a place for everything, miss. What good is it to say something if no one is ready to hear it?"

"Because silence feels like complicity and cowardice to me."

He pulls a purple blossom off the bougainvillea that runs along the railing beside the table and holds it in his palm as if he were weighing it. His face is very serious. "Miss, I think you should know. . . . The students like you, you're a good teacher and all, but some of your comments . . . about political things . . . might not always be appreciated."

It is tactfully put, but the frown lines between his eyes convey the real message. The bells for night study reach us dimly. "Yes," I sigh.

"I know. But it's hard to stay quiet when you feel strongly about something."

He pushes back his chair but does not get up. "You know, miss, a person can be completely right about something . . ."

"But?"

"A person can be completely right about something but still not have the right to say it," he says.

"So in your wonderfully diplomatic Bhutanese way, you're saying you also think I should shut up and mind my own business?" It will hurt to hear it from him. I put it harshly, hoping he will say no.

He hesitates. "Yes, miss," he says gently.

It hurts all the more for the compassion in his face. "Well, thanks for saying it, Tshewang."

"Good night, miss," he says, and places the purple flower in my hand.

When he is gone, I lay my head on my arms and send silent questions out into the night. Where did you come from. How did you get to be the way you are. Do you know that I have never met anyone like you in my life.

Lorna comes to visit for a weekend. Over supper at Pala's she tells me the latest crisis at her school, a science teacher who is convinced that other people are listening to his thoughts through some kind of "frequency device" implanted in his head. "We sent him to the Basic Health Unit," she says, "and they gave him aspirin and sent him home. His wife is really scared."

Tshewang winks as he passes and flashes my copy of *One Hundred Years of Solitude*. The sight of him makes me flush.

"Who is that?" Lorna asks.

"No one," I say, putting my head on the table. "Oh, Lorna, I think I should go home."

"He's cute," she says.

"And smart. He reads. He's funny. He's—"

"Your student."

"Well, technically he's not my student."

"Don't you 'technical' me," Lorna says. "Didn't you learn your lesson the last time?"

"Yes," I say miserably. I have told her about the student I slept with after the winter holidays. "But this is different."

"Does he feel the same way about you?"

"I have no idea, Lorna, and it's a good thing because it's the only thing that makes me behave myself. I am this close to falling in love with him."

"Well, stop," Lorna says, without much conviction.

The Map

O n an all-day walk through villages and rice paddies around Kanglung, I pick my way around the spur of a mountain, through a forest of oak and rhododendron, and emerge in a glen with a brook curling through it. The mountain wall rises up behind, and all around are trees; it is a completely sheltered and sheltering place. The sun lies thickly, like honey, over the long green grass, and I feel warm and sleepy and inexplicably content. I sit and take out my journal to describe the place, but the pen in my hand feels heavy, and I stretch out in the grass in the warm yellow light instead and sink into an intensely calm and pleasurable state, a kind of golden dreamplace, although I am not asleep, and I don't know how much time passes before I sit up, blinking. I have no idea what I've been thinking. I leave reluctantly, telling myself I can return tomorrow.

But the next day, I cannot find the glen. I walk for hours until I realize I am lost. It didn't seem possible to get lost; there are only two directions, down and up. But I do not recognize the houses or chortens I pass, and the path falls into shadow as the sun lowers itself into the western valleys. I keep walking up, certain that I will eventually hit the road. A wind rouses itself and bits of mist float past. The mist thickens as I ascend until I am walking through a soft, cold, dense fog. Finally I hit tarmac, except this is not the road. It is a runway. I know where I am now: I have heard about this out-of-service airstrip at the army camp in Yongphula, above Kanglung. It has not been used since the Indo–Chinese border skirmishes in 1962, because planes had a tendency to crash into the side of the mountain at the far end of it. In the twilight, swathed in mist, it is a strange and desolate place. Two dark figures emerge from the fog; as they approach, I see that they are

Bhutanese soldiers. Behind them they are pulling a dog, its jaws muzzled with a heavy rope. Its back legs look crippled, and its eyes have a yellow glare. The soldiers make biting motions with their hands, and I understand that the dog is rabid. I hurry back down the path until I come to the road.

I try again and again, counting the landmarks from the first visit. There was a waterfall, yes, and I passed a house just like this one, and then I went up but here the path goes down. . . .

I begin a map of the area, drawing the college buildings, the clock tower, the pine trees, the bridge. The villages around, connected by paths. Lopen Norbu's house. The old lhakhang and the village above. I draw in streams and the river where the students immersed the statue of Durga last year, boulders, a tree full of brown monkeys near the prayer wall above Kanglung. The prayer flags at the bend in the road. The place where I saw a red panda, sunning itself above a tangled bamboo thicket. And places which have revealed themselves, a small cave high up in a rock wall, uncovered when a cloud moved and the light shifted, a waterfall appearing as the mist drifted away. I think that if I finish the map, I will find the glen again. There's only so much physical space here, it's simply a matter of tracing out the paths and filling in the landmarks.

I remember things from my childhood, a love of secret places, places inside of places. I remember searching for a secret passageway in my grandparents' house, tapping on walls, squeezing past boxes and empty suitcases to explore the back of closets. "There are no secret passageways in this house," my grandmother said firmly. But I was certain there was a way to go through the mirror into a different world, or to fall through an invisible doorway into another time. Here, the folds and pleats of the mountains give me that same feeling, the places that have been forgotten in forests and the far corners of valleys. There are ruins of houses, abandoned villages, skeletons of terraces overgrown with green, and I long to know why the people left, and how long ago, and what conflict or disease sent them away. There are stories everywhere.

The map becomes its own place. I have started too small, I cannot fit everything in, and I must draw bubbles along the borders with miniature maps and symbols inside, connected to the main map with curly lines but one curly line becomes a Bhutanese cloud and another becomes a mountain, and then I give in and color in a lake that does not exist, and a river flowing out of the mouth of Tashigang Dzong, and stars wherever there is room. I look up from my map, out over the valley, north to the sharp peaks, south to the blue-shadowed ridges, up to the darkening sky with its watermelon-wedge moon and a handful of stars. My map has become a conflagration of space and memory and desire, charting the exact space where place and the experience of the place meet.

D ini and I are invited to a dance by the students in our third-year
class, a "jam session," it is called, held in the dining hall on a
Saturday night. "We don't have to be chaperones, do we?" Dini asks,
and the students laugh. "No, ma'am," they say. "Just come and dance."
We promise we will.

I put on my least teacherly clothes, a straight denim skirt and white
tee shirt, and walk over to Dini's. She offers me a shot of Dragon
Rum—"protection against an evening of Milli Vanilli," she says.
"We're still going to feel like chaperones, you know."

"Dini, do you ever feel attracted to any of the students?"

"Only twenty or thirty of them," she says, and I laugh.

In the dining hall, the tables and chairs have been pushed against
the wall, and crêpe-paper streamers and balloons are taped to the ceiling and pillars. The students, in jeans, miniskirts and leather jackets,
dance in pairs and large circles to unidentifiable dance music pounding out of a row of mismatched speakers. Two entrepreneurs sell boxes
of mango juice and plates of chips by the door. Tshewang, dressed all
in black, slides off his chair beside the DJ. "Miss," he says, bowing formally, "would you care to dance?"

We thread our way across the floor, sticking to the outer edges
because he dances as he talks, tirelessly, with frequent leaps and
bounds. He keeps closing up the distance I try to leave between us.
"Sorry, miss," he says, laughing, when we have danced ourselves into
a corner. "Would you like to sit down? Shall I get you a drink?" I slide
onto a chair against the wall, grateful for the sharp breeze from the
window behind. Tshewang returns with a box of warm mango juice
and angles his chair closer to mine. All along the left side of my body

I feel the warmth of him, and I think I should move my chair a few inches away for the sake of decorum but I cannot bring myself to move at all. A slow number comes on, and the floor clears except for three or four brave couples. Tshewang explains that they are officially "paired up," a fact which they must try to keep from the principal. "When he finds out, he'll call them to his office and make them promise to break up." His hand slides lightly down my forearm, pulling my hand out of my lap, and he holds my fingers in the tiny dark space between us. All I can think is: yes. I want only this moment, and nothing beyond matters. My body is a cold, dark shell except for my hand. Life begins at my wrist, my palm pulses gently, my fingertips glow like embers.

A strip of orange crêpe paper unravels to the floor in front of us, bringing me out of my trance. I have no idea what Tshewang is thinking, if this is merely a flirtatious diversion for him or if his desires go farther, but I feel sure he would be shocked at the extent of mine. I am too old to be perched here with streamers coming down around me, listening to some sappy Air Supply number, aching to make love with someone who isn't even allowed to date and who keeps calling me "miss." I pull my hand back into my lap. "How old are you, Tshewang?" I blurt out. I had not planned to ask it aloud, but I hope he says seventeen. That'll teach me.

"I'm twenty, miss."

"Oh yes. I—I remember when I was twenty," I say, putting a squint in my voice to make it sound like an event lost in the mists. "Well, I should find Dini. Thanks for the dance, Tshewang."

He looks at me carefully, and then he leans very close and puts his mouth to my ear. "It's up to you, miss," he says, and his fingers brush my hair away from my earlobe, burning my skin.

It is me who is shocked. I stare at him, unable to think. "We can't," I say, panicking.

"I know," he says automatically.

He is still close enough to kiss, and for a second, I think we will. Out of the corner of my eye, I notice a couple watching us curiously. "Tshewang, people are looking at us."

"I don't care."

"Then you have no more sense than a—a goose," I say helplessly. He laughs. I don't know if I am thrilled or alarmed by his audacity.

"Let's go find Dini," I say, standing up. He walks with me across the floor to where Dini is sitting on a crate, trying to convince the DJ to change the music. "Thanks, Tshewang," I say again. I dare not look at him.

"No, thank *you*, miss."

The next day, I walk the nineteen kilometers into Tashigang, praying fervently that Lorna or Leon will be in for the weekend. I have to talk to them about this. It has gone too far, I know that, and yet my strongest regret is that I didn't let it go farther. Tashigang is humid, and the sky is clotted with heavy grey cloud; the guest house smells of damp and insecticide, and there is no water. I have to haul buckets from the tap across the street for a bath and then I drink beer in the Puen Soom. Karma, the proprietor, stands at the door, watching the rain fall. "Today your friends not coming," he says. "Too much rain maybe."

The next morning I shoot out of bed, woken by a sound that I quickly identify as screaming. Leaping to the window, I see a wall of water and mud come roaring down the mountain, swallowing the bridge, uprooting trees, washing away latrines along the riverbank. Shopkeepers are fleeing up the hillside with their children and wooden cash boxes under their arms. I rush out, but the flood is already subsiding into a thick brown torrent. On the steps of a shop overlooking the river, a tearful mother is alternately scolding and kissing her drenched children. It is still raining, and I walk through mud and debris to the riverbank to watch the water churning mud and roots and leaves. Four students from the junior high school join me, pointing out the place where the barbershop used to be, now a wet muddy patch. "Lucky the barber was out having tea," one says. They tell me that this is the second of three floods predicted by a lama. The first flood happened before they were born, in the 1950s, and wiped out the lower bazaar. After that, a different lama came and performed a puja to protect the town. "See, miss, that picture?" They point to the eaves of a shop roof, under which a painting of Guru Rimpoché has been placed so that it faces the river. "The lama was putting that picture and there was no flood. But last year that lama died, and now just see, the flood again has come."

"This time no one was lost," one of them adds. "But next time will be very bad, the lama was telling like that."

I return to Kanglung, determined to end this thing with Tshewang. The more I think about it, the more disturbed I am. I realize I am actually angry, and on the long, sweaty walk uphill to the college, I try to figure out why. He took me by surprise, for one thing, speaking my secret thoughts when I had just decided he hadn't a clue what they were. I am angry at myself for misjudging him, for thinking him naïve. I am also afraid. He has brought the thing between us into the open, moving it from the realm of hopeful fantasy into the real world of decisions and consequences. All along I have been longing to know his feelings and now, when he has made them perfectly clear, I want to grab him and shake him and tell him, "It is not up to me!" I do not want it to be up to me. Yes: there is a powerful attraction and an understanding between us. But: he is a student, I am a lecturer. Real lecturers do not etc., etc. I have already made one mistake, although it seems insignificant in comparison to this. With the anonymous encounter at the beginning of the year, I put my reputation at risk, but my heart was not even remotely involved. With this relationship, I have no idea where my heart would take me.

Belief

At Pala's one morning for breakfast, I watch Amala throw buckets of water at the pack of snarling dogs that has made its home outside her kitchen. "What to do with them," she says. "Always fighting and all night barking."

Dogs are a problem all over Bhutan, especially in towns, wherever there are institutions with kitchens—schools and hospitals and army camps. The packs belong to no one and to everyone. It would be a sin in Buddhism to round them all up and kill them, since all sentient beings are considered sacred, even these horrid, diseased, deformed dogs.

"Now I will do something," Amala says grimly.

Three days later, I look up from my lunch to see her talking earnestly to a truck driver. He nods and begins rounding up the dogs, using jute sacks to pick them up and toss them, yelping and howling, into the back of his truck. When all the dogs are in, Amala hands him two hundred ngultrum, and he drives off.

"Where's he taking them?" I ask.

"Wamrong," she says.

"Why Wamrong?"

"Too far for them to walk back." She smiles into her tea.

But the next day, the truck returns. The driver leaps out and unlatches the back door. The dogs pour out, still yelping and howling, and settle themselves in front of Amala's kitchen. The driver is smiling broadly; he can hardly believe his luck. The good merchants of Wamrong gave him another two hundred rupees to take all the dogs back.

I am spending more time with Amala, who is a fountain of stories and local histories. She tells me about *pows,* people who can go visit your relatives in the afterlife, and oracles who speak through a chosen person. Amala tells me about her sister, Sonam, who returned home after many years in the West, bringing with her an anthropologist who wanted to see an oracle in action. They went to the family temple in Sakteng, where the man who could summon the oracle was called. He slumped to the floor in a trance and rose as the oracle took possession, speaking in a stern and unearthly voice. The oracle would not answer the anthropologist's questions because she was of a different faith, but had a few things to say to Sonam, accusing her of staying away from home too long and neglecting her father's temple. The oracle picked up a sword and swung it around wildly, and Sonam was terrified. Finally, it told her to throw a ceremonial white scarf around the central statue at the altar. The way the scarf fell would determine her fate. Sonam threw the scarf, which landed properly, and the oracle was placated.

Amala is surprised that I believe in the oracle. "Foreign peoples is only believing if they see with their own eyes," she says. "Not seeing, then not believing."

"But Amala, lots of people in the West believe in things they can't see," I say. "People believe in god, and ghosts, and theories that no one can prove."

"But not in Bhutanese things," she says. "They are only believing in their own things they can't see."

I think of the European woman I met having lunch here some time ago. She had been in Bhutan for three months with an international aid agency. "The Bhutanese are so superstitious, don't you find?" she had asked me. "Everything happens because of ghosts or demons."

"But Christianity has the Holy Ghost," I argued. "And the Devil."

"That's different," she said. She didn't explain how. "I really feel sorry for them. So much of their faith is based on fear."

"At least in Buddhism, hell is not forever," I countered. "I can't think of anything more frightening than the idea of eternal hell after only one lifetime." The woman ended the conversation by paying for her lunch and leaving. I hadn't meant to insult her faith. I wanted only to point out what Amala has just put so succinctly. Being in Bhutan has shown me how strong this tendency is, to think that what we believe is real and valid and what everyone else believes is fearful nonsense and superstition.

I have finished most of the Buddhist books from the library, moving from basic texts to esoteric writings such as *The Tibetan Book of Great Liberation* and back again. The first sermon of the Buddha still stuns me with its clarity; I read it and feel the world grow still and quiet around me. I read teachings on meditation and wisdom, keeping in mind Nima's summation that belief without practice is useless. Buddhist practice offers systematic tools for anyone to work out their own salvation. Here, the Buddha said, you've got your mind, the source of all your problems, but also the source of your liberation. Use it. Look at your life. Figure it out.

The teachings on compassion are particularly important to daily practice. Compassion grows out of the recognition that all sentient beings—friends, enemies, complete strangers—want the same thing. We all want to be happy, and yet again and again, we act in ways which bring suffering to ourselves, and to others, and through others back to ourselves. Seeing through the superficial differences to this core of sameness is the great equalizer, stripping away the mask of unique personal identity and revealing us one and all as simple, wanting, fearful, hopeful, bewildered beings. It is an enormous daily mental challenge to see Mr. Matthew not as my enemy but simply as my neighbor, wanting exactly what I want, and being mistaken, just like me, about how to get it.

According to Buddhism, if someone insults or hurts you, you should see their behavior as an opportunity to learn about the nature of your pride and attachment. Buddhism demands that you not only love your enemy, but see him or her as your greatest teacher. Instead of despising Mr. Matthew, I could be using each encounter with him to examine my ego and break down my own arrogance.

Buddhism requires that I take on the terrifying responsibility for myself; I am the author of my own suffering, and my own deliverance. And yet it also requires very little—only that I open my eyes right here, where I am standing, that I simply pay attention.

I ask Amala how one becomes a Buddhist, is there a ceremony, what are the requirements. She tells me to go to a lama. I feel almost ready.

Tshewang returns *One Hundred Years of Solitude* through a friend, with "thanks" scribbled on a scrap of paper inside. We have not spoken since the dance. I think this is his way of telling me he realizes that we have to stop. The unadorned note strengthens my resolve to break the spell between us. I debate the idea of discussing it with him, I write letters to him in my head. *Dear Tshewang, I am writing so that we can close what we have opened by mistake between us, and I want you to know how sorry I am that . . .* that what? That I did not kiss you the night of the dance? That I said we can't when actually I meant we can? That's what I'm really sorry about. No, it is better to leave it entirely alone. We need a complete cessation.

But I miss our disorderly discussions and wild debates, I miss that sexual charge between us, I miss the way his eyes curl up when he laughs. Without these encounters to hope for, my days are steadier and more productive, and entirely without joy.

Enter Macduff

We have finished reading *Macbeth* in the Zoo, and the students want to perform it. They have divided themselves up into groups and assigned themselves scenes, and in the evenings, I watch them rehearse on stage. They start off earnestly, standing stiffly and declaiming, but by the end they are doubled over in laughter. They are at ease with one another, shouting encouragement and insults and advice, and I think that if there are times when they forget who is north and who south, this is one of them. After rehearsal, we sometimes sit outside the auditorium, talking quietly before the bell at eight o'clock calls them back to their hostels. Night falls softly, and it is easier to talk in the dark. They remember their best and worst teachers, summer and winter holidays; they remember the first time they saw a vehicle, the first time they saw a video, the first time they met each other at boarding schools in Samtse or Khaling or Thimphu; they remember who could make even the strictest teacher laugh aloud, remember that time we got caught stealing maize from the lopen's garden, and I cannot imagine then that they actually dislike and mistrust each other. They have grown up together, and can speak each other's languages and sing each other's songs. They have a shared personal history, and perhaps this will in the end count for more than the historical divisions and facts and allegations.

On the political front, there has been no news for several weeks. Nothing in the *Kuensel,* which doesn't mean anything, but also nothing from the students. I start to believe that the crisis is over. Perhaps there is dialogue now, perhaps there will be accommodation and understanding on both sides.

The students are ready for their final performances. They have gone to great effort with costumes and makeup and special effects, and it is a travesty. "Is this a dagger that I see before me," Macbeth asks the plank of wood hanging from the stage curtains, and the alarm from a digital watch is set off to give the impression of urgency, but the persistent beepbeep flusters Macbeth who tries to wrest the watch away from the special effects team and there is a scuffle with Lady Macbeth who owns the watch; Great Birnam Wood misses its cue and there are leaves and branches everywhere; enter Macduff with Macbeth's head, a wig of black yak hair, and I laugh until I cry.

In the library the next morning, a crowd of students is pressed up against the front desk, trying to read a single copy of the *Kuensel.* I ask what's going on, and the *Kuensel* is passed silently over to me. On June 2, the anniversary of the King's coronation, in the industrial town of Gomtu in southern Bhutan, a jute sack was found near a petrol pump, containing the severed heads of two southern Bhutanese men. A letter in the sack accused the men of cooperating with the Royal Government and betraying their own people.

Ranjana, a class XII student, is led out of the library in tears. "One of them was her uncle," someone tells me.

I pass the newspaper back and leave the library. I feel sick. I stand on the balcony outside the staff room. In the fields below the college, women are weeding the rice paddies. I try to think about this labor that will feed the family, these works and days of hands, the feeling of mud between the toes, water up to the ankles, the sun on the back of the neck—it is useless, the image will not allow me entrance, and I am sent back to the mental picture of two heads in a jute sack. It seems impossible, something I have read somewhere else ("enter Macduff with Macbeth's head"), it cannot be happening here.

I force myself to read the rest of the *Kuensel* article. For the first time, the arrests of last year are mentioned. Between October and December 1989, forty-two people were arrested for anti-national activities. Thirty-nine were later released, and a general amnesty of two months was announced to enable those who had fled the country to return. A group calling itself the People's Forum for Human Rights announced that it wants to divide southern Bhutan into a separate political entity.

A northern student tells me he is leaving school to join the militia. "To fight the aunties," he says.

"The aunties?" I repeat, bewildered, and then realize he is talking about the anti-nationals. "These southerners," he explains.

"Not all southerners are anti-nationals," I say quietly.

"You don't know, miss. You don't know what they are."

Two schools in southern Bhutan are attacked and set aflame. A group of armed men attack a truck and force the driver to take off his gho. Previously, southern Bhutanese found out of national dress were fined by the Dzongkhag authorities. Now, southern Bhutanese found wearing national dress are stripped by "anti-nationals."

The time for talking and listening has disappeared, the opportunity growing smaller and smaller until it snapped shut altogether. There will only be rhetoric now, posturing and lying and violence. I want to step out sideways. I do not want to be a witness to the inevitable.

I am cleaning the bookshelf one evening in an attempt to avoid the pile of marking that awaits me. I open *One Hundred Years of Solitude* and Tshewang's thank-you note flutters out. On the other side is written LOVE IN THE TIME OF CHOLERA. I see the word "love" and I think: maybe this was the message I was supposed to respond to. Maybe this termination has been all my doing. The hand that has been holding my heart unclenches, and I can breathe deeply and it doesn't hurt. Then I crush the paper up. It is a title, not a message. What next? I wonder. Messages through a frequency device implanted in my head? I will put this desire into a stone. I will seal it up. I will make the right effort.

I make the right effort and it makes me miserable. It rains every night, and every morning the sun breaks hot and relentless through the dissipating mist. "Good for the farmers," Mr. Fantome tells me when I visit him in his garden, "good for all green growing things."

Everything swells wildly, and the forests glow eerily with gigantic ferns and luminous underbrush. *In the midst of the rainy season,* I write in my journal, *I have driven myself into this dry scorched flat place. Desire has led me to this place where there is nothing to drink or eat. I do not know how to lead myself out. I have never been so unhappy.*

Yurung

Leon invites me to his new posting in Yurung, a village in the Pema Gatshel valley. I stop at Pema Gatshel Junior High School on the way, but the kids have all gone home for the summer break. I leave a packet of letters and crayons for my former students and walk down to Gypsum, where I cross the river twice, thrice and begin to ascend to Yurung, except somehow, in the hot sun at the bottom of the valley, I have got turned around and I am actually walking back up the mountain to Pema Gatshel. A farmer turns me around. Yurung, when I finally reach it, is the prettiest village I have seen yet. The houses are clustered close together, separated by low stone walls and bramble fences and kitchen gardens, and willow and cypress line the stream that rushes through the middle. I am relieved to be in a village again, I am relieved to be away from my articulate and unreasonable students. I am relieved to be away from the possibility of meeting Tshewang and the necessity of avoiding him, the laborious battle against my heart's desire, but I cannot bring myself to tell this to Leon. I suspect that I do not want to be talked out of it for good. Somewhere in me, hope is hiding. "I don't want to think about the Situation," I say. "I just want to sit here on your front steps and watch the cows and chickens and the children. Don't ask me anything, I don't want to talk about it."

The neighborhood women show up the next morning with bottles of arra to welcome me. The arra has been cooked with butter and fried eggs, which does little to make it more palatable. We sit on the kitchen floor, drinking, but I have forgotten too much Sharchhop to participate in the conversation. After several mornings and evenings with them, however, the language returns, and they attribute my increasing fluency to the potency of their brew.

I spend a good part of each day wandering through the village, up to the temple, down to the school, across to a ridge where I sit under the prayer flags, drinking in the green of the valley below, the flowing clean spaces around me, and I thank whatever force or god or karmic link has brought me here. *Namé samé kadin chhé,* thanks beyond the sky and the earth. This is the Bhutan that I love. It seems impossible here that heads can be cut off and left in jute sacks. And yet, I know it is wrong, dishonest to separate the two things, the splendor of rural Bhutan and the political situation. Bhutan is a real place, with a real history, in which real conflicts lead to real upheaval, the real suffering of real people. As much as I would like it to be, it is not a hidden valley.

I meet the teachers at Ray's school, a mix of southern, eastern and northern Bhutanese, and Leon invites them back to his house for "Canadian drinks" one evening. In the flickering light of one candle stub, we mix up glasses of lemon squash and rum and hand them out. The teachers sip their drinks reluctantly, and adamantly refuse our offer of seconds. I think they are being polite until Leon lights more candles, and we see that we've given them mustard oil instead of rum.

We walk over to Tsebar, up to the ridge and along a mountaintop in the warm sunlight and down along a wooded slope. A thick mist squeezes its way through the trees, and the forest becomes eerie, all silent fog and shadow and hanging tangled dripping green. We are in Leech Forest. At first we stop to pull them off, but they drop from the trees and somersault off rocks, and for every one we remove, three more find their way on board, and finally we just run, clawing at branches and vines and gasping, until we are out again in a sunny meadow, where we sit and pluck them off and mop up blood with handkerchiefs. "They're clever little buggers," Leon says. "They release an anesthetic and an anti-coagulant when they latch on. You don't even know they're there." In Tsebar, we have arra and bangchang with Jangchuk and Pema, and I try to imagine Jane waking up somewhere in England, knowing that Bhutan is impossibly far away. I try to imagine myself waking up in Canada, knowing that Bhutan is closed, finished, over, and the dark line of the mountains against the dawn, the million billion trillion stars in the bowl of the sky, the faces of my students, now a memory and a grief. Leaving will be like waking from a dream, I think, the most intense and wonderful dream, knowing you'll never be able to dream it again.

The only way to avoid waking is to avoid leaving. I will not leave here until I have lived here thoroughly, until it seeps into me, into blood, bone, cell, until I am full of it and changed by it, and maybe not even then.

I tell this to Leon. He has just finished *Kiss of the Spider Woman,* and now he reads me the last line. "This dream is short but this dream is happy."

But I want it to be more.

Boils

I am marking homework in the staff room one morning when Mr. Bose sits down beside me, clears his throat, and informs me that one of my trial-exam questions is "wrong."

"What do you mean 'wrong'?"

"That business about write the letter Lady Macbeth writes in the sleepwalking scene."

"What's wrong with it?"

"What's wrong with it!" He looks dangerously close to a stroke. "I'll tell you what's wrong with it! It's not the kind of question they'll get asked on their final exam! You are not preparing them for their final exam!"

"But the questions they get on their final exams are ridiculous. 'Summarize Act I of the play.' I don't care if they can recite Act I from memory, I want them to have their own thoughts about the play."

"Never mind their own thoughts about the play! Can they answer the final exam questions? That's what you should be concerned about," Mr. Bose says, wagging a finger. "I'm going to have to monitor your work."

"Mr. Bose," I say furiously, "never tell me how to teach my class again." In a second, my anger destroys all the calm I have built up through a week of progressive meditation exercises. It breaks over me, and I indulge in it, can you believe the nerve of him, who does he think he is, etc., etc., until I feel thoroughly poisoned by it.

The sky weeps and wipes its face on the mountains. My legs break out in blisters and boils. The students tell me boils are caused by "impure blood," and if you get one, you will get nine. I have had three so far. One of my students, Kumar, develops a strange skin condition and is hospitalized in Tashigang. His bed is in an open ward, and two of his classmates stay with him, sleeping on the floor beside the bed at night, bringing his meals and arguing with the doctor over his treatment. "These college students," the doctor tells me wearily. "They think they know everything."

Kumar's face is thin and peaked. The rash makes his skin look like sandpaper. He says the hospital is not so bad, "except at night, miss, it is impossible to sleep. Everyone is groaning and praying."

On the way out, I pass by a man sitting on the stairs. A large chunk of his leg is missing, and I can see the glimmer of bone at the base of the wound. He sits quietly, waiting for someone to come and tend to him. I had meant to ask a doctor about my boils, but they seem silly now.

Everyone has them. Another student, Tashi, holds a clean handkerchief over the large angry boil on his cheek throughout class. When I pass him in the hallway the next day, I do not recognize him. "It's me, miss," he says. "Tashi." His face is swollen beyond recognition, and he has trouble speaking.

Early the next morning, the college peon knocks on my door with a notice. One of the students has died in the night, and all classes are canceled. I see a group of his classmates climbing up the embankment toward my house, and I know it was Tashi. They tell me the infection went to his brain; they took him to the hospital in Tashigang but it was too late. They wait while I put on a kira, and I follow them to the temple where Tashi's body, covered in white scarves, is laid out beneath a white canvas canopy. The Dzongkha lopens are leading the prayers, a recitation of the *Tibetan Book of the Dead,* and two students sit by Tashi's side. A plate of food has been placed beside him. His classmates will take turns sitting with him until his family arrives for the cremation. I sit with the students, the prayers rising and falling around me, and try to pray but I cry instead. "You should try not cry, ma'am," Chhoden tells me, squeezing my hand. "We say that it makes it harder for the spirit to leave, if people cry."

It takes Tashi's family three days to make the journey from their village. For three days, his classmates continue their vigil in shifts, never leaving the body alone. Two of Tashi's friends have to prepare the body for the cremation. This includes washing the body and breaking the bones to force it into a fetal position. The body is laid upon the pyre and covered with scarves and Tashi's best gho. After a long prayer and many offerings to the corpse, the wood is lit. But the body does not burn properly, and the lama heading the ceremony says it is because of the spirit's attachment to this world. Tashi's classmates bring his flute and his paints from his room and cast them onto the fire, admonishing his spirit. "You're dead now. See, all your things are gone. We don't want you here. Go now."

"How awful," I say to Chhoden.

She shakes her head. "No, madam. We have to tell like that. If we show how much we loved him, his spirit won't want to leave and then it will be stuck here. It has to know it's dead." She says some people know immediately that they are dead, but others just wander around, sitting down with their family to eat, wondering why no one will speak to them. "That's why we leave food out near the body, so that the person will not feel so bad."

More wood is added to the fire and the cloth covering the body shrivels up. Tashi's brother walks around the pyre with a bottle, pouring water into the dust. "The water is offered to the dead person, for the terrible thirst the fire causes," Chhoden says. Everyone stands and watches the flames, and what I thought would be unbearably gruesome is merely a sad fact: the flesh melts away and the bones turn grey and crumble, falling into the cinders at the bottom of the pyre. Someday that will be me, I think.

There is none of the sanitized grief that I associate with death in my own culture. Tears are hidden not for the sake of appearances—there is no need to hold up well in the eyes of the community—but for the sake of the dead, so that they will be able to leave behind this lifetime. Grief is everywhere, in the stunned expressions of Tashi's friends, in his mother's collapsed face, but there is also a stoic acceptance.

"Everyone dies," Nima tells me after the cremation. "This is what the Buddha taught." And he relates the story of the mustard seed: a woman, deranged with grief at the death of her small child, goes to the Buddha and begs him to restore her child to life. He tells her that he will, if she can bring him a handful of mustard seeds from a house in the village where no one has ever died. The woman goes from door to door, and although everyone is willing to give her a handful of mustard seeds, she can find no household that has not known death. Realizing the universality of death, she brings her son to the cremation ground, and returns to become a disciple of the Buddha.

"But the fact that everyone has to die does not make it any less sad," I tell Nima. "Because each person is unique, their personality and relationships and life."

But Nima says, "Not so unique, miss. Everyone is born, everyone grows up, everyone wants the same thing—to be happy, and everyone avoids the same things—pain and unhappiness, and in the end, everyone dies, isn't it?"

"Yes, but within those parameters, every individual's life is unique and precious, what they think and how they react."

"But see, miss. If I think how many countless times I have been reborn in this world, we say millions of times, then how many times have I been happy already? How many times have I married and had children and fulfilled all my goals, and how many times have I suffered and died? Then I think I must have experienced everything by now, but I am still here, so I have not learned anything. Then I feel tired, miss. I feel tired of this life and I think I should become a monk and go to a cave and find a way out of all this coming and going in circles."

Later, in meditation, these words come back to me. It is like something opening in my head, too fast for words. *I must have experienced everything by now, but I am still here, so I have not learned anything.* In a moment, I grasp it. Not the Buddhist theory of the self, how there is no essential Jamie Zeppa, how she is only a collection of changing conditions, attributes and desires common to all sentient beings, but the experience of that fact. Everything falls away. It is the experience of pure freedom, a momentary glimpse of how it would be—to be in the world and not be attached to it, to move through it, experiencing it and letting it go. It is impossible to put the feeling, the certainty, into words, but later, I know that this is the moment I became a Buddhist.

I come out of the meditation and the feeling dissipates slowly, dissolving into the common objects about me, straw mat, wax candle, tin cup. I am left with only the shell of the experience, the words. It was like this, like that, it was like things falling away. I feel forlorn, inconsolable—I want the feeling itself back, and then it occurs to me that I have only identified the goal. Attaining it will be a lifelong task. Not all my questions about Buddhism have been answered, but I am ready now to make a commitment to this path.

A week later, at a puja at the old lhakhang above the college, I stand in line behind mothers who have come to ask a visiting lama for blessings and names for their babies. The lama is a young man with a spiky haircut and John Lennon glasses, but the women in the line assure me that he is a very important Rimpoché. And he knows English, they tell me, so I am very lucky. I watch as he touches the forehead of each child, pausing to think of a name. When it is my turn, I prostrate and explain what I want. The lama says that to become a Buddhist, I must take refuge vows. "You take refuge in the Three Jewels," he says, "the Buddha, the Dharma, the Sangha—the Buddha, his teachings, and the religious community." He explains that taking refuge is the first step to Buddhist practice; you acknowledge that refuge cannot be found in worldly things, all of which are impermanent and incapable of leading to true liberation, and that Buddhism is your true spiritual home. It does not mean you give up living in the world and go into a monastery, the lama explains. That is the path for some people, yes, but every person has their own path. When you take the refuge vows, you commit yourself to following the Buddhist path in your daily life. You endeavor to practice nonharming in body, speech and mind, you endeavor to follow the Noble Eightfold Path.

From his briefcase, he takes a little booklet which explains the vows and the refuge prayer, and on the cover he prints a Buddhist name:

Kunzang Drolma. *Kunzang* means "all good," and *Drolma* is the Bhutanese name for Tara, the goddess of compassion.

Later that afternoon, Nima helps me set up an altar on the mantle in my sitting room. In front of pictures of the Buddha and Guru Rimpoché, he puts seven small silver bowls, which he fills with water. "We offer water because even the poorest farmer can afford to offer it," he explains. "But in our minds, we imagine that we are offering food, water for drinking and water for washing, flowers, incense, light, and perfumed oils." I must fill the water cups every morning and empty them before nightfall, he says, as an offering to the gods and to all sentient beings. Then he shows me how to twist cotton batten into a wick for the butter lamp. When he is gone, I sit cross-legged in front of the altar and watch the flame burning steady and strong above the little lamp until my mind feels quiet. I am grateful that I could take the refuge vows outside such an old and sacred temple with a Bhutanese lama who could speak English. It is apt and beautiful and undoubtedly auspicious, but the small ceremony was only a reinforcement of the powerful experience I had in meditation. In the same way that marriage vows are not the marriage, the refuge ceremony is not the practice. The practice is the practice, I think. For the rest of my life. On a small card on the altar, I have copied a verse from the Buddhist canon: "Mindfulness is the abode of eternal life, thoughtlessness the abode of death. Those who are mindful do not die. The thoughtless are as if dead already."

A Flux of Light

Perhaps enough time has passed. Perhaps it is safe now to talk. By some mutual unspoken agreement, we approach each other again, cautiously at first, shyly, exchanging neutral greetings, but within a few weeks we are back to our old rushing conversations, and with the conversations, the same old desire rises. We never mention the night of the jam session, but nothing has changed between us. I see him outside the office, waiting for the mail, or with his big blue mug and a book, on his way to the student mess for tea. "Miss, have you read that Marquez story about the sea of lost time?" he calls out, or "Miss, what's the oldest language in the world?" And I say yes, or I don't know, and we stand there, in the hall or on the lawn, and I feel the college buildings shrink around us, bells and voices echoing dimly. I always tell him more than I mean to, whole passages of my life come spilling out. He listens and then from inside his gho, he pulls out small presents: a feather, a picture of white Tara, a mango, definitions copied neatly onto pieces of paper: *aleatory—depending on random choice; a lumen is a unit of flux of light; infrangible—unbreakable.*

There is no privacy, no place or time to talk alone. I do not invite him to my house and he does not come on his own. We rely on these meetings in open corridors, trying to finish one last thought before the bell rings. They are not always happy or satisfying conversations. On the subject of the Situation, for example, we end up talking in circles, which Tshewang says proves his point, his point being that there is no point in talking about it.

"Anyway," he tells me, "I hate talking about politics with you. I haven't read what you've read. I haven't been where you've been. You always argue me into a wall, and I can never be right."

"That's not true," I say, hurt. But I fear it is. We bring too much with us into these conversations, it seems impossible to make a statement that is free of our separate pasts and upbringings and political cultures. My arguments arise from a culture that has named its own values as the highest aspirations of humanity. The fact that governments and corporations and individuals pay lip service to these values, the fact that there are grave inequalities and injustices and abuses of every sort in Western society, does not stop us—me—from pontificating in other places.

No, they are not always easy conversations, but each one adds to the ground we stand on together. In the evenings, I fall into dark fits of despair, asking myself where this can possibly go. It can't go anywhere, I tell myself. *Scalar—having magnitude but not direction.* Then I wonder if I just shouldn't give in and let it happen. Perhaps one night would quench this awful desire and then we could be free of it . . . no, no, no. One night would not be enough, and it is not one night that I want. Throw out those little scraps of paper, I tell myself. What you want is impossible.

Nima has decided to leave secular school after class XII and go to a Buddhist college in southern India, where he will become a monk. His mother, he says, is disappointed, but he has his father's blessing. "You know, miss, in Buddhism, we say that life is like housekeeping in a dream. We may get a lot done, but in the end we wake up and what does it come to, all that effort? I want to study what is really important."

"Are you sure about this, Nima?" I ask, thinking of the rigorous monastic discipline, the long periods of isolation from his family and friends.

He pulls out a book from his gho, *A Guide to the Bodhisattva's Way of Life,* and reads me a quote:

Suppose someone should wake from a dream
In which he experienced one hundred years of happiness,

And supposed another should waken from a dream
In which he experienced just one moment of happiness. . . .

"It's the same, isn't it, miss? One hundred years or just one moment. It's still a dream."

I can do nothing but nod. He is many lifetimes ahead of me in wisdom and maturity, and in my heart, I bow to him as my teacher.

We go to the temple one afternoon, bringing offerings of incense and vegetable oil for the butter lamps. A long-haired gomchen opens the door and we leave our shoes outside and enter the main room. The floor is cold beneath us as we prostrate in front of the altar on which a single butter lamp burns before a statue of Guru Rimpoché. We pause to look at the paintings on the wall, and Nima points out the six realms of existence in the wheel of life. The realms form the continuum of cyclical life, and rebirth in the worlds of gods, demigods, humans, animals, hungry ghosts, or hell, occurs in accordance with one's karma. Buddhist hell is remarkably similar to the Christian one, with its hot and cold tortures, except that it is not forever. Beings reborn in the hell realm remain until they have exhausted their negative karma. The hungry ghosts have stick arms and legs, stomachs grotesquely swollen with hunger, and twisted, knotted necks that do not permit them to swallow. They remind me of dieters in the West.

I do not believe in separate hell realms, I tell Nima. There are enough horrors right here on earth. "But what about these gods and demigods?" I ask. "They look very happy."

Nima nods. "They are happy for now, miss. Their world is very beautiful and pleasant, but they have not escaped cyclic existence, and sooner or later, they will use up their good karma and will be reborn in one of the lower realms."

I notice a black door off to the side painted with white skulls, and ask Nima if we can go in there. He says he can but I cannot. The room houses the temple's guardian deity, and women are not allowed to go in. The gomchen asks if we would like our fortunes told. Nima takes a pair of dice from a brass tray and holds them against his forehead briefly before throwing them down. The lama looks up the answer in a book and reads it aloud. Nima seems pleased. Now it is my turn, and I take the dice and look at Nima for help. "You have to think of a wish or a question," he says. I touch the dice to my forehead and drop them onto the tray. The lama reads out the answer.

"What you want will be very difficult," Nima translates. "Things will work out, but not in the way you expect."

On the way back down the hill, Nima tells me he asked about his spiritual training in India. "The answer was very positive. And miss, I know what you wished for. You wished to stay in Bhutan, isn't it?"

"Sort of," I say. Out of the starry cluster of wishes and questions that filled my head when I picked up the dice, only Tshewang's face remains clear now.

The students bring news of planned demonstrations in southern Bhutan. Arun comes to ask if I think he should go . . . down . . . to join the others, the demonstrators.

I say no. I don't want him to be hurt, trampled, run over, arrested, kidnapped, beaten up, shot, his head cut off and left in a sack. I don't want him to disappear. I don't want to lose any of them. I want them to stay here. All of them, north and south, the combination and the contradiction. I want them all to stay right here and make a final effort to talk to each other, to fight the real enemy, which is mutual mistrust and rhetoric, to find what they still hold in common beneath the cant.

I remember a verse from the Buddhist canon: *Not at any time are enmities appeased through enmity but they are appeased through non-enmity. This is the eternal law.*

The *Kuensel* reports that armed anti-nationals swept through the southern villages, rounding up people and forcing women and children to walk in front. The demonstrators grew violent, the paper reports, but the Bhutanese security forces were under orders not to fire. The crowds converged on district headquarters, stripping people of their national dress and burning office records. The militants ordered letters of their demands be carried to the central government. The contents of these letters are not reprinted.

Arun has not gone to join the demonstrators. "It could have been solved without this," he says. "If the government would only listen to what we are saying. If only they didn't make it a crime to say that we want something else. Personally, ma'am, I don't want a separate country for the southern Bhutanese, and none of my friends do, either. That's a ridiculous idea. But we don't want things to go on as they are, either. We're educated, we want our rights. We want to be able to say what we really want. And to be who we are. We are also part of Bhutan, isn't it. But they make it so that we can only be Bhutanese if we turn into them and even then we aren't real Bhutanese. It was okay before, when we only had to wear national dress in school and at office. Some of my friends say no, we shouldn't have to wear it at all, but I didn't mind. Then they made it the law and now I hate wearing it. Now just see how it has turned. After this, they will be completely right and we will all be criminals."

"I think it can still be solved, Arun."

"No, madam." His voice is hard and certain and very bitter. "This problem will never be solved."

After he leaves, I pull on shoes and run out of the house, up the driveway behind the staff quarters to the main road. The sky is dark and swollen. Lightning splits open a cloud and I am drenched in rain and sorrow. I am afraid that Arun's prediction will come true. I stand under the eaves of a shop, wiping water and tears from my face.

At a jam session to celebrate the end of the school term, Tshewang and I dance together once, and then sit outside on a bench behind the student mess. Whenever the music inside stops, we can hear the winter wind roaming wildly in the valley below us.

"What will you do in Canada?" he asks.

"See my family and friends. Go to bookstores, see movies, eat."

"You won't want to come back, maybe."

"No, I'll want to come back."

"I'll miss you," he says, looking elsewhere. In the weak yellow light of the overhead bulb, I study his profile, thinking how much I like him, his quick energy and wit and the thoughtfulness underneath. I know if I said, come back to my house with me, he would come. The burden of keeping silent is killing me. It is the only thing keeping me safe. I lean over and kiss his cheek. "Goodbye, Tshewang." He turns and we kiss again, a brief, shy, utterly delightful kiss. "Goodbye, miss."

I walk home alone, the sky full of stars, the night full of the smallest sounds, my whole self full of longing and sorrow that run clean and clear, a dark, quiet river over broken stone.

Return

A hi-lux has been sent to Tashigang to take the Canadian teachers to Thimphu at the start of the winter break. After we load our luggage into the back, we go to the Puen Soom for a last cup of tea with Karma. "Today not good for travel," he tells us. "Today is the Meeting of Nine Evils. Better you stay and go tomorrow."

"My students told me the same thing," I say. So did Kevin's; so did everyone's. Many years ago, the story goes, a man and a woman met at a crossroads. Unaware that they were actually a brother and sister who had been separated in infancy, they fell in love, and when they consummated their relationship, the nine evils descended upon them. No one could tell me exactly what the nine evils were, but everyone had warned me to stay at home in order to avoid them. We look at each other, wondering, and then Kevin says no, we have to go today, let's not be silly about this. "Maybe the Nine Evils won't bother phillingpa," Kevin tells Karma as we climb into the truck. Karma looks doubtful.

The truck roars out of town and breaks down just outside of Tashigang. The driver climbs out, cranks open the hood and bangs something, and the engine grumbles to life. This happens more times than I care to count, and we spend much of the first day sitting at the roadside, while the driver hammers away under the engine hood and curses. Finally, between Mongar and Bumthang, hours away from either, the truck chokes to a halt and the driver opens the hood, peers in, and closes it. "No chance," he says. "Engine is gone now." We are stranded. A passing flatbed stops and we pile our luggage and ourselves onto the back. There is something wrong with the flatbed's engine as well, and it cannot go faster than fifteen kilometers an hour. The low-lux, we call it. It chokes and wheezes the endless way up to

Trumseng-La, desolate with mist and snow and black ice. We huddle together, hungry and weary, wrapped in sleeping bags that feel like cellophane against the gnawing cold, and a quarrel breaks out over the use of the word "fuck" and whether freezing in the back of a fucking flatbed at four thousand meters above fucking sea level with at least six hours more in the company of a bunch of fucking uptight teachers is justification for using it in every fucking sentence, and then a jerry can of kerosene breaks open and seeps into the luggage, and someone cries out, "My silk weavings!" and someone else says, "My down sleeping bag!" and someone else says it is the Nine Evils, and everyone else says don't be ridiculous, but it is what we are all thinking. We were warned, why didn't we listen.

I close my eyes and think of the journey ahead, from Paro to Delhi to London to Toronto. I am vaguely afraid to leave Bhutan, afraid that the magic doors will snap shut and I will be on the wrong side. I am afraid that I will not find my way back. It is irrational, I know: I have extended my contract for another year, I have a return ticket, I have a visa for Bhutan in my passport, but still.

Lorna has also extended her contract. I ask her if she ever worries that something will happen and she might not get back. She tells me I am crazy.

"I can't imagine going home," I say. "I mean finishing here, and leaving for good."

"But you'll have to go home someday," Lorna says. "You can't live here forever."

I don't see why not.

When we get to Thimphu, we find that something has indeed happened: WUSC has declared bankruptcy and the program in Bhutan will begin to close down. We can all come back and finish our contract extensions, but no new teachers will be recruited under the program.

At home, everything is glossy and polished and unreal: glass-fronted shops, tinsel-bedecked displays, people's faces, all gleaming façades. In people's houses, I am overwhelmed by the number of *things*. I miss out large parts of the conversation because I am lost in looking at ornaments jostling for room on shelves, walls covered with hundreds of pictures, posters, calendars, clocks, decorative plates. Everywhere I look there is some *thing* to look at. My eyes are constantly dragged away. "Sorry, what?" I say. "Pardon?"

Television is incomprehensible. The images fly out of the screen too fast, faces phrases whole lives flash and pass and I let them; ten minutes of television exhausts me for hours. In my aunt's house, the television is always on, and it is unbearable. Come for dinner, they say, and I do, and we sit with our plates in our laps in front of the TV, my uncle clicking from channel to channel, nothing on he says but he does not turn it off.

Outside, I am shaken by the traffic, the rush, the speed at which people walk, excuse me, pardon me, are you getting on that escalator or are you just going to stand there blocking my way? A interminable line of cars on the highway, all going in the same direction, all carrying one person. I think of the gasoline consumed, the carbon monoxide produced, the money spent, the utter waste of it, one car for one person. When I suggest to my cousin that we take the bus downtown, she raises her eyebrows at me. "I don't take the *bus*," she says.

The number of stores is overwhelming, the number of things being bought and sold, things that people don't need and don't even seem to want all that much but for some reason have to have. I have never taken an economics course in my life, but after Bhutan, it is clear that this economy is not sustainable or sane. It is completely out of control, and the political prattle that links the family and democracy and small-town values to the anonymous forces of the Almighty Market is utterly absurd.

I do not do any of the things I thought I would do, go to an art gallery, the theater, a dozen movies. I meet Robert for a beer; not unexpectedly, we find we have very little to say to each other, and are both relieved when our glasses are empty and we can murmur polite wishes for a happy Christmas / life. I do the obligatory round of family visits: father in Toronto, mother and grandfather in Sault Ste. Marie, various relatives in between. I wake up tired and wander around the house, unable to breathe properly with hot stale air blasting out of the vents and all the windows sealed against the winter outside. My family's questions about Bhutan are impossible to answer. Bet you're glad to be back, aren't you? They have toilet paper in the Third World? What the hell do they use, then? Did you see our new car/electric can opener/waterbed/porcelain Dalmatian wine rack? Can you get anything like that over there? What do you do for entertainment? Thanks for the pictures you sent, geez the people sure are poor over there, aren't they? Sure makes you glad you were born here, doesn't it? Really makes you appreciate what you have, doesn't it?

I feel that I have changed and changed and changed, like Ulysses's ship changed one part at a time until every part had been replaced. It seems strange that after two years, everyone here is still talking about the same things, this aunt still not talking to that niece, that niece still saving up for a Corvette, cousin Bill and his wife are thinking about going to this new beach they opened up in Florida, someplace different, we went out to that new mall they got in Edmonton, the world's biggest mall, they got everything under the sun in there, hotels, swimming pools, skating rink, you name it they got it, Mary got married and you shoulda seen her dress, cost her somewhere up around four thousand dollars, the whole wedding must have set them back fifteen, twenty thousand but what the hey, his old man's loaded.

I tell people that I have become a Buddhist, and the responses are mixed. A few friends express concern, wondering if I am not taking this Bhutan thing a little too far; my brother is interested, and borrows my Dharma books; my parents are accepting, although my mother looks a little sad. My grandfather, however, is hostile to the idea. "You better not become a Buddhist," he says whenever the topic of religion comes up.

"It's more a philosophy than a religion," I tell him. "It has the same ethical rules as Christianity. It's not as foreign as you might think."

He says he doesn't want to hear about it.

People complain endlessly. The government this and the government that, the cost of everything, inflation, unemployment, taxes. Five minutes ago, they were telling me how lucky we are to have been born here, we have so much, we should be grateful, but they are not. What would it take to make you happy, I want to ask, but I think they do not know. A small dose of Buddhism would go a long way here.

A friend tells me how awful his mother is, she just doesn't understand him, she doesn't try to communicate with him. She always wants something from him that he just can't give. She never hugs him. "But your mother is seventy," I say. "She's from a whole other generation. They didn't hug back then."

No, that's not it, he says. It's not that she doesn't love him, it's not that she abused him or mistreated him, it's not that she was an alcoholic or anything like that. Then what is it? I ask. I am seeing it from the Bhutanese point of view: your mother raises you, she does her best, she's not perfect but it's hard to raise a child, and her mistakes arise out of the same ignorance that yours do. But this sounds hopelessly archaic and wrong when I say it, and my friend looks at me oddly and changes the subject.

I am shocked at the sheer number of claims and trivial objections and why-should-I's. Why should I give up a whole Saturday afternoon to help her move when she can hire movers. Why should I look after his cat. Why should I give her half of the furniture. In Bhutan, I often felt frustrated by the absence of questioning, and constrained by the strong social mores. In Bhutan, you should because everyone else does. You should because that's the way it has always been done. You should because if you don't, you will be criticized, perhaps ostracized, and ostracism is dangerous in a village. Here, I feel equally frustrated by the whining and the self-absorption. I can see the advantages of the mindset in Bhutan, the cohesiveness it generates, the social security net, and the disadvantages as well, the fear of critical questioning, the rigidity that stifles creativity.

It is the same with privacy. It is a relief in some ways to walk down Yonge Street thinking, "Not a single person here knows who I am and no one will ask me where I am going and why and when I will come back." But it is also frightening. If something happened, if I were attacked, or if I suddenly blacked out right here in front of this shoe store, would people continue to walk past, eyes frozen on some unattainable point in the distance? In Bhutan, the lack of privacy could infuriate me, but I always felt safe. Bhutan does not cultivate serial killers: people live too closely together, their lives are too interconnected for such atrocities to grow unnoticed and unchecked.

It seems to me that the two worlds represent extremes in many ways. Extreme individualism and extreme social conformity. Extreme privacy and extreme communalism. On one hand, a society of too many freedoms; on the other, too many constraints. My Canadian friend complaining vaguely that his mother doesn't understand him, and one of my students sobbing as she left college and her quiet, artistic boyfriend to marry a rough, domineering man twenty years her senior, because her parents said she had to and she dared not contradict them. I wonder where in the world it would be possible to have the ideal, a middle way, a balance between individuality and responsibility to the larger community. Easily named, of course, but I cannot begin to imagine where to achieve it.

What appeals to me most strongly about Bhutan is that daily life still makes sense. It runs on a comprehensible scale. A small farm with a few cows, a few chickens, a kitchen garden, a few cash crops, and the family has a place to live, food to eat. The mountains still have their forests intact, which means few floods, little soil erosion and enough fuelwood and timber for the small population. Small things still make a difference: a pipe to bring clean water down to a village, a basic health unit offering vaccinations and prenatal care.

Sometimes, when I am describing a typical Bhutanese village, people sigh and say oh how lovely. They want to believe in the Bhutan I used to believe in, a lost world in the mists of time, the fairy-tale place I first imagined two years ago, looking at black-and-white pictures in the library. But fairy tales don't have villages without a clean water supply, or four year olds dying of dysentery or tuberculosis. People don't want to hear this. Nor do they want to hear my criticisms of life in Canada. Everyone wants a cleaner, simpler, safer, saner world but no one wants to give up anything. No one wants to take the bus.

My grandfather is upset that I am going back. "You can't tell me that life is better over there," he says. "I saw those pictures you sent."

"But it is better in *some* ways," I say. It is safer, it is smaller, it is more real.

"They don't have anything," he says.

"They have what they need."

He shakes his head. "I just don't understand why you're going back," he says. "After all, it's not like you're not getting anything out of it."

Even with friends, it is difficult. They talk about their work, their plans, academic conferences, the split in the department. I sit politely at the edge of the conversation, and when it is my turn to talk, about Bhutan, my work, my students, I tell too much or not enough, and it is impossible to explain my love for the place, and how it has changed me utterly. Everyone seems sharp, impatient, aggressive, cynical, all raised eyebrows and ironic smiles.

I feel slow. I think slowly, I talk slowly, I react slowly. In the blur and rush of everything around me, I am more mindful. The mindfulness has grown quietly and surely, perhaps more a result of my slow, sparse environment in Kanglung than my own efforts. I can see how it would evaporate here without a consistent daily practice.

I scan the horizon from every window: grey city, frozen sky, smoke stacks belching yellow smog. I close my eyes and I can see the mountains from my window in Kanglung, the first pale light entering the valley, a raven circling a chorten. I count the days until I can go home, and there are too many, so I call the airline and change the date of my return.

The world seems smaller on the return trip, through transit lounges and security checks from Toronto to India, and then into the deep, forested valleys of Bhutan. Here are the mountains in their bleached winter raiment still rising to meet the sky, the calm streets of Thimphu, the quiet fields and forests, the prayer flags adrift in the air that smells of pine trees in sunlight, the strings of dried red chilies hanging from the eaves of mud and wood houses, here are the roofs shingled with wooden slats held down with white stones from the river, here are the haystacks and cowherds and the calling of crows, here I am, home again, home.

I unpack my luggage in the Thimphu guest house, shop for supplies to take to Kanglung, drink thick bitter coffee at the Swiss Bakery and write in my journal. The sky turns milky white one morning and heavy clotted snow flakes begin to fall. By early evening, the town is ghostly white, and a hard, lean moon hangs in the pale wintry sky. I return to the guest house and am startled to find an American woman in the kitchen, boiling water for tea. Her name is Julie, and she is visiting her cousin, an engineer working in Thimphu. We sit in front of the electric heater, watching steam curl out of our mugs and I tell her about my trip to Canada.

"I can see how you would feel displaced after here," she says. "It's so beautiful and so quiet. It must have been a shock to the system after two years."

It takes a long time to find the true words, to put them in order, to tell the whole story. It is not just this or that, the mountains the people, it is me and the way I can be here, the freedom to walk unafraid into the great dark night. It is a hundred thousand things and I could never trace or tell all the connections and reflections, the shadows and echoes and secret relations between them.

The snow melts the next day, water dripping everywhere in the brilliant light. Julie asks if I will come with her to visit a monastery at the north end of the Thimphu valley. We ride out in a taxi, past the dzong and the walled palace of Dechencholing, around a mountain to the end of the road where we sit on a rock by the river beneath Cheri monastery. The sun warms our cold stiff fingers and a raven in an oak tree calls to its mate. There is something magical about the place, Julie says, it reminds her of a wishing place she knew as a child. We try to figure out what makes it so: the end of the road, the bluegreen river, the narrow path that leads north through forested valleys to the snow-peaks, the temple built into the face of the mountain, the deep and complete silence of the rocks, the earth, the trees. I pick up a small blue stone and examine it, smiling to myself. "I wish to stay in Bhutan," I say, and I see Tshewang's face exactly.

"Really?" Julie says. "Do you think that will happen? I mean . . ." She takes a big breath. "Look, Jamie, I hope you won't mind if I say this, but I don't think that's a very wise thing to wish for. For one thing, you'll never really belong here. Even if you got married to a Bhutanese, even if you stay here for years and years. It won't ever be your place, if you know what I mean."

I don't. "It's home to me now," I say.

"Well, yes, it might feel like that, and I know I've only been here a few weeks, and you've been here for two years, but it seems to me that this might be a hard place to belong to, I mean really belong to. I think you would have to change profoundly in order to live here."

"People emigrate all the time," I say. "They leave their homes, their identities, they pack up and start new lives in countries far away. People do it every day. They leave their homes, go forth from their countries, the sons of the Buddhas all practice this way," I quote from a Buddhist prayer.

"No," she says. "People don't emigrate here. At least not that I know of. The way you feel now—well, I can understand the way you feel now, because it's so beautiful and it's so different from where you came from, but that feeling won't last, and then—"

"Why shouldn't it last?"

"How can it?" she says. "Someday, you will wake up and ask yourself, what am I doing here? Don't wish to stay here forever. If what you've been telling me about Buddhism is right, you shouldn't want to hold on to it, right? You should enjoy it and then let it go. I know you didn't ask me for advice, but I feel this so strongly I just have to tell you."

And she has a point, I can see that, from some other part of myself, perhaps from some distant future place, looking back, I can hear that she is offering very sound advice. Unfortunately or fortunately, I do not know right now, I cannot take it. I close my eyes and throw my stone and make my wish.

Love

*Un paysage
quelconque est un
état de l'ame.*

—*H. F. Amiel,*

Journal Intime

Love Is a Big Reason

Behind the frosted glass sky, the sun is a blurry orb of weak light. A tenuous blue-tinged mist like woodsmoke lies over Kanglung. The bare branches of trees tremble in the cold; the ground is rusted and blighted by frost. Inside my house, my bags are scattered over the sitting room floor, half-unpacked. Presents for various people are piled up on the altar, magazines and books for students, chocolate and newspapers for the Canadians who didn't go home. I arrived in Kanglung a week ago, heart singing to be home. Now I am weeping into a cup of black tea. I don't know why I have come back. I don't know where I belong. I don't know what to do.

I have come back because I have not had enough of these mountains. Because I have not finished with Bhutan. Because Bhutan is not finished with me. Because I am under a spell. Because I am in love.

Today I picked up my timetable. I will teach Tshewang's class this year, which should not have been a surprise to me, but the sight of his name on the class list was a jolt. I don't want him in my class. Before, we had that small, dubious, precarious space. A relationship would have been difficult but not impossible. Now it is unthinkable. Except I am still thinking it.

I swallow the last of the cold bitter tea, and put on a sweatshirt. Outside the college gate, I begin to run slowly uphill, fighting against the slope, my feet pounding on the tarmac. I run until my lungs are full of knives and then I stagger back.

At home, I swab the grimy floors with a virulent mixture of hot water and kerosene. I drag mattresses and quilts outside and drape them over chairs to air. Mrs. Chatterji waves from the balcony upstairs, where she sits reading in a cane chair. From the college store I bring three tins of paint and a paintbrush; I paint the walls in the sitting room and the bedroom. I move the divans, the desk, change the order of the books on the shelves.

I sort through stacks of notebooks and paper and photographs. I burn boxes of old letters. I make lesson plans for my first class on William Blake. I go to a staff party and make a strenuous effort to converse with Mr. Matthew. This is where I belong, in the staff room, talking with colleagues. I have come to my senses.

I stay up late reading a history of the English language. I turn off the lights and my senses betray me. I pull the blankets over my head, roll and twist and turn. I want to see him, I want to talk to him. I want to hear him laugh. I want I want I want. I meditate on the cycle of desire, the endless wanting and grasping that lead us to wrong understanding, wrong speech and wrong action, and the negative karma they generate. I meditate on the body, breaking it down into bone and hair and fat, *decay is inherent in all component things*. I meditate on the certainty of death. I fall asleep, empty at last, wanting nothing, free.

I wake up in the morning with his name in my head. Tshewang. It means the Power of Life. A crow flaps noisily into the pine tree outside my window, regards the world intently with its black-bead eyes, then lifts itself effortlessly up, and I watch as it wings its way toward the mountains at the far end of the valley, stark outlines in the cold north light. I remain rooted, caught. I cannot extinguish this hunger, this hope. *If any should desire what he is incapable of possessing, despair must be his eternal lot.*

He does not come to the first class. I stand at the front of the room and make a slow careful X beside his name, unsure if what I feel is blessed relief or crushing disappointment.

He comes instead to my house, just as night is falling. I begin to babble. "Come in, Tshewang, it's good to see you, sit down over there, move that stuff aside, yeah, just push it over—would you like some, some coffee? Tea? Lemon squash? I have some books for you, did I tell you that already? Just let me find them here in this mess . . ."

"Miss," he says in a small, tight voice, "I can't go on like this."

I cannot go on like this, either. I will have to go back to Canada. There is no other option. "Tshewang, this is all my fault. I should have—"

"Miss," he says loudly, and I wince. "Listen. Just listen." His gaze is frozen on the cuff of his gho. "I love you."

I want to weep.

"Well?" he says in a voice as hushed as dust. "Have I ruined everything now?"

"No. No." I sit down beside him and hold his hand. We are both trembling. I tell him that I've been in love with him since I don't know when, that I tried my best not to be, but I am. He nods, squeezes my hand tightly.

"But there's nowhere for us to go. We can't see each other, we can't be together. We're just —just *stuck* here. We can't have a relationship."

"We already have a relationship."

"But it can't go beyond this. I mean, we can't sleep together."

"Oh," he says. "No. I knew that." He goes to the window and pulls the curtain edge over the bit of night showing through. "But, miss?"

"Yes?"

"It's up to you. I told you that before. And I'll accept whatever you say. But the truth is, I don't see why not." He smiles wickedly. "Aside from all the obvious reasons."

"The obvious reasons are pretty big reasons, Tshewang."

"Well, yes," he says slowly. "But love is a big reason."

"Don't you care that I'm your English teacher? And a foreigner? Don't you care what might happen? Don't say you don't care—it makes me crazy. It's just not true."

"Well, of course it's not true," he says, exasperated. "Of course I care. I wish you were the shopkeeper's daughter down the road, but you're not. So what to do."

I could say we should do nothing. It is too risky, too difficult, I could say it is all wrong, and it would never work out, and we would regret it in the end, so let's turn back now. But I am tired of pretending to myself and fighting with myself. Underneath all my efforts at detachment was this singular, driving, persistent attachment. I want Tshewang far more than I ever wanted to give him up.

I pretended that I was resisting out of the ethical considerations but the truth is I resist because I am afraid. My time in Bhutan, my whole journey in fact, from the day I first read the name in the newspaper until this very moment, has been a coming to these edges, these verges, high places where I am buffeted by winds and dazed by the view, by the risks and the possibilities I never imagined could exist in my life, where I am astonished that I could get so high up, how on *earth* did I get so high up, where a voice whispers JUMP and another cries DON'T. Where I could turn back and walk down to safer ground, or I could throw myself over that edge, into *what,* what is out there, what *is* it that I am so afraid of beyond this last safe step where I am now standing? It is only my own life, I realize, that I am afraid of, and at each high point I am given the chance to throw myself over and back into it.

I am sobbing with the realization, and Tshewang is panicked, telling me shh, shhh, he is sorry, he will go, and I tell him to stay, it is not that at all. He puts his arms around me and I cry into his gho until the tears stain a dark lake in the wool, until I am exhausted and lighter than air, and then I take his hand and lead him out of the sitting room into the hallway where we stop to kiss, and I feel a million tiny windows flying open in my skin. We look into the bedroom. "Not here," Tshewang whispers, and pulls the mattress and quilt off the bed and into the dining room, where the single window can be easily covered with one piece of cloth. He lights a candle stub and sets it on the floor under the table. The shadows grow and shrink crazily, and then the flame burns steadily, and the room becomes still. In a moment of painful awkwardness, we stand side by side, looking at the bed on the floor. The only remedy is to take off all our clothes as quickly as possible. Once we have plunged directly into nakedness, shyness is impossible, and we curl up on the mattress beside the candle, wrapped in the quilt, whispering. Outside, the night has deepened, and we are held in a rich dark silence. He is a warm and ardent lover, completely uninhibited. It is as if we have been lovers for years.

"Tshewang, there's just one thing."

"Hmmm?"

"You absolutely have to stop calling me 'miss'."

He snorts with laughter. "You prefer ma'am? Shall I call you that?"

I hide my face in the quilt and laugh. I am safe here, with him; in the middle of the biggest risk I have ever taken in my life, I am safe. "Jamie," he says. "How is that?" I like the way it falls from his tongue into two clear, neatly balanced syllables. "Don't let me go to sleep," he says, "I have to leave before morning." But we both drift off and awaken to daylight sounds: a broom scraping concrete steps, windows being unlatched upstairs, Miss Dorling muttering to her two snapping, yapping Apsoos as she passes by. I don't know how he'll get out unseen now. In the kitchen, he pins a towel up over the window and makes sweet tea which we drink from one mug. I ask him if he wants toast, and he pulls an alarmed face, as if I had just offered him something insane for breakfast. He says he will eat rice at Pala's, thanks. I watch as he dresses, pulling on his gho, crossing one side over the other, aligning the seams, checking the hems. Grasping the sides, he raises the hem to his knees, then folds the sides back into two neat pleats. One hand holds the pleats in place, the other wraps the belt around his waist.

"How do I look?" he asks, smoothening down his hair. "Guilty?"

"No," I laugh. "Do you feel guilty?"

"No. I feel happy."

I wait at the back door to let him out but he heads into the sitting room. "Tshewang, you aren't going to walk out the front door!"

"No one will know that I haven't just stopped by this morning to get a book," he says, and grabs one from the shelf. A last kiss behind the door and then I wrench it open. We are suddenly separate, he standing on the steps outside, I in the shadow of the door frame inside. I am shocked at the sunlight, the bright trees, flowers, voices, the whole ordinary world awake below us, the same as it was yesterday, except that I feel I am seeing it from a perilous angle and my heart is pounding wildly, and I wonder if I will regret this. "Thanks, miss," he says loudly, formally, becoming Tshewang, student proper again. He raises the book. "This should help my writing."

"Oh yeah, that'll really help," I say, biting my lip. He looks down at the book for the first time, and throws his head back and laughs. I love him. I regret nothing. He strolls off, stuffing *Recipes for a Small Planet* into his gho. I close the door and lean against it, feeling the wood against my back, blood running in my veins, warmth in my palms, the trace of the last kiss.

Energy is eternal delight.

A Secret in Eastern Bhutan

He leaves his hostel room at night, after eleven, taking the most circuitous routes across campus. He must avoid students returning late from Pala's, the hostel dean, the night watchman, houses with lights still on, and the dogs. The dogs are the worst, he says, and we are glad when it rains, because the dogs take shelter under the hostels and the black curtains of rain hide him as he sprints down the road to my house. He turns the handle of the unlocked door slowly, and pads across the floor. We go into the dining room, now our room, where we lie on the mattress on the floor, beside the candle burning under the table. Sometimes he returns to his room before dawn, gliding out the back door into the wide night, but often he stays until morning, and then he walks out the front door with a book or a sheaf of papers in his hand. His boldness terrifies me, but no one seems to notice. "People come to your house all the time," he says. "Of course people will suspect something if I sneak out the back door. The trick is to walk out like everyone else."

Often, we don't sleep until dawn. I doze uneasily, waking every twenty minutes to look at the changing light. I have to teach at nine o'clock. I shake him awake but he burrows deeper into the quilt, his limbs heavy with sleep. Many mornings, I go off to teach and he sleeps through his economics class.

One night, he wakes up shouting in Nepali. "Tshewang! Shhhh!" I hiss, shaking him and pointing upwards.

"What? What?" he asks, bewildered.

"You were shouting! In Nepali, no less!"

We stare at the ceiling in horror, and then fall back onto the mattress, shaking with laughter at the thought of explaining, at the thought of merely trying to explain, to Mr. Chatterji.

We are both terrified of someone finding out. We don't know exactly what would happen, but if the principal is raging against students having relationships with *each other*, he certainly won't be amused by this, and the other lecturers—well, I can just hear them now. Tshewang dreads Monday morning assembly when the principal addresses the students. "It has come to my attention," each speech begins, and Tshewang is certain that one morning, he will say it has come to his attention that an improper relationship has developed between one of the lecturers and one of the students. Then we say we should stop this, we decide that it cannot go on, there is too much at risk. We lie on our mattress on the floor, holding each other, staring into the shadows, searching for a way, finding none. Okay, last time, we say. This is the last night. After tonight, it's over.

But he always returns, and my door is always open.

It is an affair housed in one tiny room, window closed, curtains drawn, door bolted, a relationship conducted in whispers and gestures, by candle light, in the uncounted hours of the night. Laughter is stifled in pillows, cries are swallowed or buried in flesh. I long to go outside with him, into ordinary daylight, walk down the road, laugh out loud. We talk about going to India during the winter holidays, to Calcutta where we will be two among ten million. We will walk down Sudder Street, hold hands in bookshops, we will go into a restaurant and sit at a table and no one will know us, no one will care.

But inside this room we have another kind of freedom. We live outside of scheduled time, according to our immediate wants. We get up in the middle of the night to cook packets of instant noodles. We mix up spicy salads of tomatoes, chilies, cucumbers and crumbled cheese, which we eat from a cooking pot with tablespoons. We make love and sleep, wake up and read, we talk and fall silent. I write a love letter on his thigh, he writes me a long musical dirty message in his sharp minute script on the wall above the mattress. We discuss how many children we would like to have, and whether we would give them Bhutanese or English names, and what kind of house we would like best, we tell each other family stories, secrets. There is time to talk about nothing, to lie with our limbs entwined, absorbed in our separate books. In this room, our everywhere, there is time to spare, time to waste, time to play. When we are together here, we feel disrobed of nationality, personal history, past betrayals and future anxieties. We are pared down to simpler, more lucid selves. In this room, we are two people who love each other. I have never known a flow of affection as pure and as easy as this.

But the moment we get up, dress, prepare ourselves to separate, time contracts painfully, shrinks around us, becomes tight and inelastic. When he has gone, I remember all the things we do not talk about, like is it true that Bhutanese who marry foreigners can not be promoted past a certain level, and could he ever be happy outside of Bhutan, and will this relationship work outside of this room, in real time. In this room there are few causes for quarrel, no push no pull, no stress, no others. We have few misunderstandings, but this means only that we know each other in this one place, in this one way. Outside this room, we have no idea who we are, who we would be together.

Outside this room, we are actors, cool and distant, nodding politely when we pass each other in the corridors of the college. In class, he is just Tshewang, taking notes, asking questions, muttering asides in Dzongkha that make his friends laugh. We become good at the split, the deception. We watch each other without ever looking. I am aware of him in the corner of the auditorium, I hear his voice through concrete walls, feel him moving down the hall outside the classroom I am in.

We are careful to do nothing to arouse suspicion. He is an excellent student, but I am careful when marking his homework. Not that it matters—his final exams will be marked in Delhi. I will have nothing to do with the grades on his certificate.

Except he misses so many early-morning classes that he fails economics.

Spring flourishes into summer and we barely notice.

When we cannot be together, we write letters, a dangerous practice considering how disorganized Tshewang is, shedding bits of paper, dropping books, losing notes. He leaves for his summer break and time without him is so painfully slow and barren that I don't know how I will get through it. It turns out I don't have to—he returns early, and we spend the next nine days in our room. We tell each other all the fears we can think of. "I am afraid you will get tired of this," I say. "I am afraid you will want a real relationship."

"Isn't this real?"

"I mean a relationship with a woman you can go outside with. Go to Pala's with. You know what I mean."

"I'm afraid you'll go to Canada and abandon me."

"I'm afraid you'll tell your parents, and they'll beg you to put a stop to this."

"I'm afraid you'll tell *your* parents, and they'll beg *you* to put a stop to this."

"What would your parents really say, Tshewang?"

He thinks about it. "Honestly, I don't know. They wouldn't understand if I converted to another religion, I know that, but about other things, they're very tolerant. Now, what I'm really afraid of is that I'm going to die if I don't eat a green vegetable soon."

We have been living on noodles, eggs and chocolate for a week.

"I'm afraid I can't do anything about that."

"You could go get some spinach from the Matthews' garden."

"Or you could go."

"Or I could go, and they could look out their window and see me sneaking out of your house."

"All right, all right. I'll go." I creep out stealthily, casting nervous glances at the windows of the upstairs flats as I collect an armful of vegetables. Tshewang cooks a sumptuous meal of red rice, spinach in butter and garlic, and a salad of green chilies, spring onions and tomatoes.

We stand at the backdoor after we have eaten, drinking in the air and eating raisins for dessert until a door opening upstairs sends us scurrying back inside.

The monsoon unleashes itself in a cloudy fury, the students return to the college, and still no one has found out. There are no secrets in eastern Bhutan, except this one.

Furniture

I am boiling water for the filter and cleaning the kitchen when I hear Lorna walk through the front door. She is singing, "Why, why, why, Delila." We meet in the back hallway. "Hi," she says. "I'm pregnant. What's up with you?"

"Tshewang and I are in love."

We collapse on the floor, laughing. She tells me about Darren in Canada. "I had no idea when I left that I was pregnant," she said. "Poor Darren. I sent him a letter. The kid'll be in high school by the time he gets it."

"Are you going to have the baby here?"

"No, I'll finish up early and go home. Home! You know what this means, don't you?"

"No, what?"

"Furniture!" Lorna equates furniture with settling down. Her voice is grumpy but the happiness comes off her in waves. She makes me promise not to tell anyone, especially the field director. "He'll pack me off home, and I want to stay as long as I possibly can."

"I won't tell if you won't," I say.

"I knew this would happen," she says. "I mean you and Tshewang. I knew that day we saw him at Pala's. Well, are you happy now?"

"I don't know, Lorna. I'm happy, all right. I'm ecstatic, except when I think of the future. We want to get married, but we don't know if it's even allowed. Tshewang has already told his parents about us, and says they are fully supportive, but of course there are a thousand other things to consider." I go through the List of Unresolved Issues and Unanswerable Questions, and she throws in a few of her own. Cultural differences, conflicting expectations about marriage (she has observed that marital fidelity does not seem to be considered a great virtue in Bhutan), power imbalances caused by money, education, experience. "I don't think Bhutan allows dual citizenship," she says. "If he emigrates to Canada, he'll have to give up his Bhutanese passport. And would you really be content to stay in Bhutan for the rest of your life?"

I can't say for certain about the rest of my life in *any* one place. After all, I only know two places, Canada and Bhutan. "I love Bhutan," I tell her.

"Yes, I know. I love Bhutan, too, but I know I couldn't live here forever."

"Anyone can live anywhere," I say.

"For a time, sure. But I think part of the reason we love Bhutan so much is that it's not permanent. We know we have a limited time here, that's what makes it so precious. And it's a difficult place to get to. Remember how you felt going home this winter, how you were so worried you wouldn't get back? It's one of those impossible places that everyone dreams about. The forbidden kingdom."

"That's all true, Lorna, but it doesn't really have anything to do with Tshewang."

"I'm not questioning your feelings for Tshewang, but these things form the background of your relationship and you should think about them."

I do think about all these things. They go around and around in my head in a whirlwind of fear and hope. I write lists, For the Future and Against, For the Relationship and Against, I have arguments in my head as different people, Ann Landers debates P. B. Shelley, my grandfather contends with Florentino Ariza. I thought Bhutan was all I would want, I tell Lorna. Just more time in Bhutan, enough time, until I was full up with it, saturated, satiated. I thought that would be the end of it, but it seems there is no end to wanting. Now there is a whole new desire. Now I want Tshewang.

"Well, you have him," Lorna says.

"I have him now, yes, but I want him tomorrow and next year

and the next. We want to have a future together. We want to have furniture."

"Why can't you just be happy with what you have now and say goodbye when it's time to leave?"

Because I cannot bear the thought of that. Because the thought of never seeing him again paralyzes me with grief. It's not that kind of love, and I'm not that kind of person, and it's too late for that now, anyway. "I want what I want," I say. "And I don't want to come to the end of my time here and say to Tshewang, 'Well, sweetie, that was nice. Have a happy life.' "

"Well, given the circumstances," Lorna says, "and I don't mean to discourage you, but given the circumstances, I think you should at least think about it."

I say that I will but I know that I won't. I haven't told her the other thing I want: a baby.

I think of all the relationships and circumstances in which children can be conceived, and I think of Tshewang and me in our little room, the pure flame of our love and our time together, and I want a child to come out of it. There will never be another time like this.

Outside our room, there are changes. Two new Canadian lecturers arrive, part of a new project that links Sherubtse with a Canadian university. One is a warm sunny man whose house is instantly full of the students and lecturers he befriends effortlessly; the other is an odd, older man who manages to stand erect in spite of the heavy white man's burden he is carrying. He moves into the flat next to mine, and we take an instant dislike to each other. He has come, he announces gravely to Dini and me, to develop the college. He has the tools to do this because he has spent many, many years in undeveloped countries. I wince at the word but he doesn't notice. Dini laughs outright, but no, he is serious. She engages him in vitriolic arguments about development and imperialism, but he doesn't get it.

Southern students begin to leave. Some say their families are being pressured by the army and local authorities to get out. They could not find a land tax receipt from 1958 to prove they are citizens. Others say they are leaving because everyone else is. Others say the south is too dangerous, they are caught between the security forces and the armed groups that raid their houses. "If we wear this dress," Arun tells me, fingering his gho, "we will be caught by the anti-nationals. If we don't wear it, the government will think we support the anti-nationals." He has come to say goodbye; his family sent a message for him to come home. "But where will you go?" I ask. He says to a refugee camp in Nepal, where many others have already gone. He does not know if he will ever come back.

Once again it is news by I-hear-that. I hear that large numbers of southerners are leaving their homes in the south. I hear that they are selling their land back to the government and heading to camps in Nepal. I hear that they are being forced into leaving but that authorities capture the moment on videotape to document this "voluntary migration." I hear that the emigration is part of a careful plot by the anti-nationals, a propaganda ploy to win international sympathy. They intend to bring out as many people as possible, accusing the Bhutanese government of oppression and human rights abuses. Their plan is to bring down the Bhutanese government, and march back in to a new Nepali state which they will rule. I hear the army is dismantling houses, I hear that heads of families are taken out into fields at night where they are beaten by soldiers and asked, "Now will you leave?" I hear that southerners who cannot prove they are citizens are being labeled F-7s. F-1 means both mother and father are Bhutanese. F-7 means non-national. What is in between, I ask. F-2 to F-6. No one knows. I hear this is being done to rid Bhutan of thousands of illegal immigrants. I hear this is affecting bona fide southern Bhutanese as well. I hear it is winding down, I hear it is just beginning.

I am distraught beyond tears when Arun leaves, and then a cold numbness sets in. I am disgusted by both sides. The worst are full of passionate intensity, the best lack all conviction.

In a staff meeting, the principal makes reference to The Procession of Seventy-Five, and it takes me a few minutes to realize he is talking about the Durga Puja incident from two years ago, when about seventy-five southern students refused to wear national dress at the college gate. He makes reference to two southern staff members who have absconded. This is the new buzzword. Villagers voluntarily emigrate; government employees abscond. He makes reference to non-national staff members getting involved when they don't really understand the situation. I don't know if this is a reference to me for having been in The Procession of Seventy-Five, or for talking to the southern students about the situation, or if it refers to something else altogether. I pretend to be least bothered. It has nothing to do with me. I am an outsider, I have no stake in this, it means nothing to me at all.

Tashigang Tsechu

Tshewang wakes me in the middle of the night. "Let's go to Tashigang tsechu," he says. The tsechu is a series of masked dances, performed annually at dzongs and temples across the country to convey Buddhist teachings and history. Each dzong and important temple has its own, and people from all over the district come to watch, dressed in their best, most colorful clothes.

"What, now?" I burrow back into the blanket.

"The *thongdrel* is coming down today. We have to be there early."

The thongdrel is a large religious scroll, usually of Guru Rimpoché, appliquéd in bright silk. It is lowered on the last or second-last day of the tsechu in the early hours of the morning, and is rolled back up before direct sunlight touches it. Thongdrel means liberation upon sight; seeing one is enough to bring the faithful into an enlightened state.

"Come on," Tshewang says, tying on his gho.

"How are we getting there?" I yawn, but I already know. "Don't forget the flashlight and batteries," I tell him, pulling a kira out of the closet.

He forgets the batteries, and the flashlight dies the minute we leave the road and embark on a long steep descent though thick scrub, "a shortcut," Tshewang says, "we'll be in Tashigang in an hour," but without light, it takes forever to feel our way down the hill. Tshewang has to hold my hand as we inch our way through the darkness. We stop to rest under a tree, lying on our backs, watching the stars through the leaves. It is the first time we have been together, just ourselves, outside. "It feels like the ends of the earth," Tshewang says. "Listen." We strain our ears for a sound in the vastness of the night, but there is nothing, not one. By the time we reach the road again, the stars have withdrawn and the darkness is lifting. Tshewang pulls me down into the grass at the side of the road, and we make love while the world grows gold and bright around us. No sooner have we finished than we hear the unmistakable whine of an approaching vehicle. We untangle ourselves and jump over the embankment, scattering clothes into the thorn bushes as the truck passes. After, laughing hysterically, we search for our things, finding everything except Tshewang's underwear.

Inside the dzong, the thongdrel is down, covering the entire wall of the temple; dozens of butter lamps flicker on the altar set up below it. The rippled cry of gyalings rises up, raising the hair on the back of my neck, and a drum beats like a heart as hundreds of people prostrate in the flagstone courtyard. We watch the masked dancers in wooden masks and skirts made out of bright yellow strips of silky cloth as they bend and sway and twirl slowly to the accompaniment of drums and cymbals. The dance ends, another begins with dancers wearing deer masks. A hunter appears with a crown of leaves and a bow, followed by a dancer in a long white dress and tall white hat. The white dancer admonishes the hunter, showing him the hell that awaits him; the hunter is eventually converted and throws down his bow.

In between dances, the joker appears, a strange figure in rags and an ugly, red mask, brandishing a huge wooden phallus. He chases young girls, old men, kids, a chicken, pointing and jabbing lewdly. His gait is exaggerated, loose and drunken, as he pitches himself forward and whirls around wildly, but when the next dance begins, he rests soberly on the temple steps.

Tshewang sits beside me throughout, explaining the dances, making a point of calling me "miss." But I still forget and once I lay my hand on his arm. He nudges it off and frowns at me, and I am annoyed although I know he is right. I am sick of this. I want to go where we can sit together in public, come home and leave the curtains and windows open, answer the door, invite friends for dinner. The magic space we create in our dark little room is precious and sacred, and it is not enough. I want a love that lives in the plain light of day.

We take the Comet back to Kanglung, sitting in separate seats. The bus stops to pick up someone a hundred meters from where we made love this morning, and Tshewang hurries to the front of the bus and talks to the driver. The driver opens the door for him and he disappears. He reappears a few moments later, stuffing a ball of maroon cotton into his gho as he gets back onto the bus: he has found his underwear.

Jomolhari

An early-morning thunderstorm. We are crouched at the window, peering around the flap of the curtain, watching clouds move over Brangzung-la. The thunder fades, the clouds and rain remain. Every word you can use for cloth you can use for the monsoon: soft, heavy, swath, silk, cotton, wool, faded, splotched, woven, washed, rinsed, wrap, blanket, mantle, quilt, stuff, ruff, swaddle, muffle, cover, layer, stratum, sheet, shroud. I will miss the monsoon when I leave. I squeeze my brain shut at the thought of leaving, blocking out the image of the plane lifting itself above the Paro valley, soaring out. I have six weeks left.

I have been in Bhutan for over three years, and my contract ends in June. I have decided not to extend it. Tshewang and I cannot go on in our little room forever. People are starting to ask questions. During a meeting to discuss possible editors for the college's newsletter, the principal sent the peon to call Tshewang from his hostel. I sat, frozen, in my seat. Tshewang was not in his hostel. I had left him, naked and asleep, in my house. The peon returned, shaking his head. "Tshewang is very hard to find," the student beside me said. "He just disappears!" I am certain that my Canadian neighbor knows about our relationship, and disapproves, and it will be just a matter of time before he mentions it casually to someone.

Moreover, I am pregnant. I know because every morning at ten o'clock, I must excuse myself from class and rush to the staff toilet, where I am violently but briefly sick. (Once, I stay home from class and hear Mrs. Chatterji being sick upstairs at the same time as me. Later, when I have gone to Canada, several students will write to tell me the happy news: after all these years, Mrs. Chatterji is pregnant.)

My body has taken charge, it is engaged in this secret activity and will brook no interference from me. It refuses coffee, tea, alcohol, and for some reason, kidney beans. It demands sleep and fresh fruit and meat. I tell Tshewang, and he walks to his family village, two hours north of Tashigang, and brings back strips of dried pork fat that he boils into an oily chili-flecked curry. I am revolted, but my body says eat it. Tshewang watches me devour two plates with rice. In Bhutan, he says, people believe that eating lots of pork will cause the baby to have good, thick, black hair. He brings me tamarind and urges me to eat it raw. "Pregnant women are supposed to crave this," he tells me.

"No they're not, they're supposed to crave ice cream," I say, my face puckering up painfully as I chew one of the sticky pods. "I'm sure the baby would prefer ice cream."

"She," Tshewang guesses, rubbing my stomach, which is beginning to thicken. "She wouldn't."

"He." I have dreamed of the baby already, a boy with curly brown hair in spite of the pork. "He would."

I will return to Canada to have the baby, due in December. Tshewang will visit during his winter holidays, and return to Bhutan to finish his last semester at college. Then we will decide what to do. It will be a test, we tell each other, it will give us some perspective. We will use the time to think. We will wait and see. When we are together, I love the sound of these words, cool and unassailably rational. But when we are apart, I am caught in the most terrible despair imaginable. I don't want to wait and see, I want to know now, for certain, whether we will be together, in Canada or Bhutan or anywhere, it doesn't matter where, whether we will be a family and have a future together. I want the unequivocal Answer to How Will It All Turn Out. I fill the water cups on my altar and sit in meditation, remembering my practice. I cannot eradicate my worries entirely but, with effort, manage to attain some measure of mental stillness.

In my last weeks in Bhutan, I decide to accompany a few other volunteer teachers on a trek to Jomolhari in northwestern Bhutan. We drive to the end of the road in Paro, to the ruins of Drukgyal Dzong, and then, hoisting up our rucksacks, we set off along the path I saw that first week in Bhutan, the centuries-old trading route. We walk through summer meadows filled with white butterflies, past large comfortable farmhouses surrounded by prayer flags, following the river, a constant rush and surge of white and blue water over stone. A forest envelopes us, thorny oak, luminous larch, a dozen kinds of rhododendron, red, cream, pink, flame-shaped, bell-shaped, tiny white star-shaped. Across wooden bridges, up a path that used to be a river. A chorten marks the way to the old pass that leads down into the Chumbi Valley in Tibet, but we veer right, stay close to the river, leaving behind the fields and farmhouses. The ascent is slow, almost imperceptible. We turn a corner, and the soft round hills and oak forests of Paro close behind us. Ahead are sheer-sided mountains, black and bare, the peaks pinched and crimped by frozen snowy fingers. Above, the sky is the color of wind and cold whipped into froth. We walk deeper into the emptiest, cleanest landscape I have ever seen. Snow pigeons are wheeling in bright arcs, swooping up, free falling down and into a current that carries them over a ridge. We are already above the tree line, and three days from the nearest shop. Five houses are strung out along the valley, built of grey stone, a year's supply of deadwood piled up along the fences. Yaks watch us disinterestedly as we pass, picking our way through enormous boulders fingered and dropped by glaciers along the valley floor. Even here, chortens and faded prayer flags stuck into rock mark the path. We arrive as the sun disappears, leaving the valley in cold blue shadow, and sit, exhausted and breathless, on lichen-blistered rocks at the base of a ruined dzong, thin branches rising out of the broken stone walls like pencil marks. A wall of cloud hides the mountain from us.

At five the next morning, we wake to see it, huge and white, impossible, as if the moon had fallen to earth. We walk toward it, climbing over boulders and splashing through an icy river. Over a moraine, down into soft wet sand, shallow cloudy green river winding through. We climb another moraine and then we can see the base of the mountain, rock falls, snow and ice, pieces of the mountain smashed into gravel, gravel crushed into grey sand. We can see the remains of a glacial lake, bottle-green. Even this close to the mountain, there are yaks pulling up bits of grass. We climb up a slope until we can see another upthrust spire of mountain, Jichu Draké. In the brilliant light, I cannot tell the mountain from the cloud.

At first I think, this awful, awful place. An icy, windy desert. But then I realize it is not wasteland, land used up and useless, it is not the end of life, but the beginning of it. Here are the great mother mountains and the watersheds, the beginning of the river that grows the forests and rice in the fertile valleys downstream. This is primeval land, belonging to itself. It is not a landscape of many choices. It is immaculate, spare, sparse, parsed into its primary elements. The grammar of mountains. Stone, ice, time. The wind sounds like the ocean. Nothing I have with me would help me here for very long. There is little here, and little to want. But there is space and time to think.

Tshewang and I have made separate, discreet inquiries; it *is* possible for us to marry and stay in Bhutan. It *is* possible for us to marry and leave Bhutan. These are the only options we have spoken of. I have not voiced the third, not to marry, to go our separate ways. Because I do not know if either of us is ready to make the sacrifices that the future will require. I don't know if I have brought Tshewang further into this than he ever wanted to be. I worry that I am asking him for a commitment that he may not be ready for. He says he is, has said from the beginning that he only thought about this relationship in one way, heading toward one conclusion, marriage, a family, but I am not entirely convinced that at twenty-two, he is ready to make that kind of decision.

Sitting on a stone looking up at Jomolhari, I let myself think. I came to Bhutan to find out if the careful life I had planned, the life of waiting, watching, counting, planning, putting into place, was the life I really wanted. I can still go back to that life, even now, even after everything. Here I am, in another high place, the highest edge I have come to so far. I can still say goodbye to Tshewang, go home, find an apartment, have the child, go back to school. In some ways, it is the least risky, most sensible option. I can turn these last three and a half years into a neatly packaged memory, pruned by caution, sealed by prudence. I can still turn back. But I will not. I will go over the edge and step into whatever is beyond.

Lotus Thunderbolt

"J esus Christ, Jamie Lynne!" my grandfather says when I tell him. If he were not so visibly, angrily, intensely upset, I might laugh. I had written to him about Tshewang, and he had written back telling me not to be foolish, to think of my future. "It will all blow over," he wrote. "You'll forget each other the minute you're back here. Where you belong." He thought I was coming home to do my Ph.D. When I tell him I have come home to have a baby, he doesn't believe me.

"Grandpa," I say gently, "I wanted a baby. I want this baby. I love Tshewang very much."

For a few weeks, he says nothing. He is thinking, turning it over and over in his mind, looking for something to salvage, a piece upon which he can build a future for me.

"All right," he begins one morning, stirring sugar into his coffee. "So you have the baby. Fine. Lots of people have babies when they're studying at that level. You can apply now, and start after the baby is born."

"I don't want to go back to school now, Grandpa. I'm going to wait for Tshewang to finish school, and then we'll decide what to do."

"Forget him —"

"I can't *forget* him, Grandpa."

"Why make your life more complicated than you've already made it? You have to simplify it now."

"I agree. That's why I'm not making any decisions right now."

"You won't ever really belong in Bhutan, and he won't ever feel at home here."

"Well, I don't know about that, Grandpa. He's a pretty adaptable person, and I love Bhutan."

"You aren't even the same religion," he says. "How in hell do you expect this to work?"

I mumble unhappily and get up to clear the dishes. I don't know how to tell him, he is already so upset. "Don't tell me you've gone and become a—a—"

"A Buddhist."

Now he is furious. "You were raised a Catholic!"

"Yes, but I've chosen to be something else, Grandpa. Anyway, you used to say that all religions are the same underneath."

"Then why can't you stay a Catholic? That's a cult, that's all that is. Buddhism!"

I enlist the help of my brother, father and mother. Please talk to him, I ask them. Tell him that you're not upset about it, you think it will all work out fine. The phone rings and rings, and I try not to listen to my grandfather explaining patiently why I never should have gone to Bhutan in the first place. "Everything will change after the baby is born," my mother tells me. "Your grandfather will come around. They always do."

I try talking through it with him, I try not talking about it at all, I try ignoring his comments, I try snapping back at him. I come home one day from a walk and find that the small altar I have set up in my room has been dismantled and packed away. "I don't want that nonsense in my house!" he shouts. When my father calls and offers me an alternative place to stay, I accept and move to Toronto.

I spend my time reading, swimming at the Y, seeing films, and writing to Tshewang. I miss him hugely, and sometimes I fret about the future, but mostly I am calm. I take refuge in the Dharma community in Toronto, visiting a Tibetan Buddhist temple regularly, and attending a series of teachings given by a visiting Tibetan Rimpoché. The temple is in a downtown building; the downstairs lobby is all mirrors and polished brass, but several floors up, in a bright, airy room, there is an altar, butter lamps and water cups set before a statue of the Buddha, and every time I go in, it is a homecoming. I stay in touch with my Bhutan friends in Canada, visiting Tony and Margaret (who returned home, got married, and settled in Vancouver), Leon, who has begun a postgraduate degree in international affairs in Ottawa, and Lorna and her new family in Saskatchewan. Lorna does indeed have furniture, and seems very happy with it.

Friends working in Thimphu write to tell me that the political situation, or the "southern problem" as it is now called, continues along the same course it started out on, two sides, two stories, parallel lines. There is no resolution in sight.

The baby is born on the ninth day of the tenth month of the Water Monkey Year, December 3, 1992, a boy with curly brown hair, dark eyes, golden-brown skin, and a bluish mark at the base of his spine which the doctor calls a Mongolian Blue Spot. I have to wait for Tshewang to get a name for the baby from a lama. He will phone me from Thimphu with the name, and then he will come to Canada for six weeks. In the meantime, I call the baby Dorji, and the baby does not complain. Tshewang finally calls from Thimphu—he has been to Taktsang, he announces excitedly, the baby has a name, and it is Sangha Chhophel.

"Sangha?"

"Sangha," he corrects me.

"Sangha."

"No, not Sang-ha," he says. "Sang-ngha. Can you hear the difference?"

"Yes," I lie. "But listen, Tshewang, maybe we should call him something easier for Canadians to pronounce. Is that allowed?" I do not tell him that no one in my family can pronounce "Tshewang." My brother refers to him as Say-Wrong, and my mother's mother calls him Sam. I don't know what they'll do to Sangha.

"It's allowed, I think. How about Pema? Pema Khandu?"

I like Pema, but in Canada, Khandu would inevitably be pronounced Candu. I explain the nuclear associations, and suggest Dorji. Pema means lotus, a symbol of enlightenment because the white flowers bloom out of mire, the same way the mind blossoms out of samsara into enlightenment. Dorji means thunderbolt, a symbol of enduring truth.

My grandfather calls, wanting to know do I need any money, am I sure I don't need any, well okay then, he just wanted to make sure . . . and how is the baby? And when is *he* going to arrive, the baby's father? "Soon, grandpa," I say. "We'll be coming up to see you after Christmas."

"Well," my grandfather says, "have you done anything about winter clothes for him?"

"No." I haven't even thought about winter clothes for Tshewang.

"Well, I don't suppose you saw—they had a special on boots at the K-Mart," my grandfather says. "I picked him up a size eight."

Revenue Stamps

Tshewang and I were married at the Thimphu District Court in September 1993. We wore matching clothes, a gho and kira cut from one piece of red-and-gold cloth woven by his mother. Pema Dorji, nine months old, wore a Blue Jays outfit. At the courthouse, we waited around for most of the morning before a clerk informed us that Bhutanese needed permission from the Home Ministry to marry foreigners. Across town we went to the Home Ministry, where we waited around a few more hours for our letter of permission. Back to the court with the letter. More waiting. The clerk emerged again from the judge's chamber and said, "You do have revenue stamps, don't you? For the marriage certificate?" We didn't bother asking what a revenue stamp was, or why we needed them to get married; we just went off to the revenue-stamp office to buy some. By the time we got back, it was almost five o'clock, and the clerk informed us that the judge was going home. One of our witnesses whispered something, and the clerk looked us up and down, nodded sympathetically and went back into the judge's chamber. "What did you tell him?" we asked our friend.

"I told him you were wearing borrowed clothes and had to return them tonight," he said. I began to straighten my kira in anticipation of the actual event. How would the Bhutanese ceremony go? What would the judge say exactly? I checked my camera: film, flash, batteries. The clerk came out and said the judge had agreed to marry us. In fact, he had *already* married us. "What do you mean?" I asked.

"You're married," said the clerk. "You just have to sign the certificate."

"But we weren't even in the room!" I wailed.

The clerk shrugged. "Do you have the stamps?"

We signed the certificate, giggling, and stuck on the stamps. As wedding ceremonies go, it wasn't much, but with the mountains rising up to the violet sky outside and the river turning gold in the last drop of light, it was enough.

Postscript

Tshewang and I lived in Thimphu for several years, and Pema's first words were an equal balance of English and Sharchhop. During our time in Thimphu, Tshewang and I found some of the cultural differences between us to be even greater than we had expected, and had to make some difficult decisions about our future. Eventually, I decided to return to Canada, at least "for some time," as the Bhutanese say, and the future, well, we will see what it brings.

One of the questions I am most often asked about my life in Bhutan is, "But does it feel like home to you?" In many ways, it does. I can stand on a ridge, looking at those mountains and forests and clouds forever, feeling wholly at ease, wholly at home. But I use the word "home" to refer to Canada as well. I go "home" to visit, "home" for a holiday. My grandfather phoned me often in Thimphu to see how I was, and always asked when I was coming "home." He meant for good, not for a holiday. It was hard for him to understand that home could be, for me, two radically different places and cultures, and it remained a source of sadness and difficulty between us. He was too old to make his own journey into Bhutan, which was unfortunate, because I knew that if he could see me there, he would know that I was already home. On a November afternoon in 1996, I was having lunch at my friend Dechen's house, and I had a sudden strong impression of my grandfather, as if he could somehow see me sitting cross-legged on the floor amongst friends, drinking warm salty butter tea and laughing as our children chased each other under the brilliant autumn sky outside. It was such a peculiar feeling that when my brother Jason phoned later to tell me that Grandpa had died that day in his sleep, I already knew.

Namé samé kadin chhé, Grandpa.

Beyond the sky and the earth, thank you.

ABOUT THE AUTHOR

Jamie Zeppa spent several years teaching and living in Bhutan. Her letters home were featured on "Morningside," and in 1996 she won the CBC–*Saturday Night* Canadian Literary Award for Memoir. Zeppa currently spends time in both Toronto and Thimpu.